™

ADVANCED
TOPICS

Be™

ADVANCED
TOPICS

The Be Development Team

O'REILLY™

Cambridge · Köln · Paris · Sebastopol · Tokyo

Be™ Advanced Topics

Be, Inc.
800 El Camino Real
Suite 300
Menlo Park, CA 94025
http://www.be.com

ISBN: 1-56592-396-0

Table of Contents

PREFACE

If you use a computer everyday, chances are good that your hardware is no more than five years old. And if you actually *like* computers, it's more likely that you own a box that's less than two years old. How old is your operating system? Updates help, certainly, but how old is the *core* software technology behind your "Version X" or "UltraLimp '96" OS?

In the last five years, the computer hardware industry has undergone drastic changes. CPU speeds and disk capacities have shot through the roof while the price per megahertz and gigabyte has fallen dramatically. Computers now boast two, four, even eight CPUs on a single motherboard. The major OS vendors try to keep up with this change, but they have other concerns, such as maintaining backwards compatibility and supporting their loyal following. They can't make the clean break with the past that new hardware demands.

The BeOS is a fresh start. Be likes hardware—the faster the better. If you've seen it running, then you know what a computer can do when the dead weight is removed.

But the BeOS isn't just about speed. It's also about the things that a modern OS should give you automatically, with no outboard equipment, and without having to reboot your computer everytime you make a change. Like networking, true parallel processing, real-time response in the user interface, recognition of standard data formats. Intelligent design that recognizes and knows how to use the capacities of the hardware to its fullest: That's the reason for the BeOS.

About the Be Books

There are two books that make up the Be developer's reference bible. They contain descriptions of every C++ class, every function, every constant that the BeOS defines, and let you know how and when to use them. If you want to design an application that will run on the BeOS, you'll need these books.

The first book, the *Be Developer's Guide*, describes the foundation "kits" in the OS. These are the kits that every developer will need to understand:

- *The Application Kit*. This is the kit that gets you started.
- *The Storage Kit*. An interface to the file system.
- *The Interface Kit*. Windows, views, buttons, controls—everything you need to design a graphic user interface.
- *The Kernel Kit*. Access to the lowest programmable level of the BeOS.
- *The Support Kit*. A catchall for common functionality and definitions.

Be Advanced Topics—the "geek" book—is about special topics. There you'll find the kits that don't pertain to every application. But most developers will need to know at least a little bit about some of them:

- *The Network and Mail Kits*. An interface to the network and e-mail.
- *The Translation Kit*. Lets you convert your data from one format to another.
- *The Media Kit*. Real-time processing of audio data.
- *The Midi Kit*. MIDI data generation and processing, including the Headspace® General MIDI synthesizer.
- *The Game Kit*. Lets your application take over the machine.
- *The OpenGL Kit*. An implementation of the OpenGL® 3D graphics interface.
- *The Device Kit*. Software that controls hardware.
- The book also contains chapters on writing device drivers, network add-ons, and controlling the Tracker.

Support Information

Be provides as much information as possible about the BeOS via the Web and other electronic means. For basic customer and technical support, visit the Support section of the Be Web site at *http://www.be.com/support*.

The Support section offers Frequently Asked Questions (FAQs), software updates, and documentation in both on-line and downloadable formats. You can also find information about Be's electronic mailing lists.

Be FAQs: *http://www.be.com/support/qandas*

BeOS Updates: *http://www.be.com/support/updates*

Be Documentation: *http://www.be.com/documentation*

Be Internet Mailing Lists: *http://www.be.com/aboutbe/mailinglists.html*

Also available on our Web site is an Assistance Request form. Use this when you need help from our Customer Technical Support group: *http://www.be.com/support/assist/custsupport.html*.

If you can't submit a help request via a Web form, send e-mail to one of our support addresses. Include as much information about your problem as possible, such as the configuration of your system, what you were doing, what happened, what you expected to have happen and why, and anything else about your configuration or problem that you think we should know.

For BeOS users in the Americas or Pacific Rim:

- *custsupport@be.com* — for questions regarding set up, installation, configuration and compatibility of the BeOS, or other technical questions that are not about programming or coding.
- *custservices@be.com* — for assistance with obtaining any of our products.

For BeOS users in Europe:

- *custsupport@beeurope.com* — for questions regarding set up, installation, configuration and compatibility of the BeOS, or other technical questions that are not about programming or coding.
- *custservices@beeurope.com* — for assistance with obtaining any of our products.

If Web searching and e-mail don't do the trick, or if you would rather talk to a human, you can call us. We're available Monday through Friday, between 6 AM and 6 PM (Pacific time) for callers in the Western hemisphere and 8 AM to 6 PM GMT for those of you in the Eastern Hemisphere. Be's support phone numbers can be found on our Web site at *http://www.be.com/support*.

CHAPTER ONE

Introduction

Introduction

This book tells you how to use the BeOS to play sounds, draw in 3D, talk to the net, build a kernel device driver—in other words, it describes parts of the OS that are more narrowly focused than the material in the first Be book, the *Be Developer's Guide*. To understand this book, you'll need to be aware of many of the fundamental concepts (and C++ classes) introduced in the first book. For example, if you simply want to put a window on the screen, you have to look in the first book. But if you want to stream live video into that window, you would then augment your fundamental window knowledge by looking in Chapter 7 of this book ("The Game Kit").

The descriptions in this book correspond to BeOS Release 3 for Intel and PPC. The rest of the chapters in this book are:

- *Chapter 2: The Network Kit.* How to connect to the network, find out who else is connected, and send and receive data.

- *Chapter 3: The Mail Kit.* How to talk to the Be mail daemon, setup mail accounts, and how to use the BMailMessage class to compose and send mail.

- *Chapter 4: The Translation Kit.* How to convert data of particular media (bitmaps, sounds, etc.) from one format to another. This kit really deserves to be among the fundamental software described in the *Be's Developer Guide*—except it didn't exist when that book was written.

- *Chapter 5: The Media Kit.* How to record and playback sounds (despite the name, the Media Kit only handles sound). Be aware that BeOS Release 4 will include a new kit (which handles video as well as sound) that will replace the Media Kit described here. However, the present Media Kit will continue to be supported.

- *Chapter 6: The Midi Kit.* How to read, store, and play MIDI data. The Midi Kit includes a General MIDI software synthesizer designed by the philosopher kings at Headspace Inc.

- *Chapter 7: The Game Kit.* Not just for games, the Game Kit shows you how to take over the entire screen, and how to stream video into a window.

- *Chapter 8: The OpenGL Kit.* This is an interface to our implementation of the OpenGL language. Note that the Kit won't teach you OpenGL, nor does it make the language any easier. It's designed, primarily, to let you port existing OpenGL code with a minimum of fuss.

- *Chapter 9: The Device Kit.* Software that controls hardware. Specifically, serial ports, joysticks, and the GeekPort. The last of these is for BeBox owners only.

- *Chapter 10: Playing with Tracker.* The Tracker is the filing cabinet for the BeOS. It shows you what disks are mounted, lets you open folders, lets you query for files, and so on. Here we show you how to add your own file-processing gizmos to the Tracker, and how to drive the Tracker through the use of scripts.

- *Chapter 11: Graphics Card Drivers.* How to write a graphics card driver. Fun.

- *Chapter 12: Device Drivers.* How to write a kernel-loaded driver that can talk to an external piece of hardware. Even more fun—although scheduled to be replaced by new driver API in BeOS Release 4.

- *Chapter 13: Network Add-ons.* The Network Kit is way up there...what's this thing down here? A network add-on is a piece of software that's loaded and run by the BeOS Network Server. To add support for a new network device or protocol to the BeOS, you have to create and install an appropriate network add-on.

Conventions

This section looks at the typography and naming conventions used in this book

Typography

Individual API elements are presented in a distinct font—for example, `system_time()`, `be_synth`, and `B_STRING_TYPE`. The only exceptions are class names, which appear in the same font as surrounding text—for example, BDirectWindow and BMidiSynth.

Each component of a more complicated syntax is given in a different font style. For example:

```
virtual status_t Invoke(BMessage *message = NULL)
typedef char font_family[B_FONT_FAMILY_LENGTH + 1]
```

Four different fonts are used:

- The API element being defined is bold—for example, **Invoke()** and **font_family**.

- The names of other API elements that enter into the definition (such as default arguments) are in a less bold version of the API font—for example, NULL and B_FONT_FAMILY_LENGTH.

- The names of parameters are italic—for example, *message*.

- Data types are in plain (roman) text—status_t, BMessage, and char in the examples above—as are other keywords like typedef and virtual.

Naming Conventions

All our class names begin with the prefix "B". The rest of the name is in mixed case; for example:

```
BTextView

BFile

BDACStream

BMessageQueue

BScrollBar

BList
```

The simplest thing you can do to prevent namespace collisions is to refrain from putting the "B" prefix on class names you invent.

Other names associated with a class—the names of data members and member functions—are also in mixed case. The names of member functions begin with an uppercase letter—for example, `AddResource()` and `UpdateIfNeeded()`. The names of data members begin with a lowercase letter (`what` and `bottom`). Member names are in a protected namespace and won't clash with the names you assign in your own code; they therefore don't have—or need—a "B" prefix.

All other names in the Be API are single case—either all uppercase or all lowercase—and use underbars to mark where separate words are joined into a single name.

The names of constants are all uppercase and begin with the prefix "B_". For example:

```
B_LONG_TYPE

B_OP_OVER

B_PULSE
```

The only exceptions are common constants not specific to the Be operating system. For example:

```
true
false
NULL
```

All other names—global variables, macros, nonmember functions, members of structures, and defined types—are all lowercase. Global variables generally begin with "be_",

```
be_app
be_roster
be_clipboard
```

but other names lack a prefix. They're distinguished only by being lowercase. For example:

```
rgb_color
system_time()
app_info
```

To summarize:

Category	Prefix	Spelling
Class names	B	Mixed case
Member functions	*none*	Mixed case, beginning with an uppercase letter
Data members	*none*	Mixed case, beginning with a lowercase letter
Constants	B_	All uppercase
Global variables	be_	All lowercase
Everything else	*none*	All lowercase

Occasionally, private names are visible in public header files. These names are marked with prefixed underbars, and often postfixed ones as well—for example, _pthread_ and _remove_volume_(). Don't rely on these names in the code you write. They're neither documented nor supported, and may change or disappear in the next release.

An underbar prefix is also used for kit-internal names that may intrude on an application's namespace, even though they don't show up in a header file. For example, the kits use some behind-the-scenes threads and give them names like "_pulse_task_" and they may put kit-internal data in public messages under names like "_button_". If you were to assign the same names to your threads and data entries, they might conflict with kit code. Since you can't anticipate every name used internally by the kits, it's best to avoid all names that begin in underbars.

CHAPTER TWO

The Network Kit

CHAPTER TWO

The Network Kit

The Network Kit provides a collection of global C functions that let you communicate with other computers through the TCP and UDP protocols. With a few exceptions, the names, protocols, and intents of these functions adhere to the precedent set by the 4.2BSD network/socket implementation. Note, however, that some BSD-defined functions are not yet implemented.

There are two sections to this chapter:

- "Network Sockets" describes how to create a "socket" onto the network, and how to send and receive data.

- "Network Names, Addresses, and Services" describes the functions you use to look up other machine names and addresses and user account information.

For information on e-mail services, see Chapter 3, "The Mail Kit."

For information on creating and installing your own network device driver, see Chapter 13, "Network Add-ons."

Network Sockets

A socket is an entry onto a network. To transmit data to another machine, you create a socket, tell it how to find the other computer, and then tell it to send. To receive data, you create a socket, tell it who to listen to (in some cases), and then wait for data to come pouring in.

Socket concepts are mixed in with regular function descriptions; the `socket()` function, which is where any socket user must start, is described first. The description gives a general overview of the different types of sockets, how you use them, and where to go to next.

The socket implementation (and philosophy) follows the precedent established by 4.2BSD. In particular, the API presented here bends many of the Be naming and calling conventions in order to make porting existing programs easier.

WARNING

Although the API desribed in this section is very similar to the 4.2BSD sockets implementation, it is *not* 100% compatible, so be aware of the occasional differences when you're porting UNIX code to the BeOS. Many of these differences are called out specifically in this section.

Socket Functions

Declared in: be/net/socket.h

Library: libnet.so

socket(), closesocket()

int **socket**(int *family*, int *type*, int *protocol*)

int **closesocket**(int *socket*)

The `socket()` function returns a token (a non-negative integer) that represents the local end of a connection to another machine (0 is a valid socket token). Freshly returned, the token is abstract and unusable; to put the token to use, you have to pass it as an argument to other functions—such as `bind()` and `connect()`—that know how to establish a connection (however temporary) over the network. (The function's arguments are examined in a separate section, below.)

NOTE

Network Kit socket tokens are *not* file descriptors (this violates the BSD tradition).

`closesocket()` closes a socket's connection (if it's the type of socket that can hold a connection) and frees the resources that have been assigned to the socket. When you're done with the sockets that you've created, you should pass each socket token to `closesocket()`—no socket, no matter how abstract or how you use it, is exempt from the need to be closed. In regard to this universal need, you should be aware that this extends to sockets that are created through the `accept()` function.

`closesocket()` returns a negative value if its argument is invalid.

The socket() Arguments

`socket()`'s three arguments, all of which take predefined constants as values, describe the type of communication the socket can handle:

- *family* takes a constant the describes the network address format that the socket understands. Currently, it must be `AF_INET` (the Internet address format).

- The *type* constant must be either `SOCK_STREAM` or `SOCK_DGRAM`. The constant describes the "persistence" of the connection that can be formed through this socket. The `SOCK_STREAM` constant means the impending connection (which is formed through a `connect()` or `bind()` call) will remain open until told to close. `SOCK_DGRAM` describes a "datagram" socket; the connection through a datagram socket is open while data is being sent (typically through `sendto()`) or received (`recvfrom()`). It's closed at all other times (note, however, that you still have to call `closesocket()` on a datagram socket when you're done with it).

- *protocol* describes the "messaging" protocol, a description that's closely related to the socket type. Although there are three *protocol* constants (`IPPROTO_TCP`, `IPPROTO_UDP`, and `IPPROTO_ICMP`), values that you would actually use are either 0 or, less commonly, `IPPROTO_ICMP`. More specifically, if you set the *type* to be `SOCK_STREAM`, then a *protocol* of 0 automatically sets the messaging protocol to `IPPROTO_TCP`—this is the "natural" messaging protocol for a stream socket. Similarly, `IPPROTO_UDP` is the natural protocol for the `SOCK_DGRAM` type. Note that it's an error to ask for a "udp stream" or a "tcp datagram"—in other words, you can't specify `SOCK_STREAM` with `IPPROTO_UDP`, or `SOCK_DGRAM` with `IPPROTO_TCP`.

As implied by the preceding description, the most typical socket calls are:

```
/* Create a stream TCP socket. */
long tcp_socket = socket(AF_INET, SOCK_STREAM, 0);

/* Create a datagram UDP socket. */
long udp_socket = socket(AF_INET, SOCK_DGRAM, 0);
```

ICMP messages are normally sent through "raw" sockets; however, the Network Kit doesn't currently support raw sockets, so you should use a datagram socket instead:

```
/* Create a datagram icmp socket. */
long icmp_socket = socket(AF_INET, SOCK_DGRAM, IPPROTO_ICMP);
```

Sorts of Sockets

There are only two socket type constants: `SOCK_STREAM` and `SOCK_DGRAM`. However, if we look at the way sockets are used, we see that there are really five different categories of sockets, as illustrated below.

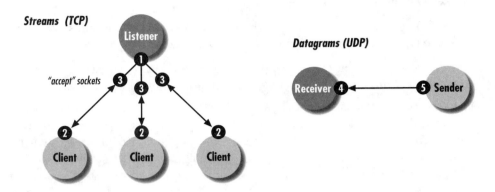

The labelled ovals represent individual computers that are attached to the network. The solid circles represent individual sockets. The numbers near the sockets are keys to the socket categories, which are:

1. **The stream listener socket.** A stream listener socket provides access to a service that's running on the "listener" machine (you might want to think of the machine as a "server.") The listener socket waits for client machines to "call in" and ask to be served. In order to listen for clients, the listener must call `bind()`, which "binds" the socket to an IP address and machine-specific port, and then `listen()`. Thus primed, the socket waits for a client message to show up by sitting in an `accept()` call.

2. **The stream client socket.** A stream client socket asks for service from a server machine by attempting to connect to the server's listener socket. It does this through the `connect()` function. A stream client can be bound (you can call `bind()` on it), but it's not mandatory.

3. **The "accept" socket.** When a stream listener hears a client in an `accept()` call, the function call creates yet another socket called the "accept" socket. Accept sockets are valid sockets, just like those you create through `socket()`. In particular, you have to remember to close accept sockets (through `closesocket()`) just as you would the sockets you explicitly create. Note that you can't bind an accept socket—the socket is bound automatically by the system.

4. **The datagram receiver socket.** A datagram receiver socket is sort of like a stream listener: It calls `bind()` and waits for "senders" to send messages to it. Unlike the stream listener, the datagram receiver doesn't call `listen()` or `accept()`. Furthermore, when a datagram sender sends a message to the receiver, there's no ancillary socket created to handle the message (there's no UDP analog to the TCP accept socket).

5. **The datagram sender socket**. A datagram sender is the simplest type of socket—all it has to do is identify a datagram receiver and send messages to it, through the `sendto()` function. Binding a datagram sender socket is optional.

Returning to the illustration, notice that the paths connecting the stream socket clients to the stream listener (through the accept sockets) are "double arrow-headed." This indicates that TCP communication is two-way: once the link between a client and the listener has been established (through `bind()`/`listen()`/`accept()` on the listener side, and `connect()` on the client side), the two machines can talk to each other through complementary `send()` and `recv()` calls.

Communication along a UDP path, on the other hand, is one-way, as indicated by the direction of the arrow. The datagram sender can send messages (through `sendto()`), and the datagram receiver can receive them (through `recvfrom()`), but the receiver can't send message back to the sender. However, you can simulate a two-way UDP conversation by binding both sockets. This doesn't change the definition of the UDP path, or the capabilities of the two types of datagram sockets, it simply means that a bound datagram socket can act as a receiver (it can call `recvfrom()`) or as a sender (it can call `sendto()`).

NOTE

To be complete, it should be mentioned that datagram sockets can also invoke `connect()` and then pass messages through `send()` and `recv()`. The datagram use of these functions is a convenience; its advantages are explained in the description of the `sendto()` function.

Return values:
Upon failure, `socket()` returns a negative value and sets `errno` to...
`EAFNOSUPPORT`. *format* was other than `AF_INET`.
`EPROTOTYPE`. *type* and *protocol* mismatch.
`EPROTONOSUPPORT`. Unrecognized *type* or *protocol* value.

bind()

int **bind**(int *socket*, const struct sockaddr *interface, int *size*)

The `bind()` function creates an association between a socket and an "interface," where an interface is a combination of an IP address and a port number. Binding is, primarily, useful for receiving messages: When a message sender (whether it's a stream client or a datagram sender) sends a message, it tags the message with an IP address and a port number. The receiving machine—the machine with the tagged IP address—delivers the message to the socket that's bound to the tagged port.

The necessity of the bind operation depends on the type of socket; referring to the five categories of sockets enumerated in the `socket()` function description (and illustrated in the charming diagram found there), the "do I need to bind?" question is answered thus:

1. **Stream listener sockets must be bound**. Furthermore, after binding a listener socket, you must then call `listen()` and, when a client calls, `accept()`.

2. **Stream client sockets can be bound**, but they don't have to be. If you're going to bind a client socket, you should do so *before* you call `connect()`. The advantages of binding a stream client escape me at the moment. In any case, the client doesn't have to bind to the same port number as the listener—the listener's binding and the client's binding are utterly separate entities (let alone that they are on different machines). However, the client does *connect* to the interface that the listener is bound to.

3. **Stream attach sockets must not be bound**.

4. **Datagram receiver sockets must be bound**.

5. **Datagram sender sockets don't *have* to be bound**...but if you're going to turn around and use the socket as a receiver, then you'll have to bind it.

Once you've bound a socket, you can't unbind it. If you no longer want the socket to be bound to its interface, the only thing you can do is close the socket (`closesocket()`) and start all over again.

Also, a particular interface can be bound by only one socket at a time and a single socket can only bind to one interface at a time. If your socket needs to bind to more than one interface, you need to create more than one socket and bind each one separately. An example of this is given later in this function description.

WARNING

The 1-to-1 binding differs with the BSD socket implementation, which expects a socket to be able to bind to more than one interface. Consider it a bug that will be fixed in a subsequent release.

The bind() Arguments

`bind()`'s first argument is the socket that you're attempting to bind. This is, typically, a socket of type `SOCK_STREAM`. The *interface* argument is the address/port combination (or "interface") to which you're binding the socket. The argument is typed as a `sockaddr` structure, but, in reality, you have to create and pass a `sockaddr_in` structure cast as a `sockaddr`. The `sockaddr_in` structure is defined as:

```
struct sockaddr_in {
    unsigned short sin_family;
    unsigned short sin_port;
```

```
    struct in_addr sin_addr;
    char sin_zero[4];
};
```

- `sin_family` is the same as the address format constant that was used to create the socket (the first argument to `socket()`). Currently, it's always `AF_INET`.

- `sin_port` is the port number that the socket will bind to, given in network byte order. Valid port numbers are between 1 and 65535; numbers up to 1024 are reserved for services such as *ftp* and *telnet*. If you're not implementing a standard service, you should choose a port number greater than 1024. The actual value of the port number is meaningless, but keep in mind that the port number must be unique for a particular address; only one socket can be bound to a particular address/port combination.

NOTE

Currently, there's no system-defined mechanism for allowing a client/sender machine to ask a listener/receiver machine for its port numbers. Therefore, when you create a networked application, you either have to hard-code the port numbers or, better yet, provide default port numbers that the user (or a system administrator) can easily change.

- `sin_addr` is an `in_addr` structure that stores, in its `s_addr` field, the IP address of the socket's machine. As always, the address is in network byte order. You can use an address of 0 to tell the binding mechanism to find an address for you. By convention, binding to address 0 (which is conveniently symbolized by the `INADDR_ANY` address) means that you want to bind to *every* address by which your computer is known, including the "loopback" (address 127.0.0.1, or the constant `INADDR_LOOPBACK`).

WARNING

The BeOS does not currently implement global binding. When you bind to `INADDR_ANY`, the `bind()` function binds to the first available interface (where "availability" means the address/port combination is currently unbound). Internet interfaces are considered before the loopback interface. If you want to bind to all interfaces, you have to create a separate socket for each. An example of this is given later.

- `sin_zero` is padding. To be safe, you should fill it with zeros.

The *size* argument is the size, in bytes, of the second argument.

If the `bind()` call is successful, the *interface* argument is set to contain the actual address that was used. If the socket can't be bound, the function returns a negative value, and sets the global `errno` to `EABDF` if the *socket* argument is invalid; for all other errors, `errno` is set to -1.

The following example shows a typical use of the `bind()` function. The example uses the fictitious `gethostaddr()` function that's defined in the description of the `gethostname()` function.

```
struct sockaddr_in sa;
int sock;
long host_addr;

/* Create the socket. */
if ((sock = socket(AF_INET, SOCK_STREAM, 0)) < 0) {
   /* error */
}

/* Set the address format for the imminent bind. */
sa.sin_family = AF_INET;

/* We'll choose an arbitrary port number translated to network byte order. */
sa.sin_port = htons(2125);

/* Get the address of the local machine. If the address can't
 * be found (the function looks it up based on the host name),
 * then we use address INADDR_ANY.
 */
if ((host_addr = (ulong)gethostaddr()) == -1) {
   host_addr = INADDR_ANY;
}
sa.sin_addr.s_addr = host_addr;

/* Clear sin_zero. */
memset(sa.sin_zero, 0, sizeof(sa.sin_zero));

/* Bind the socket. */
if (bind(sock, (struct sockaddr *)&sa, sizeof(sa)) < 0) {
   /* error */
}
```

As mentioned earlier, the bind-to-all-interfaces convention (by asking to bind to address 0) isn't currently implemented. Thus, if the `gethostaddr()` call fails in the example, the socket will be bound to the first address by which the local computer is known.

But let's say that you really do want to bind to all interfaces. To do this, you have to create separate sockets for each interface, then call `bind()` on each one. In the example below we create a series of sockets and then bind each one to an interface that specifies address 0. In doing this, we depend on the "first *available* interface" rule to find the next interface for us. Keep in mind that a successful `bind()` rewrites the contents of the `sockaddr` argument (most importantly, it resets the 0 address component). Thus, we have to reinitialize the structure each time through the loop:

```
/* Declare an array of sockets. */
#define MAXSOCKETS
```

```
int socks[MAXSOCKETS];
int sockN;
int bind_res;

struct sockaddr_in sock_addr;

for (sockN = 0; sockN < MAXSOCKETS; sockN++)
{
    (socks[sockN] = socket(AF_INET, SOCK_STREAM, 0));
    if (socks[sktr] < 0) {
        perror("socket");
        goto sock_error;
    }

    /* Initialize the structure. */
    sa.sin_family = AF_INET;
    sa.sin_port = htonl(2125);
    sa.sin_addr.s_addr = 0;
    memset(sa.sin_zero,0,sizeof(sa.sin_zero));

    bind_res = bind(socks[sockN],
                (struct sockaddr *)&sa,
                sizeof(sa));

    /* A bind error means we've run out of addresses. */
    if (bind_res < 0) {
        closesocket(socks[sockN--]);
        break;
    }
}

/* Use the bound socket (listen, accept, recv/send). */
...

sock_error:
    for (;sockN >=0; sockN--)
        closesocket(socks[sockN]);
```

To ask a socket about the address and port to which it is bound you use the getsockname() function, described later in this section.

Return values:
   Upon failure, bind() returns a negative value and sets errno to...
   EABDF. The *socket* argument is invalid.
   B_ERROR. All other errors.

connect()

   int **connect**(int *socket*, const struct sockaddr **remote_interface*, int *remote_size*)

The meaning of the connect() function depends on the type of socket that's passed as the first argument:

- If it's a stream client, then `connect()` attempts to form a connection to the socket that's specified by *remote_interface*. The remote socket must be a bound stream listener. A client socket can only be connected to one listener at a time. Note that you can't call `connect()` on a stream listener.

- If it's a datagram socket (either a sender or a receiver), `connect()` simply caches the *remote_interface* information in anticipation of subsequent `send()` and `recv()` calls. By using `connect()`, a datagram avoids the fuss of filling in the remote information that's needed by the "normal" datagram message functions, `sendto()` and `recvfrom()`. Note that a datagram may only call `send()` and `recv()` if it has first called `connect()`.

The *remote_interface* argument is a pointer to a `sockaddr_in` structure cast as a `sockaddr` pointer. The *remote_size* value gives the size of *remote_interface*. See the `bind()` function for a description of the `sockaddr_in` structure.

Currently, you can't disconnect a connected socket. If you want to connect to a different listener, or reset a datagram's interface information, you have to close the socket and start over.

When you attempt to `connect()` a stream client, the listener must respond with an `accept()` call. Having gone through this dance, the two sockets can then pass messages to each other through complementary `send()` and `recv()` calls. If the listener doesn't respond immediately to a client's attempt to connect, the client's `connect()` call will block. If the listener doesn't respond within (about) a minute, the connection will time out. If the listener's acceptance queue is full, the client will be refused and `connect()` will return immediately.

If the socket is in no-block mode (as set through `setsockopt()`), and blocking would occur otherwise, connect() returns immediately with a result of `EWOULDBLOCK`.

Return values:
Upon failure, `connect()` returns a negative number and sets `errno` to...
`EWOULDBLOCK`. The connection attempt would block.
`EISCONN`. The socket is already connected.
`ECONNREFUSED`. The listener rejected the connection.
`ETIMEDOUT`. The connection attempt timed out.
`ENETUNREACH`. The client can't get to the network.
`EBADF`. The *socket* argument is invalid.
`B_ERROR`. All other errors.

getpeername(), getsockname()

int **getpeername**(int *socket*, struct sockaddr **interface*, int **size*)

int **getsockname**(int *socket*, struct sockaddr **interface*, int **size*) `getpeername()` returns, in the structure pointed to by the *interface* parameter, a `sockaddr_in` structure that describes the remote interface to which the *socket* is connected.

`getsockname()` returns, by reference in *interface*, a `sockaddr_in` structure that contains the interface information for the bound socket given by *socket*.

In both cases, the **size* argument gives the size of the *interface* structure; **size* is reset, on the way out, to the size of the interface argument as it's passed back. Note that the `sockaddr_in` pointer that you pass as the second argument must be cast as a pointer to a `sockaddr` structure:

```
struct sockaddr_in interface;
int size = sizeof(interface);

/* We'll assume "sock" is a valid socket token. */
if (getsockname(sock, (struct sockaddr*)&interface, &size) < 0)
   /* error */
```

Return values:

Upon failure, `getsockname()` and `getpeername()` return negative numbers and set `errno` to...

EINVAL. The **size* value (going in) wasn't big enough.

EBADF. The *socket* argument is invalid.

B_ERROR. All other errors.

listen(), accept()

int **listen**(int *socket*, int *acceptance_count*)

int **accept**(int *socket*, struct sockaddr **client_interface*, int **client_size*)

After you've bound a stream listener socket to an interface (through `bind()`), you then tell the socket to start "listening" for clients that are trying to connect. You then pass the socket to `accept()`; this function blocks until a client connects to the listener (the client does this by calling `connect()`, passing it a description of the interface to which the listener is bound).

When `accept()` returns, the value that it returns directly is a new socket token; this socket token represents an "accept" socket that was created as a proxy (on the local machine) for the client. To receive a message from the client, or to send a message to the client, the listener must pass the accept socket to the respective stream messaging functions, `recv()` and `send()`.

A listener only needs to invoke `listen()` once; however, it can accept more than one client at a time. Often, a listener will spawn an "accept" thread that loops over the `accept()` call.

NOTE

Only stream listeners need to invoke `listen()` and `accept()`. None of the other socket types (enumerated in the `socket()` description) needs to call these functions.

`listen()` takes two arguments: The first is the socket that you want to have start listening. The second is the length of the listener's "acceptance count." This is the number of clients that the listener is willing to accept at a time. If too many clients try to connect at the same time, the excess clients will be refused—the connection isn't automatically retried later.

After the listener starts listening, it must process the client connections within a certain amount of time, or the connection attempts will time out.

If `listen()` succeeds, the function returns 0; otherwise it returns a negative result and sets the global `errno` to a descriptive constant. Currently, the only `errno` value that `listen()` uses, other than -1, is `EBADF`, which means the socket argument is invalid.

The arguments to `accept()` are the socket token of the listener (*socket*), a pointer to a `sockaddr_in` structure cast as a `sockaddr` structure (*client_interface*), and a pointer to an integer that gives the size of the *client_interface* argument (*client_size*).

The *client_interface* structure returns interface information (IP address and port number) of the client that's attempting to connect. See the `bind()` function for an examination of the `sockaddr_in` structure.

The *client_size* argument is reset to give the size of *client_interface* as it's passed back by the function.

The value that `accept()` returns directly is a token that represents the accept socket. After checking the token value (where a negative result indicates an error), you must cache the token so you can use it in subsequent `send()` and `recv()` calls.

When you're done talking to the client, remember to call `closesocket()` on the accept socket that `accept()` returned. This frees a slot in the listener's acceptance queue, allowing a possibly frustrated client to connect to the listener.

Return values:
Upon failure, `listen()` and `accept()` return negative numbers and set `errno` to...
`EBADF`. The *socket* argument is invalid.
`EINVAL`. (`accept()` only) The listener socket isn't bound.
`EWOULDBLOCK`. (`accept()` only) The acceptance queue is full.
`B_ERROR`. All other errors.

select()

> int **select**(int *socket_range*, struct fd_set **read_bits*, struct fd_set **write_bits*,
> struct fd_set **exception_bits*, struct timeval **timeout*)

The `select()` function returns information about selected sockets. The *socket_range* argument tells the function how many sockets to check: It checks socket numbers up to (*socket_range* - 1). Traditionally, the *socket_range* argument is set to 32.

The `fd_set` structure that types the next three arguments is a 32-bit mask that encodes the sockets that you're interested in; this refines the range of sockets that was specified in the first argument. You should use the `FD_OP()` macros to manipulate the structures that you pass in:

- `FD_ZERO`(*set*) clears the mask given by *set*.
- `FD_SET`(*socket*, *set*) adds a socket to the mask.
- `FD_CLEAR`(*socket*, *set*) clears a socket from the mask.
- `FD_ISSET`(*socket*, *set*) returns non-zero if the given socket is already in the mask.

The function passes socket information back to you by resetting the three `fd_set` arguments. The arguments themselves represent the types of information that you can check:

- *read_bits* tells you if a socket is "ready to read." In other words, it tells you if a socket has an in-coming message waiting to be read.
- *write_bits* tells you if a socket is "ready to write."
- *exception_bits* tells you if there's an exception pending on the socket.

WARNING

Currently, only *read_bits* is implemented. You should pass `NULL` as the *write_bits* and *exception_bits* arguments.

`select()` doesn't return until at least one of the `fd_set`-specified sockets is ready for one of the requested operations. To avoid blocking forever, you can provide a time limit in the final argument, passed as a `timeval` structure.

In the following example, we check if a given datagram socket has a message waiting to be read. The `select()` times out after two seconds:

```
bool can_read_datagram(int socket)
{
    struct timeval tv;
    struct fd_set fds;
    int n;
```

```
    tv.tv_sec = 2;
    tv.tv_usec = 0;

    /* Initialize (clear) the socket mask. */
    FD_ZERO(&fds);

    /* Set the socket in the mask. */
    FD_SET(socket, &fds);
    select(s + 1, &fds, NULL, NULL, &tv);

    /* If the socket is still set, then it's ready to read. */
    return FD_ISSET(socket, &fds);
}
```

Return values:

If `select()` fails, it returns -1; if the function times out, it returns 0. Otherwise (i.e. if *any* of the selected sockets was found to be ready) it returns 1.

send(), recv()

ssize_t **send**(int *socket*, const void **buf*, size_t *size*, int *flags*)

ssize_t **recv**(int *socket*, void **buf*, size_t *size*, int *flags*)

These functions are used to send data to a remote socket, and to receive data that was sent by a remote socket. `send()` and `recv()` calls must be complementary: after socket A sends to socket B, socket B needs to call `recv()` to pick up the data that A sent. `send()` sends its data and returns immediately. `recv()` will block until it has some data to return.

The `send()` and `recv()` functions can be called by stream or datagram sockets. However, there are some differences between the way the functions work when used by these two types of socket:

- For a stream listener and a stream client to transmit messages, the listener must have previously called `bind()`, `listen()`, `accept()`, and the client must have called `connect()`. Having been properly connected, the two sockets can send and receive as if they were peers.

  For stream sockets, `send()` and `recv()` can both block: `send()` blocks if the amount of data that's sent overwhelms the receiver's ability to read it, and `recv()` blocks if there's no message waiting to be read. You can tell these functions to be non-blocking by setting the sending socket's no-block socket option (see `setsockopt()`).

- If you want to call `send()` or `recv()` through a datagram socket, you must first `connect()` the socket. In addition, a receiving datagram socket must also be bound to an interface (through `bind()`). See the `connect()` description for more information on what that function means to a datagram socket.

Datagram sockets never block on `send()`, but they can block in a `recv()` call. As with stream sockets, you can set a datagram socket to be non-blocking (for the `recv()`, as well as for `recvfrom()`) through `setsockopt()`.

The Arguments

The arguments to `send()` and `recv()` are:

- *socket* is, for datagrams and stream client sockets, the local socket token. In other words, when a datagram or stream client wants to send or receive data, it passes its own socket token as the first argument. The recipient of a `send()`, or the sender of a `recv()` is, for these sockets, already known: It's the socket that's identified by the previous `connect()` call.

  For a stream listener, *socket* is the "accept socket" that was previously returned by an `accept()` call. A stream listener can send and receive data from more than one client at the same time (or, at least, in rapid succession).

- *buf* is a pointer to the data that's being sent, or is used to hold a copy of the data that was received.

- *size* is the allocated size of *buf*, in bytes.

- *flags* is currently unused. For now, set it to 0.

Return values:

A successful `send()` returns the number of bytes that were sent; a successful `recv()` returns the number of bytes that were received. Upon failure, the functions return negative numbers and set `errno` to...

EWOULDBLOCK. The call would block on a non-blocking socket.

EINTR. The local socket was interrupted.

ECONNRESET. The remote socket disappeared (`send()` only).

ENOTCONN. The socket isn't connected.

EBADF. The *socket* argument is invalid.

EADDRINUSE. The interface is busy (datagram sockets only).

B_ERROR. All other errors.

sendto(), recvfrom()

ssize_t **sendto**(int *socket*, const void **buf*, size_t *size*, int *flags*,
            struct sockaddr **to*, int *toLen*)

ssize_t **recvfrom**(int *socket*, const void **buf*, size_t *size*, int *flags*,
            struct sockaddr **from*, int **fromLen*)

These functions are used by datagram sockets (only) to send and receive messages. The functions encode all the information that's needed to find the recipient or the sender of the desired message, so you don't need to call `connect()` before invoking these functions. However, a datagram socket that wants to receive messages must first call `bind()` (in order to fix itself to an interface that can be specified in a remote socket's `sendto()` call).

The four initial arguments to these function are similar to those for `send()` and `recv()`; the additional arguments are the interface specifications:

- For `sendto()`, the *to* argument is a `sockaddr_in` structure pointer (cast as a pointer to a `sockaddr` structure) that specifies the interface of the remote socket that you're sending to. The *toLen* argument is the size of the *to* argument.

- For `recvfrom()`, the *from* argument returns the interface for the remote socket that sent the message that `recvfrom()` received. *fromLen* is set to the size of the *from* structure. As always, the interface structure is a `sockaddr_in` cast as a pointer to a `sockaddr`.

`sendto()` never blocks. `recvfrom()`, on the other hand, will block until a message arrives, unless you set the socket to be non-blocking through the `setsockopt()` function.

You can broadcast a message to all interfaces that can be found by setting `sendto()`'s target address to `INADDR_BROADCAST`.

As an alternative to these functions, you can call `connect()` on a datagram socket and then call `send()` and `recv()`. The `connect()` call caches the interface information provided in its arguments, and uses this information the subsequent `send()` and `recv()` calls to "fake" the analogous `sendto()` and `recvfrom()` invocations. For sending, the implication is obvious: The target of the `send()` is the interface supplied in the `connect()`. The implication for receiving bears description: when you `connect()` and then call `recv()` on a datagram socket, the socket will only accept messages from the interface given in the `connect()` call.

You can mix `sendto()`/`recvfrom()` calls with `send()`/`recv()`. In other words, connecting a datagram socket doesn't prevent you from calling `sendto()` and `recvfrom()`.

Return values:
  A successful `sendto()` returns the number of bytes that were sent; a successful `recvfrom()` returns the number of bytes that were received. Upon failure, the functions return negative numbers and set `errno` to...
  EWOULDBLOCK. The call would block on a non-blocking socket.
  EINTR. The local socket was interrupted.
  EBADF. The *socket* argument is invalid.
  EADDRNOTAVAIL. The specified interface is unrecognized.
  B_ERROR. All other errors.

setsockopt()

int **setsockopt**(int *socket*, int *level*, int *option*, const void **data*, uint *size*)

`setsockopt()` lets you set certain options that are associated with a socket. Currently, the Network Kit only recognizes one option: It lets you declare a socket to be blocking or non-blocking. A blocking socket will block in a `recv()` or `recvfrom()` call if there's no data to retrieve.

A blocking socket will block in a `send()` or `sendto()` call if the send would overrun the network's ability to keep up with the data.

A non-blocking socket returns immediately, even if it comes back empty-handed or is unable to send the data.

The function's arguments are:

- *socket* is the socket that you're attempting to affect.
- *level* is a constant that indicates where the option is enforced. Currently, *level* should always be `SOL_SOCKET`.
- *option* is a constant that represents the option you're interested in. The only option constant that does anything right now is `SO_NONBLOCK`. (Two other constants—`SO_REUSEADDR` and `SO_DEBUG`—are recognized, but they aren't currently implemented.)
- *data* points to a buffer that's used to toggle or otherwise inform the option. For the `SO_NONBLOCK` option (and other boolean options), you fill the buffer with zeroes if you want to turn the option off (the socket will block), and non-zeros if you want to turn it on (the socket won't block). In the case of a boolean option, a single byte of zero/non-zero will do.
- *size* is the size of the *data* buffer.

Return values:

Upon failure, `setsockopt()` returns a negative number and sets `errno` to...
`EINTR`. The local socket was interrupted.
`EBADF`. The *socket* argument is invalid.
`ENOPROTOOPT`. Unknown *option*.

Network Names, Addresses, and Services

The functions described below let you look up the names, addresses, and other information about the computers and services that the local computer knows about, and let you retrieve information about the current user's account. Also defined here are functions that perform *Internet Protocol* (IP) address format conversion.

You use the functions defined here to find the information you need so you can form a connection to some other machine. Connecting to other machines is described in "Network Sockets".

Terms and Tools

Throughout the following function descriptions, an *IP address* is the familiar four-byte, dot-separated numeric identifier. For example,

192.0.0.1

The bytes in a multi-byte address are always given in *network byte order* (big-endian). You should always run your addresses through the appropriate host/network conversion. See the group of functions with the obsessively shortened names (`ntohs()`, `htohl()`, etc.) for more information on such transformations.

An *IP name* is the two-or-three-element "[machine.]domain.extension" case-insensitive text name. For example:

- be.com
- decca.be.com

The two most important functions described below, `gethostbyname()` and `gethostbyaddr()`, retrieve information about computers ("hosts") that can be reached through the network. Host information is typically (and primarily) gotten from the *Domain Name Server* (DNS), a service that's usually provided by a server computer that's responsible for tasks such as mail distribution and direct communication with the *Internet Service Provider* (ISP).

You can also provide host information by adding to your computer's */boot/beos/etc/hosts* file. This is a text file that contains the IP addresses and names of the hosts that you want your computer to know about. Each entry in the file lists, in order on a single line, a host's IP address, IP name, and other names (aliases) by which it's also known. For example:

```
# Example /boot/beos/etc/hosts entries
192.0.0.1 phaedo.racine.com fido phydough
204.123.5.12 playdo.mess.com plywood funfactory
```

The amount of whitespace separating the elements is arbitrary. The only killing point is that there mustn't be any leading whitespace before the IP address.

If you're connected to DNS, then you shouldn't need the *hosts* file. If you're not connected to a network at all, the only way to get information about other machines is through the *hosts* file, but it won't do you much good—you won't be able to use the information to connect to other machines. The archetypal situation in which the *hosts* file becomes useful is if your computer is connected to some other machine that's supposed to be connected to a DNS machine, but this latter connection is down (or the DNS machine isn't running). If you have an entry in your *hosts* file that identifies the other machine, you'll still be able to look up the machine's address and connect to it, despite the absence of DNS.

Functions

Declared in: be/net/netdb.h

Library: libnet.so

gethostbyname(), gethostbyaddr(), herror()

    struct hostent *gethostbyname(const char *name)
    struct hostent *gethostbyaddr(const char *address, int length, int type)

    void herror(const char *string)

The gethostbyname() and gethostbyaddr() functions retrieve information about a particular host machine, stuff the information into a global "host entry" structure, and then return a pointer to that structure. To get this information, the functions talks to the Domain Name Server. If DNS doesn't respond or doesn't know the desired host, the functions then look for an entry in the file */boot/beos/system/etc/hosts*. See "Terms and Tools" for more information on DNS and the *hosts* file.

herror() generates a human-readable message that describes the most recent gethostby...() error, and prints it to standard error.

NOTE

Because gethostbyname() and gethostbyaddr() use a global structure to return information, the functions are *not* thread safe.

The gethostbyname() Function

gethostbyname()'s *name* argument is a NULL-terminated, case-insensitive host name that must be no longer than MAXHOSTNAMELEN (64) characters (not counting the NULL). The name can be:

- An entire "machine.domain.extension" IP name—"mybox.me.com", for example.

- Just the machine name portion—"mybox" (DNS only). In this case, the domain and extension of the local machine are automatically appended. (If you're looking up an IP name in the *hosts* file, the domain and extension *aren't* appended for you.)

- A host name alias. Aliases are alternate names by which a host is known. Your DNS should provide a means for declaring aliases; you can also declare them in your *hosts* file.

The gethostbyaddr() Function

`gethostbyaddr()`'s *address* argument is a pointer to a complete IP address given in its natural format (but cast to a `char *`; note that the argument's type declaration doesn't mean that the function wants the address converted to a string). *length* is the length of *address* in bytes; *type* is a constant that gives the format of the address.

For IP format, the first argument is a four-byte integer, *length* is always 4, and type is `AF_INET` ("Address Format: InterNET"). The following gets the `hostent` for a hard-coded address:

```
/* This is the hex equivalent of 192.0.0.1
ulong addr = 0xc0000001;
struct hostent *theHost;
theHost = gethostbyaddr((const char *)&addr, 4, AF_INET);
```

If you have an address stored as a string, you can use the `inet_addr()` function to convert it to an integer:

```
ulong addr = inet_addr("192.0.0.1");
struct hostent *theHost;
theHost = gethostbyaddr((const char *)&addr, 4, AF_INET);
```

The hostent Structure

If a `gethostby...()` function fails, it returns `NULL`; otherwise, it returns a pointer to a global `hostent` structure. The `hostent` structure (which isn't `typedef`'d) looks like this:

```
struct hostent
   char *h_name;
   char **h_aliases;
   int h_addrtype;
   int h_length;
   char **h_addr_list;
};
```

The fields are:

- `h_name` is the IP name of the host (or the "official" name given in the *hosts* file).

- `h_aliases` is a `NULL`-terminated array of other names by which the host is known. These names aren't necessarily in IP name format; typically, they're single-word names.

- `h_addrtype` identifies the format of the addresses listed in `h_addr_list`. Currently, the type is always `AF_INET`.

- **h_length** is the length, in bytes, of the host's address. In **AF_INET** format, the address is four bytes long

- **h_addr_list** is a **NULL**-terminated array of pointers to the addresses by which the host is known. Host addresses are given in network byte order.

As a convenience, the global **h_addr** constant is a fake field that points to the first item in the **h_addr_list** field. Keep in mind that **h_addr** must be treated as a structure field—it must point off a **hostent** structure. Also, make sure you dereference the **h_addr** "field" properly. For example:

```
ulong ip_address;
struct hostent *theHost;

theHost = gethostbyname("fido");
ip_address = *(ulong *)theHost->h_addr;
```

As a demonstration of the **h_addr** definition, the final line is the same as

```
ip_address = *(ulong *)theHost->h_addr_list[0];
```

Keep in mind that the hostent structure that's pointed to by the **gethostby...()** functions is global to your application's address space. If you want to cache the structure, you should copy it as soon as it's returned to you.

h_errno and the herror() Function

The host look-up functions use a global error variable (an integer), called **h_errno**, to register errors. You can look at the **h_errno** value directly in your code after a host function fails (the potential **h_errno** values are listed below). Alternatively, you can use the **herror()** function which prints, to standard error, its argument followed by a system-generated string that describes the current state of **h_errno**.

The values that **h_errno** can take, and the corresponding **herror()** messages, are:

Value	Message
HOST_NOT_FOUND	"unknown host name"
TRY_AGAIN	"host name server busy"
NO_RECOVERY	"unrecoverable system error"
NO_DATA	"no address data is available for this host name"
anything else	"unknown error"

Note that while **h_errno** is set when something goes wrong, it isn't cleared if all is well. For example, if **gethostbyname()** can't find the named host, **h_errno** is set to **HOST_NOT_FOUND** and the function returns **NULL**. If, in an immediately subsequent call, the function succeeds, a pointer to a valid **hostent** is returned, but **h_errno** will *still* report **HOST_NOT_FOUND**.

The moral of this tale is that you should only check **h_errno** (or call `herror()`) if the network function call has failed, or clear it yourself before each `gethostby...()` call. Or both:

```
struct hostent *host_ent;

h_errno = 0;
if ( !(host_ent = gethostbyname("a.b.c")) {
   herror("Error");
}
```

Furthermore, **h_errno** might be legitimately set to a new error code even if the `gethostby...()` function succeeds. For example, if DNS can't be reached but the desired host is found in the *hosts* file, **h_errno** will be set to **TRY_AGAIN**, yet the returned **hostent** will be legitimate (it won't be **NULL**).

Be aware that **TRY_AGAIN** is used as a blanket "DNS doesn't know" state, regardless of the reason why. In other words, **h_errno** is set to **TRY_AGAIN** if DNS is actually down, if your machine isn't connected to the network, or if DNS simply doesn't know the requested host. You can use this fact to tell whether a (successful) look-up was performed through DNS or the *hosts* file:

```
struct hostent *host_ent;

h_errno = 0;
if ( !(host_ent = gethostbyname("a.b.c")) {
   herror("Error");
}
else {
   if (h_errno == TRY_AGAIN)
      /* The hosts file was used. */
   else
      /* DNS was used. */
}
```

Keep in mind that **h_errno** is global; be careful if you're using it in a multi-threaded program.

gethostname(), getusername(), getpassword()

> int **gethostname**(char *name*, uint *length*)
> int **getusername**(char *name*, uint *length*)
> int **getpassword**(char *password*, uint *length*)

These functions retrieve, and copy into their first arguments, the name of the local computer, the name of the current user, and the current user's encoded password, respectively. In all three cases, *length* gives the maximum number of characters that the functions should copy. If the length of the desired element is less than *length*, the copied string will be **NULL**-terminated.

The functions return the number of characters that were actually copied (not counting the NULL terminator). If there's an error—and such should be rare—the gethostname() and getusername() functions return 0 and point their respective name arguments to NULL. getpassword(), sensing an error, copies "*" into the password argument and returns -1 (thus you can tell the difference between a NULL password—which would legitimately return 0—and an error).

All three bits of information (host name, user name, and password) are taken from the settings that are declared through the Network preferences application.

A typical use of gethostname() is to follow the call with gethostbyname() in order to retrieve the address of the local host, as shown below:

```
/* To fill a need, we invent the gethostaddr() function. */
long gethostaddr(void) {
   struct hostent *host_ent;
   char host_name[MAXHOSTNAMELEN];

   if (gethostname(host_name, MAXHOSTNAMELEN) == 0) {
      return -1;
   }

   if ((host_ent = gethostbyname(host_name)) == NULL) {
      return -1;
   }

   return *(long *)host_ent.h_addr;
}
```

Keep in mind that since host name information is taken from Network preferences, there's no guarantee that the name that's returned by gethostname() will match an entry that DNS or the *hosts* file knows about.

getservbyname()

struct servent *getservbyname(const char *name, const char *protocol)

You pass in the name of a service (such as "ftp") that runs under a particular protocol (such as "tcp"), and getservbyname() returns a pointer to a servent structure that describes the service.

The servent structure is:

```
struct servent {
   char *s_name;
   char **s_aliases;
   int s_port;
   char *s_proto;
};
```

- `s_name` is the name of the service.

- `s_aliases` is a NULL-terminated array of other names by which the services is known.

- `s_port` is the port number on which the service runs (given in network byte order).

- `s_proto` names the protocol ("tcp", "udp", etc.) that supports the service.

Currently, the function recognizes only two services: "ftp" and "telnet". Both run under the "tcp" protocol; thus, the only valid calls to `getservbyname()` are:

```
getservbyname("ftp", "tcp");
```

and

```
getservbyname("telnet", "tcp");
```

Such calls point to (separate) pre-defined `servent` structures that look like this:

Field	ftp structure	telnet structure
s_name	"ftp"	"telnet"
s_aliases	NULL	NULL
s_port	21	23
s_proto	"tcp"	"tcp"

If you ask for a service other than these two, the function returns NULL. Although the two `servent` structures are separate entities, they are both global to your application. In theory, this means the `getservbyname()` function isn't thread-safe. However, since the structures are hard-coded and separate, there's little danger in using them unprotected in a multi-threaded program.

inet_addr(), inet_ntoa()

uint **inet_addr**(const char *addr)
char ***inet_ntoa**(struct in_addr addr)

These functions convert addresses from ASCII to IP format and vice versa. Neither of them consults the DNS or the *hosts* file to perform the conversion—in other words, they perform the conversions without regard for an address' correspondence to an actual machine.

`inet_addr()` converts from ASCII to IP:

```
ulong addr = inet_addr("192.0.0.1");
```

The result of this call (`addr`) would be appropriate as the initial argument to `gethostbyaddr()` (for example). The returned address is in network byte order.

`inet_ntoa()` converts the other way: It takes an IP address and converts it into an ASCII string. Note that the address that you pass in must first be placed in the `s_addr` field of the argument `in_addr` structure (`s_addr` is the structure's only field). For example:

```
in_addr addr;
char addr_buf[16];

addr.s_addr = 0xc0000001;
strcpy(addr_buf, inet_ntoa(addr));
```

Here, `addr_buf` will contain the (NULL-terminated) string "192.0.0.1". `inet_ntoa()` isn't thread-safe; if you want to cache the string that it returns you must copy it, as shown in the example. Given the IP format, the string that `inet_ntoa()` returns is guaranteed to be no more than 16 characters long (four 3-character address components, three dots, and a NULL).

ntohs(), ntohl(), htons(), htonl()

Declared in: be/support/ByteOrder.h

> short **ntohs**(short *val*)
> long **ntohl**(long *val*)
> short **htons**(short *val*)
> long **htonl**(long *val*)

These macros convert values between host and network byte order; `ntohs()` and `ntohl()` convert 16-bit and 32-bit integers from network byte order to host byte order, and `htons()` and `htonl()` convert from host byte order to network byte order.

There are other functions available for converting between big-endian and little-endian form, but these four guarantee that the correct network and host order is used, regardless of the processor for which your application is compiled.

The Mail Kit

The Mail Kit

The Mail Kit, which consists of an interface to the *mail daemon* and the BMailMessage class, provides Internet e-mail messaging services. These services include:

- Configuration of the user's mail accounts.
- Sending messages using the Simple Mail Transfer Protocol (SMTP).
- Receiving messages via the Post Office Protocol (POP).
- Automatic, timed sending and receiving of messages.
- Encoding and decoding base-64 encoded data.

An assortment of global C functions are provided by the Mail Kit to configure the mail daemon and process base-64 data. See "The Mail Daemon" for information on how to use these functions.

Outgoing mail messages are constructed and sent using the BMailMessage class.

Mail Message Files

Every mail message is stored in an individual file with attached attributes that describe the message in detail; you can query the file system to obtain information about the sender, subject, and receiver of the message, among other things. See "Querying Mail Messages" below for more detailed information and an example program.

Every message the user writes is saved in a file until it's sent by the mail daemon (and may or may not be deleted after being sent). Likewise, messages that the mail daemon has retrieved are also stored in files on a local disk.

The process of sending a mail message works something like this:

- The user writes a new mail message and chooses the mail writing program's "Send" option.

- The mail writing program creates a BMailMessage object and configures it based on the user's input by setting the "To," "Subject," and other header fields appropriately, and by storing the message content in the BMailMessage.

- The program then calls the BMailMessage object's Send() function to tell the mail daemon to send the message.

- The mail daemon creates a disk file that contains the message. The message content is stored in the file itself, and attributes are created to contain the "To," "Subject," and other relevant header fields. See "Querying Mail Messages" for more information. The message's status attribute is set to "New".

- The next time the mail daemon's check_for_mail() function is called (either automatically or explicitly), the daemon sends the message via SMTP, then changes the message's status attribute to "Sent". This is done for all mail messages whose status is "New".

After sending outgoing messages, the mail daemon will also check to see if any incoming mail is waiting to be retrieved. If there is, it proceeds something like this:

- The mail daemon fetches the first message from the mail server via POP.

- The daemon creates a new mail message file, and the message is written into the file. The file contains the Internet headers, message content, and all enclosures (if any).

- The mail daemon scans the message and adds attributes to the message file for each of the header fields, as well as a couple of extra attributes. These are described in detail in "Querying Mail Messages" below.

- The daemon continues reading mail messages from the mail server until there aren't any left.

Querying Mail Messages

The Mail Kit takes full advantage of the BeOS attribute and query system. Each message received is parsed by the mail daemon and important information about it is converted into a defined collection of attributes attached to the file. This makes it extremely easy to create applications that search for messages meeting specific parameters. In an example to follow shortly, we'll create a program that lists all unread messages.

Once the mail daemon has received a message and saved it to disk, any application can query the file system to locate messages that meet certain parameters, then read the attributes and message content to present information about that message to the user.

The following attributes are provided by the Mail Kit:

Constant	Attribute Name	Description
B_MAIL_ATTR_NAME	MAIL:name	Name of the mail file.
B_MAIL_ATTR_STATUS	MAIL:status	Message status.
B_MAIL_ATTR_PRIOIRITY	MAIL:priority	"Priority" field value.
B_MAIL_ATTR_TO	MAIL:to	"To" field value.
B_MAIL_ATTR_FROM	MAIL:from	"From" field value.
B_MAIL_ATTR_SUBJECT	MAIL:subject	"Subject" field value.
B_MAIL_ATTR_REPLY	MAIL:reply	"Reply-to" field value.
B_MAIL_ATTR_WHEN	MAIL:when	"When" field value.
B_MAIL_ATTR_FLAGS	MAIL:flags	Message flags.
B_MAIL_ATTR_RECIPIENTS	MAIL:recipients	List of message recipients.
B_MAIL_ATTR_MIME	MAIL:mime	The MIME version used.
B_MAIL_ATTR_HEADER	MAIL:header	Length of the message header.
B_MAIL_ATTR_CONTENT	MAIL:content	Length of the message content.

B_MAIL_ATTR_NAME is a string that identifies the name of the sender.

B_MAIL_ATTR_STATUS is a string that identifies the status of the message. Possible values are:

Status String	Description
"Error"	An error occurred trying to send the message.
"New"	The message has not been read yet.
"Pending"	The message has not been sent yet.
"Read"	The message has been read.
"Sent"	The message has been sent.

B_MAIL_ATTR_PRIORITY is a string that contains the value of the Priority field in the message.

B_MAIL_ATTR_TO, B_MAIL_ATTR_FROM, and B_MAIL_ATTR_REPLY are strings that contain the primary recipient's e-mail address, the sender's e-mail address, and the sender's reply-to address.

B_MAIL_ATTR_SUBJECT is a string containing the subject of the message.

B_MAIL_ATTR_WHEN is a BeOS time field (B_TIME_TYPE) containing the message's "When" field.

B_MAIL_ATTR_FLAGS contains 32-bit integer (int32) flags which can be any combination of the following values:

Flag	Description
B_MAIL_PENDING	Message is waiting to be sent.
B_MAIL_SENT	Message has been sent.
B_MAIL_SAVE	Mail will be saved after being sent.

The B_MAIL_ATTR_FLAGS attribute is BeOS-specific.

B_MAIL_ATTR_RECIPIENTS contains a list of all recipients of the message, but is only valid for outgoing messages (this attribute doesn't exist on incoming messages).

B_MAIL_ATTR_MIME contains a string that defines the version number of the MIME specification used to transmit any enclosures attached to the file. This attribute is only present if the file has one or more enclosures.

B_MAIL_ATTR_HEADER and B_MAIL_ATTR_CONTENT contain the lengths, in bytes, of the header and content portions of the message. They're both int32 type data.

The following attributes are indexed:

```
B_MAIL_ATTR_NAME
B_MAIL_ATTR_STATUS
B_MAIL_ATTR_PRIORITY
B_MAIL_ATTR_TO
B_MAIL_ATTR_FROM
B_MAIL_ATTR_SUBJECT
B_MAIL_ATTR_REPLY
B_MAIL_ATTR_WHEN
B_MAIL_ATTR_FLAGS
```

The headers, the contents of the message, and the enclosures (in base-64 encoded form) can all be found in the file itself and can be read using a BFile object. See "The Storage Kit" in the *Be Developer's Guide* for further information on reading files.

Queries and Mail Messages

Now that you know which attributes are available on mail message files, and which attributes are indexed, you can consider all the clever things you can use them for. Let's look at an example program that, from a Terminal window, lets you see a list of the unread mail you have.

```
void main(void) {
  BQuery query;
  BNode node;
```

```
BVolume vol;
BVolumeRoster vroster;
entry_ref ref;
char buf[256];
int32 message_count = 0;

vroster.GetBootVolume(&vol);
query.SetVolume(&vol);
```

The program begins by establishing needed variables, then using a BVolumeRoster to set the query's search volume to the boot disk. This is covered in more detail in the Storage Kit chapter.

```
if (query.SetPredicate("MAIL:status = New") != B_OK) {
    printf("Error: can't set query predicate.\n");
    return;
}
```

Then the query is configured to search for new mail. New messages can be identified by the B_MAIL_ATTR_STATUS attribute (called "MAIL:status") having a string value of "New". If an error occurs, the program prints an error end returns.

```
if (query.Fetch() != B_OK) {
    printf("Error: new mail query failed.\n");
    return;
}
```

The query is told to fetch. Again, if this fails, an error message is displayed and the program returns.

```
while (query.GetNextRef(&ref) == B_OK) {
    message_count++; // Increment message counter
```

The loop scanning through the fetched new messages begins by incrementing the counter of new messages received.

```
    if (node.SetTo(&ref) != B_OK) {
        printf("Error: error scanning new messages.\n");
        return;
    }
```

Then a BNode is set to reference the message file. If this fails, the program displays an error message and quits.

```
    buf[0] = '\0'; // If error, use empty string
    node.ReadAttr(B_MAIL_ATTR_FROM, B_STRING_TYPE, 0, buf, 255);
    buf[20] = '\0'; // Truncate to 20 characters
    printf("%3d From: %-20s", message_count, buf);
```

The buffer we're using to receive the attribute values is initialized to an empty string, then we call BNode's ReadAttr() function to read the B_MAIL_ATTR_FROM attribute into the buffer. We then truncate the read string to 20 characters for display purposes (to make it fit into the table we're outputting) and print the message number and sender information.

```
        buf[0] = '\0';// If error, use empty string
        node.ReadAttr(B_MAIL_ATTR_SUBJECT, B_STRING_TYPE, 0, buf, 255);
        buf[40] = '\0';// Truncate to 40 characters
        printf("   Sub: %s\n", buf);
    }
```

The buffer is reset to an empty string and the **B_MAIL_ATTR_SUBJECT** attribute is read into it. This string is truncated to 40 characters, then printed.

This loop continues until no more new messages are found; this is detected when **GetNextRef()** returns an error.

```
    if (message_count) {
        printf("%d new messages.\n", message_count);
    }
    else {
        printf("No new messages.\n");
    }
}
```

Finally, the number of new messages is printed. If there aren't any messages, we very politely print "No new messages." rather than "0 new messages," for a little added panache.

This simple example demonstrates how you can use the attributes provided by the Mail Kit to create mail message reading applications. The message body and attachments are stored within the file itself, and can be read using the functions described in the BFile section in the Storage Kit chapter of the *Be Developer's Guide*.

The E-mail File Type

The mail daemon ensures, when it's first launched at system boot time, that the BeOS File Type database includes an entry for e-mail files. E-mail files have the MIME string "text/x-email", which is represented by the constant **B_MAIL_TYPE**.

The E-mail entry in the File Type database includes a list of the attributes on which you can search. You can look up this information using the BMimeType class's **GetAttrInfo()** function:

```
BMimeType mime;
BMessage message;

mime.SetTo(B_MAIL_TYPE);
mime.GetAttrInfo(&message);
```

After running this code, the *message* contains the description of the attributes available on e-mail files. The message has three useful arrays of items:

Message Item	Description
"attr:public_name"	The user-readable name of the attribute.
"attr:name"	The attribute as it's known to attribute-accessing API (defined by the Storage Kit).
"attr:type"	The type of data the attribute contains.

You can examine the items in each of these arrays in the message to get useful information about the attributes you can reference on the e-mail files. For example:

```
printf("Public name: %s\n", FindString("attr:public_name", 1));
printf("Name: %s\n", FindString("attr:name", 1));
```

This code will print the public name and the attribute name of the second attribute registered in the File Type database entry for e-mail files. In the current implementation of the Mail Kit, this would print:

```
Public name: Subject
Name: MAIL:subject
```

The number of (and order of) attributes in the database entry might change in the future—and that's where the File Type database comes in handy. If, a year from now, Be adds more attributes to e-mail files, your File Type database-savvy application won't have to be updated to support them.

At this time, the File Type database has attribute information records for each of the following attributes:

```
B_MAIL_ATTR_NAME
B_MAIL_ATTR_STATUS
B_MAIL_ATTR_PRIORITY
B_MAIL_ATTR_TO
B_MAIL_ATTR_FROM
B_MAIL_ATTR_SUBJECT
B_MAIL_ATTR_REPLY
B_MAIL_ATTR_WHEN
```

You can obtain information on these attributes, their formats, and their user-readable names by looping through the arrays in the message until the BMessage:Find...() function returns NULL or B_BAD_INDEX.

For more information on the BMimeType class and the File Type database, see BMimeType in The Storage Kit.

The Mail Daemon

Declared in: be/mail/E-mail.h

Library: libmail.so

Every computer running the BeOS has a *mail daemon*; this is a local process that's responsible for sending e-mail to and receiving e-mail from a mail server. The mail server that the daemon talks to is a networking application that's either part of your Internet Service Provider's services, or that's running on a local "mail repository" machine.

The functions described in this section tell you how to manage the mail daemon's connection with the mail server—how to tell the daemon which mail server to communicate with, how to tell the mail daemon to send and retrieve e-mail, how to automate mail retrieval, and so forth.

Many of the functions described here are user-accessible through the E-mail preference application. These functions should generally not be used; the settings they control belong to the user, and your application should usually avoid changing the user's settings. The only legitimate reason to use these configuration setting functions is if you want to build your own E-mail preference application.

The other functions, such as `forward_mail()`, `check_for_mail()`, `encode_base64()`, and `decode_base64()`, might be legitimately used by your e-mail program.

The Mail Daemon and the Mail Server

The mail daemon can talk to two different kinds of mail server:

- The *Post Office Protocol* (POP) server manages individual mail accounts. When the BeOS mail daemon wants to retrieve mail that's been sent to a user, it must tell the mail server which POP account it's retrieving mail for.

- The *Simple Mail Transfer Protocol* (SMTP) server manages mail that's being sent out onto the network. Messages sent through an SMTP server will eventually find their way to a POP server to be received by the destination user.

The POP and the SMTP servers are identified by their hosts' names (in other words, the names of the machines on which the servers are running). The mail daemon can only talk to one POP and one SMTP server at a time, but can talk to the two of them simultaneously. Usually—but not always—the POP and SMTP servers reside on the same machine, and so are identified by the same name.

To set the identity of the POP host, you fill in the fields of a `mail_pop_account` structure and pass the structure to the `set_pop_account()` function. As the name of the structure implies, `mail_pop_account` encodes more than just the name of the POP host. It also identifies a specific user's POP mail account; the complete definition of the structure is this:

```
typedef struct
{
   char pop_name[B_MAX_USER_NAME_LENGTH];
   char pop_password[B_MAX_USER_NAME_LENGTH];
   char pop_host[B_MAX_HOST_NAME_LENGTH];
   char real_name[128];
   char reply_to[128];
   int32 days;
   int32 interval;
   int32 begin_time;
   int32 end_time;
} mail_pop_account;
```

The `pop_name`, `pop_password`, and `pop_host` fields in the `mail_pop_account` structure represent the username, password, and POP server host of the e-mail user. The `real_name` is the user's real name, and `reply_to` is the e-mail address to which replies should be sent.

The `days` field can contain any of the following flags to specify which days of the week the mail daemon should automatically check mail for the described account:

Constant	Meaning
B_CHECK_NEVER	Don't automatically check the account's mail.
B_CHECK_WEEKDAYS	Check the mail only on weekdays.
B_CHECK_DAILY	Check the mail every day.
B_CHECK_CONTINUOUSLY	Check continuously every day.

The `interval` specifies how many seconds apart each e-mail retrieval should be, and the `begin_time` and `end_time` specify the time of day (in seconds) that automatic retrieval should begin and end.

The SMTP server can be selected by calling `set_smtp_host()`, passing in a pointer to the SMTP host's name.

Sending and Retrieving Mail

Messages that are retrieved (from the mail server) by the mail daemon are stored as individual files on the user's hard disk, from whence they are plucked and displayed by a mail-reading application (a "mail reader"; Be supplies a simple mail reader called BeMail). Similarly, messages that the user composes (in a mail composition application) and sends are stored as individual files until the mail daemon comes along and passes them on to the mail server.

Sending and retrieving mail is the mail daemon's most important function. Both actions (server-to-database and database-to-server transmission) are performed through the `check_for_mail()` function.

The BMailMessage class provides a convenient means for creating and sending new mail messages; visit the section on that class for further information and a simple example.

Mail that has been retrieved by the mail daemon can be identified and queried using the mail attributes defined by the Mail Kit. By using the BQuery class, you can scan all newly-received mail messages and parse the message file to present each message to the user. For a more in-depth discussion of the mail attributes and how to use them to your benefit, read "Querying Mail Messages".

Other Mail Daemon Features

The other mail structures and functions define the other features that are provided by the mail daemon. These features are:

- **Mail notification.** The `mail_notification` structure (passed through the `set_mail_notification()` function) lets you tell the daemon how you would like it to tap you on the shoulder when it has new mail for you to read. Would you like it to display an alert panel? Squawk at you? Both? This can be configured by the user in the E-mail preference application.

- **Mail forwarding.** The `forward_mail()` function lets you ask the Mail Kit to forward a message to one or more other accounts.

- **Base-64 encoding and decoding.** The `encode_base64()` and `decode_base64()` functions let you easily handle ASCII-encoded file attachments.

Functions

check_for_mail()

    status_t check_for_mail(int32 *incoming_count = NULL)

Sends and retrieves mail. More specifically, this function asks the mail daemon to retrieve incoming messages from the POP server and send any queued outgoing messages to the SMTP server. The number of POP messages that were retrieved are stored in the variable pointed to by incoming_count. If you specify NULL for incoming_count, check_for_mail() won't return the number of messages retrieved. You should specify NULL unless you really want to know how many messages were retrieved, since requesting this information could potentially slow down the retrieval process.

If all is well in the mail world, this function returns B_OK; otherwise, it returns a highly useful result code.

Return values:

B_OK. Mail was sent and retrieved without incident.

B_MAIL_NO_DAEMON. The mail daemon isn't running.

B_MAIL_UNKNOWN_USER. The POP server doesn't recognize the user name.

B_MAIL_WRONG_PASSWORD. The POP server doesn't recognize the password.

B_MAIL_UNKNOWN_HOST. The POP or SMTP server can't be found.

B_MAIL_ACCESS_ERROR. The connection to the POP or SMTP server failed.

count_pop_accounts()

int32 **count_pop_accounts**(void)

Returns the number of POP accounts that have been configured.

NOTE

The mail daemon currently supports only one POP account, so this function will always return 1. You shouldn't assume there will only be one POP account, though, as this will probably change in the future.

decode_base64()

ssize_t **decode_base64**(char *out*, char *in*, off_t *length*, bool *replace_cr* = false)

Decodes the base-64 data pointed to by *in*, which is *length* bytes long, and writes the decoded output into the buffer pointed to by *out*. If *replace_cr* is true, carriage return characters in the output are converted into newlines, otherwise the data is returned in its original, unaltered, form.

You would typically specify *replace_cr* as true if you're decoding an ASCII text document, and as false if decoding a binary file.

This function returns the size of the output data that's been stored in the *out* buffer.

WARNING

You must be certain, in advance, that the output buffer is large enough to hold the decoded data, or this function will do bad things.

encode_base64()

> ssize_t **encode_base64**(char *_out_, char *_in_, off_t _length_)

Encodes the data pointed to by _in_, which is _length_ bytes long, and writes the base-64 encoded output into the buffer pointed to by _out_.

This function returns the size of the output data that's been stored in the _out_ buffer.

WARNING

> You must be certain, in advance, that the output buffer is large enough to hold the encoded data, or this function will do bad things.

forward_mail()

> status_t **forward_mail**(entry_ref *_message_ref_, const char *_recipients_,
> bool _now_ = true)

Forwards the mail message specified by _message_ref_ to the list of users given by _recipients_. The list of user names specified in _recipients_ must be separated by commas and/or whitespace, and must be null-terminated.

If the _now_ parameter is `true`, the message will be sent immediately; if `false`, the message will be queued up to be sent the next time `check_for_mail()` is called, or the next time the mail daemon performs an automatic mail check.

Return values:
> B_OK. The message was forwarded without error.
> B_MAIL_NO_RECIPIENT. No valid recipients were specified.
> Errors returned by `send_queued_mail()`, if _now_ is `true`.

get_mail_notification(), set_mail_notification()

> status_t **get_mail_notification**(mail_notification *_notification_settings_)

> status_t **set_mail_notification**(mail_notification *_notification_settings_,
> bool _save_ = true)

`get_mail_notification()` fills the specified `mail_notification` structure with information describing how the user is currently being notified of received e-mail. There are two possible notification signals: the mail alert panel and the system beep. The `mail_notification` structure looks like this:

```
typedef struct
{
   bool alert;
   bool beep;
} mail_notification;
```

`get_mail_notification()` always returns `B_OK`. If the current settings can't be checked (for example, if the user has never configured mail), *alert* will be returned as the default value of `false`, and *beep* will be `true`.

`set_mail_notification()` accepts a pointer to a `mail_notification` structure and configures the system to report incoming mail using the methods specified therein. If the *save* argument is `true`, the change is set as the new default and will be remembered when the computer is shut down. If `false`, the change is temporary.

Return values:

B_OK. The notification was successfully set or retrieved.

B_NO_REPLY. The mail daemon didn't respond to the request.

get_pop_account(), set_pop_account()

status_t **get_pop_account**(mail_pop_account **account_info*, int32 *index* = 0)

status_t **set_pop_account**(mail_pop_account **account_info*, int32 *index* = 0)

Get and set the specified POP account's information. The `mail_pop_account` structure is defined as follows:

```
typedef struct
{
   char pop_name[B_MAX_USER_NAME_LENGTH];
   char pop_password[B_MAX_USER_NAME_LENGTH];
   char pop_host[B_MAX_HOST_NAME_LENGTH];
   char real_name[128];
   char reply_to[128];
   int32 days;
   int32 interval;
   int32 begin_time;
   int32 end_time;
} mail_pop_account;
```

The `pop_name`, `pop_password`, and `pop_host` fields in the `mail_pop_account` structure represent the username, password, and POP server host of the e-mail user. The `real_name` is the user's real name, and `reply_to` is the e-mail address to which replies should be sent.

The `days` field can contain any of the following flags to specify which days of the week the mail daemon should automatically check mail for the described account:

Constant	Meaning
B_CHECK_NEVER	Don't automatically check the account's mail.
B_CHECK_WEEKDAYS	Check the mail only on weekdays.
B_CHECK_DAILY	Check the mail every day.
B_CHECK_CONTINUOUSLY	Check continuously every day.

The `interval` specifies how many seconds apart each e-mail retrieval should be, and the `begin_time` and `end_time` specify the time of day (in seconds) that automatic retrieval should begin and end. If `begin_time` and `end_time` are the same, the daemon checks mail round-the-clock.

NOTE

Eventually these functions will support multiple POP accounts; at this time, the Mail Kit only supports one POP account, so you must use an *index* of 0. Any other index will result in a `B_BAD_INDEX` error.

`get_pop_account()` fills the specified `mail_pop_account` structure with the information on the POP account, and `set_pop_account()` takes the information in the buffer and saves it as the new default.

Return values:
 B_OK. The notification was successfully set or retrieved.
 B_BAD_INDEX. An index other than 0 was specified.
 B_NO_REPLY. The mail daemon didn't reply to the request.

get_smtp_host(), set_smtp_host()

 status_t **get_smtp_host**(char *smtp_host*)
 status_t **set_smtp_host**(char *smtp_host*, bool *save* = true)

`get_smtp_host()` returns in the buffer pointed to by *smtp_host* the name of the SMTP host as currently configured. The buffer should be at lest `B_MAX_HOST_NAME_LENGTH` bytes long.

`set_smtp_host()` sets the SMTP host through which mail will be sent in the future to the specified host. If *save* is `true`, the new setting becomes the default and will persist through a reboot of the computer; otherwise, the change is only temporary.

Return values:
 B_OK. The notification was successfully set or retrieved.
 B_NO_REPLY. The mail daemon didn't respond to the request.

send_queued_mail()

 status_t **send_queued_mail**(void)

Tells the mail daemon to send all pending outgoing mail.

Return values:
 B_OK. Mail transfer initiated successfully.
 Errors from BMessage::SendMessage().

BMailMessage

Derived from: none

Declared in: be/mail/E-mail.h

Library: libmail.so

The BMailMessage class provides an easy way to send e-mail messages. If you want to do it the hard way, look up the SMTP RFC and start plodding your way through the Network Kit documentation. You'll get it working one of these days.

Or you can sail right on through and be sending e-mail from your own applications in a matter of minutes using your friend, the BMailMessage.

Constructing a Mail Message

To send an e-mail, you simply construct a new BMailMessage object, add a "To" header field, add the content, and send the message on its way. For example:

```
BMailMessage *mail;
char *message;

mail = new BMailMessage();
mail->AddHeaderField(B_MAIL_TO, "bob@uncle.com");
mail->AddHeaderField(B_MAIL_SUBJECT, "Hi");
message = "Hi, Uncle Bob!";
mail->AddContent(message, strlen(message));
```

This is a pretty basic message. The subject is "Hi," the message is sent to "bob@uncle.com," and the message body is "Hi, Uncle Bob!"

You can add other fields, including carbon-copy (CC) and blind-carbon-copy (BCC) fields, and you can add attachments. For example, if you want to also attach a file called "/boot/home/file.zip," you can do the following:

```
mail->AddEnclosure("/boot/home/file.zip");
```

Once your message has been constructed, you can send it by calling `Send()`:

```
mail->Send();
```

That's the basic technique behind sending e-mail under the BeOS. The mail daemon also fetches incoming mail from a POP server, but you can't use the BMailMessage class to read these messages; you use the BeOS BQuery and BNode classes to locate messages of interest and obtain information about them. See "Querying Mail Messages" for more information.

Constructor and Destructor

BMailMessage()

> BMailMessage(void)

Creates and returns a new BMailMessage object, which is empty. You need to call other functions defined by this class to fill out the message.

~BMailMessage()

> ~BMailMessage()

Destroys the BMailMessage, even if the object's fields are "dirty." For example, if you create a new BMailMessage object with the intention of sending a message, fill out some or all the fields, and delete the object, the object is destroyed without being sent.

Member Functions

AddContent()

> status_t **AddContent**(const char *text*, int32 *length*,
>   uint32 *encoding* = B_ISO1_CONVERSION, bool *replace* = false)

> status_t **AddContent**(const char *text*, int32 *length*, const char *encoding*,
>   bool *replace* = false)

Adds the specified *text* (which contains *length* characters) to the BMailMessage object's content. The text's encoding is specified by the *encoding* parameter, either directly or by pointer.

If *replace* is true, any existing text is deleted before the new content is added; otherwise, the specified text is appended to the end of the existing message content.

Return values:
> B_OK. The content was changed without error.
> B_ERROR. Unable to add the new content.

AddEnclosure()

> status_t **AddEnclosure**(entry_ref *enclosure_ref*, bool *replace* = false)
> status_t **AddEnclosure**(const char *path*, bool *replace* = false)
> status_t **AddEnclosure**(const char *mime_type*, void *data*, int32 *length*,
>   bool *replace* = false)

Adds an attachment to the message. The first two forms of `AddEnclosure()` add a file to the message, given either an `entry_ref` pointer or a pathname. The third form adds a block of memory (of the given *length*) to the message as an enclosure, with the specified MIME type.

If *replace* is `true`, any existing attachments—including the body of the message—are removed before the new one is added; otherwise the new enclosure is added, leaving previous attachments intact.

WARNING

If you specify `true` for *replace*, not only will all existing enclosures be discarded, but so will the content of the message body itself.

Return values:
   B_OK. The enclosure was added without error.
   B_ERROR. Unable to add the new enclosure.

AddHeaderField()

   status_t **AddHeaderField**(const char **field_name*, const char **field_str*,
                  bool *replace* = false)

Adds a header field to the BMailMessage object. The value of the field whose name is specified by *field_name* is set to the string specified by *field_str*.

If *replace* is `true`, all existing header fields of the specified name are deleted before adding the new header field; if *replace* is `false`, a new header whose field is named *field_name* is added.

Return values:
   B_OK. The header was changed without error.
   B_ERROR. Unable to add the new header field.

Send()

   status_t **Send**(bool *send_now* = false, bool *remove_when_sent* = false)

Queues the message for transmission. If *send_now* is `true`, the message is sent immediately; otherwise, it is placed in the queue to be sent the next time `check_for_mail()` is called or the mail daemon performs an automatic mail check. If the *remove_when_sent* argument is `true`, the message will be deleted from the user's disk drive after it has been sent; otherwise, it will be saved for posterity.

Return values:
   B_OK. The message was sent without error.
   B_MAIL_NO_RECIPIENT. Missing "To" or "Bcc" field in the message.
   Errors from BMessage::SendMessage().

The Translation Kit

The Translation Kit

The Translation Kit provides a framework for converting data streams between different media formats. A word processor, for example, could use the Translation Kit to import and export documents in a variety of formats, including HTML, PostScript, and plain ASCII, while working in its own native format. The Translation Kit uses add-ons called *translators* to carry out the conversions, defining a protocol to which these add-ons adhere. Applications use a utility class in the Translation Kit to invoke the translators.

The Translation Kit operates on BPositionIO objects and their descendents. Since `BFile` derives from BPositionIO, the Translation Kit is naturally suited for importing and exporting files. However, it's far more general: The Translation Kit could be used, for example, to translate input directly to or from a network connection, provided a suitable BPositionIO subclass was available. More importantly, BMemoryIO and BMallocIO can be used to load data directly into or out of memory.

Applications primarily interact with the Translation Kit through the BTranslatorRoster class. This class encapsulates the functionality required to load and unload translators, discover their capabilities, configure the translators, and execute the translations.

Applications may also use the BTranslationUtils class, a collection of static utility functions designed to simplify access to the Translation Kit. Currently, the class only defines members for loading bitmap images from files, resources, and general BPositionIO data streams.

Where to Go From Here

The next section, "Media Formats", describes the types of media that the Translation Kit is designed to handle. A later section, "Default Media Formats", fills in the media format details. All Translation Kit users need to know about the media formats.

The three middle sections, "BTranslatorRoster", "BBitmapStream", and "BTranslationUtils", describe the Translation Kit classes. You use these classes when you're converting data.

The final section, "Creating a Translator Add-on", gives instructions for creating your own translator. To understand this section, you must first read about the BTranslatorRoster class. If you're not creating a translator add-on, you can ignore this section.

Media Formats

The Translation Kit identifies a particular media format by a *media group* and *format type*. Media groups identify the class of media represented by a format. Definitions for the common media groups can be found in *be/translation/TranslatorFormats.h*:

Media Group	Constant
Bitmap	B_TRANSLATOR_BITMAP
BPicture data	B_TRANSLATOR_PICTURE
Text	B_TRANSLATOR_TEXT
Sound	B_TRANSLATOR_SOUND
Standard MIDI	B_TRANSLATOR_MIDI
Streaming media	B_TRANSLATOR_MEDIA
nothing	B_TRANSLATOR_NONE

A format type is a type constant identifying the specific data format, such as tiff, aiff, mpeg. The standard type constants can be found in *be/support/TypeConstants.h*.

It is often convenient to define a baseline format to which all translators of a given media group adhere. An application that understands the baseline format could then use all the translators for that group. This also simplifies the job of the translator, which minimally needs only to translate between the baseline and the new formats. Well-behaved translators will always be able to translate to and from the default media format (if one exists for its media group).

The Translation Kit defines a default media format for each existing media group. They are explained at length in the section "Default Media Formats". The format type constant for each default format is the same as the media group constant; for example, the format type for the default bitmap format is B_TRANSLATOR_BITMAP.

BTranslatorRoster

Derived from: public BArchivable

Declared in: be/translation/TranslatorRoster.h

Library: libtranslation.so

BTranslatorRoster is the main mechanism through which applications interact with the Translation Kit. An application using the Translation Kit doesn't need to worry about explicitly loading or calling add-ons; BTranslatorRoster transparently handles all the niggling details. The class provides four categories of service: initialization, information, translation, and configuration.

Initialization

You can create an empty BTranslatorRoster (one which has no translators loaded) by instantiating it in the usual fashion:

```
BTranslatorRoster *roster = new BTranslatorRoster();
```

You can then load translators into the newly-created BTranslatorRoster with the `AddTranslators()` method (all paths must be absolute):

```
// load all translators in a given directory
roster->AddTranslators("/boot/home/config/add-ons/viewer/");

// load a specific translator
roster->AddTranslators("/system/add-ons/Translators/photos");
```

More commonly, you want a BTranslatorRoster with the default translators (those in */boot/home/config/add-ons/Translators*, */boot/home/config/add-ons/Datatypes*, and */system/add-ons/Translators*). The static member `Default()` returns just such a beast:

```
BTranslatorRoster *roster = BTranslatorRoster::Default();
```

However, not all BTranslatorRosters are created equal: The object returned by `Default()` is global to the application and controlled by BTranslatorRoster. Therefore, you should never `delete` it. Furthermore, if you want to load additional translators, you're better off creating a new instance of BTranslatorRoster rather than using the default one:

```
BTranslatorRoster *roster = new BTranslatorRoster();
roster->AddTranslators(NULL); // load default translators
roster->AddTranslators(...);  // load additional translators
```

Information

Applications typically ask the following questions of the Translation Kit:

- Which translators are installed?
- Which translations can a particular translator carry out?
- Which translator is best suited for handling my conversion?

An application can determine the installed translators by calling `GetAllTranslators()`. `GetAllTranslators()` returns an array of `translator_id` values for the installed translators. A `translator_id` is an application-wide value assigned by BTranslatorRoster identifying a specific translator. The following snippet prints out the names of the default translators:

```
BTranslatorRoster *roster = BTranslatorRoster::Default();
int32 num_translators, i;
translator_id *translators;
const char *translator_name, *translator_info;
int32 translator_version;

roster->GetAllTranslators(&translators, &num_translators);
for (i=0;i<num_translators;i++) {
    roster->GetTranslatorInfo(translators[i], &translator_name,
        &translator_info, &translator_version);
    printf("%s: %s (%.2f)\n", translator_name, translator_info,
        translator_version/100.);
}

delete [] translators; // clean up our droppings
```

The `translator_id` is very valuable; it can be used to query BTranslatorRoster for specific information about a translator's capabilities. This information comes in two nearly identical flavors: `translation_format` and `translator_info`. They're defined in *be/translation/TranslationDefs.h*:

```
struct translation_format {
    uint32 type;
    uint32 group;
    float  quality;
    float  capability;
    char   MIME[251];
    char   name[251];
}

struct translator_info {
    uint32        type;
    translator_id translator;
    uint32        group;
    float         quality;
    float         capability;
    char          name[251];
    char          MIME[251];
}
```

The common fields:

- `group`. Defines the type of media the format represents, i.e. bitmap image, sound, or video. Constants for common media types can be found in *be/translation/TranslatorFormats.h*.

- `type`. Type constant defining the specific data format. For example, the type constant for tiff bitmaps differs from the constant for jpeg bitmaps.

- `quality`. Ability of the format to represent data of its media group. This value ranges from a low of 0.0 (utter inability) to a high of 1.0 (encodes all relevant information).

- `capability`. Ability of translator to decode the format. As with the quality, the value ranges from 0.0 (unable to decode) to 1.0 (can decode all variants and extensions).

- `MIME`. MIME type of the format. This is a more reliable indicator of the data format than the *type* field for those formats that have standard MIME names.

- `name`. Human-readable string describing the format. May include information about the translator as well.

Additionally, `translator_info` defines an additional field:

- `translator`. The `translator_id` for the translator associated with the structure.

To find the media formats supported by a particular translator, call `GetInputFormats()` or `GetOutputFormats()` as appropriate. These methods return a list of the supported input and output formats in a `translation_format` array.

Many times, however, you don't really care about individual translators; you just want the translator best suited for handling your media stream. In these cases, you can just call `Identify()` on the BPositionIO. BTranslatorRoster will then return, in a `translator_info` structure, the translator most suited for carrying out the translation. If, instead, you're interested in finding all the translators capable of handling the data in your stream, use `GetTranslators()` instead.

Note that some translators do not publish their input and output formats. In these cases, `GetInputFormats()` and `GetOutputFormats()` return an empty list of formats. The only way to tell if such a translator supports a particular input or output format is to pass it to `Identify()`.

Translation

Although the function of BTranslatorRoster is to provide translation services, carrying out the translation is simple. All it requires are the input and output BPositionIO streams and the type constant for the desired output. In the simplest case, if you know the type constant you want to convert the data into, you can let the BTranslatorRoster decide which translator to use:

```
BPositionIO *in = ..., *out = ...;
BTranslatorRoster *roster = BTranslatorRoster::Default();
uint32 desired_format_constant = ...;

roster->Translate(in, NULL, NULL, out, desired_format_constant);
```

Sometimes, however, you'd like the services of a specific translator. In these cases, you can use the alternate form of `Translate()`:

```
BPositionIO *in = ..., *out = ...;
BTranslatorRoster *roster = BTranslatorRoster::Default();
uint32 desired_format_constant = ...;
translator_id desired_translator_id = ...;

roster->Translate(desired_translator_id, in, NULL, NULL, out,
    desired_format_constant);
```

Configuration

BTranslatorRoster provides two mechanisms for configuring the behavior of translators: *ioExtension* and `MakeConfiguationView()`.

ioExtension is a BMessage that can be passed to most BTranslatorRoster members. It is used by the application to communicate format-specific information to the translator. For example, it could be used to ask a video translator to only translate the first 15 frames of the movie. The *ioExtension* message is also used by the translator to communicate information back to the application. The translator may use it, for example, to tell the application that it's returning a greyscale image.

A translator need not support any particular extension and there's no way for an application to tell if a translator supports any extensions.

A set of standard *ioExtension* message field can be found in *be/translation/TranslatorFormats.h* and are explained below:

Name	Type	Direction	Description
kCommentExtension	`string`	n/a	Text comment about data.
kTimeExtension	`bigtime_t`	app to translator	If one exists, it specifies a single instant in time. If two exist, they specify a range in time. Time is measured in microseconds.

Name	Type	Direction	Description
kFrameExtension	uint32	app to translator	Same as kTimeExtension, except the unit of time is frames.
kBitsRectExtension	BRect	app to translator	Specifies subsection of a bitmap.
kBitsSpaceExtension	color_space	both	Specifies desired/actual color space of bitmap.
kHeaderExtension	bool	app to translator	Only output header if true.
kDataExtension	bool	app to translator	Only output data if true.
kNoisChannelExtension	uint32	app to translator	Only output specified channel of sound.
kNoisMonoExtension	bool	app to translator	Mix all audio channels to a single mono channel if true.
kNoisMarkerExtension	uint32	both	Specifies markers in sound data. Units are in frames. "1" specifies marker between first sample of last channel and second sample of first channel.
kNoisLoopExtension	uint32	both	If there is one value, loop from the end of the sound data to the loop point. If there are two values, loop from the second value to the first. If there are more than two values, then there is a release loop.

BTranslatorRoster contains two methods to facilitate configuration of translators. The first method, MakeConfigurationView(), instructs the translator to create a BView in which configuration options may be changed. It's the responsibility of the application calling MakeConfigurationView() to attach the view to a BWindow. The second method, GetConfigurationMessage(), fills in a BMessage with the current settings for a specified translator. This BMessage can then be passed to Translate() to request a translation with the settings contained within.

Example

The task of translating data often boils down to finding the right type constant. The following function will print the format type constants associated with a MIME string given a BTranslatorRoster:

```
void find_constant(BTranslatorRoster *roster, const char *mime)
{
    translator_id *translators;
    int32 num_translators;

    roster->GetAllTranslators(&translators, &num_translators);

    for (int32 i=0;i<num_translators;i++) {
        const translation_format *fmts;
```

```
        int32 num_fmts;

        roster->GetOutputFormats(translators[i], &fmts, &num_fmts);

        for (int32 j=0;j<num_fmts;j++) {
            if (!strcasecmp(fmts[j].MIME, mime))
                printf("match: %s type %8.8x (%4.4s)\n",
                    fmts[j].name, fmts[j].type, &fmts[j].type);
        }
    }
}
```

Constructor and Destructor

BTranslatorRoster()

BTranslatorRoster()
BTranslatorRoster(BMessage *model)

Creates a new container for translators. The no-argument constructor creates an empty container. The BMessage constructor loads all the translators from the directories specified in the "be:translator_path" field in *model*.

If you just want to load the translators from the standard directories, you can instead use the static member `Default()` described below.

See also: `Default()` static function, `AddTranslators()`

~BTranslatorRoster()

~BTranslatorRoster()

Unloads any translators that were loaded and frees all memory allocated by the BTranslatorRoster.

Static Functions

Default()

BTranslatorRoster *Default()

This returns a default set of translators, loaded from the colon-separated list of files and directories found in the environment variable **TRANSLATORS**. If no such variable exists, the translators are loaded from the default locations */boot/home/config/add-ons/Translators*, */boot/home/config/add-ons/Datatypes*, and */system/add-ons/Translators*.

The instance of BTranslatorRoster returned by this function is global to the application and should not be deleted. Although you can add translators to the returned BTranslatorRoster, this is not recommended. It's better to use a new instance of the class.

See also: `AddTranslators()`

Version()

> const char ***Version**(int32 *outCurVersion, int32 *outMinVersion,
>   int32 *inAppVersion = B_TRANSLATION_CURRENT_VERSION)

Sets *outCurVersion* to the Translation Kit protocol version number and *outMinVersion* to the minimum protocol version number supported. Returns a human-readable string containing version information. Currently, *inAppVersion* must be `B_TRANSLATION_CURRENT_VERSION`.

Member Functions

AddTranslators()

> virtual status_t **AddTranslators**(const char *load_path = NULL)

Loads all the translators located in the colon-separated list of files and directories found in *load_path*. All specified paths must be absolute. If *load_path* is NULL, it loads the translators from the locations specified in the `TRANSLATORS` environment variable. If the environment variable is not defined, then it loads all the files in the default directories   */boot/home/config/add-ons/Translators*, */boot/home/config/add-ons/Datatypes*, and */system/add-ons/Translators*.

Return values:
> B_NO_ERROR. Identification of *inSource* was successful.
> B_BAD_VALUE. Error parsing *load_path*.
> *Anything else.* Error loading add-ons.

See also: `Default()` static function

GetAllTranslators()

> virtual status_t **GetAllTranslators**(translator_id **outList, int32 *outCount)

Returns, in *outList*, an array of all the translators loaded by the BTranslationRoster. The number of elements in the array is placed in *outCount*. The application assumes responsibility for deallocating the array.

Return values:
> B_NO_ERROR. Success.
> B_NOT_INITIALIZED. Internal Translation Kit error.
> B_BAD_VALUE. *outList* or *outCount* is NULL.

See also: `Identify()`, `GetTranslators()`, `GetAllTranslators()`

GetConfigurationMessage()

> virtual status_t **GetConfigurationMessage**(translator_id *forTranslator*, BMessage
> **ioExtension*)

Saves the current configuration information in *ioExtension*. This information may be flattened, unflattened, and passed to `Translate()` to configure it.

Return values:
> B_NO_ERROR. Success.
> B_NO_TRANSLATOR. *forTranslator* not a valid `translator_id`.
> B_NOT_INITIALIZED. Internal Translation Kit error.
> B_BAD_VALUE. *ioExtension* is NULL.
> *Anything else.* Error passed on from add-on.

See also: `GetConfigurationView()`, `Translate()`

GetInputFormats()   see **GetOutputFormats**

GetTranslatorInfo()

> virtual status_t **GetTranslatorInfo**(translator_id *forTranslator*, const char **outName,
> const char **outInfo, int32 *outVersion)

Returns public information about translator *forTranslator*. Sets *outName* with a short description of the translator, *outInfo* with a longer description, and *outVersion* with the translator's version number.

Return values:
> B_NO_ERROR. Success.
> B_NO_TRANSLATOR. *forTranslator* not a valid `translator_id`.
> B_NOT_INITIALIZED. Internal Translation Kit error.

See also: `GetInputFormats()`, `GetOutputFormats()`

GetTranslators()

virtual status_t **GetTranslators**(BPositionIO *inSource*, BMessage *ioExtension*,
translator_info ***outInfo*, int32 *outNumInfo*,
uint32 *inHintType* = 0, const char *inHintMIME* = NULL,
uint32 *inWantType* = 0)

Identifies the media in *inSource*, returning an array of valid formats and translators equipped to handle them in *outInfo*. *outNumInfo* holds the number of elements in the array. If *inHintType* or *inHintMIME* is specified, only those translators that can accept data of the specified type are searched. If *inWantType* is specified, only those translators that can output data of that type are searched. *ioExtension* offers an opportunity for the application to specify additional configuration information to the add-ons. The application assumes responsibility for deallocating the array.

Return values:

B_NO_ERROR. Identification of *inSource* was successful.
B_NO_TRANSLATOR. No suitable translators found.
B_NOT_INITIALIZED. Internal Translation Kit error.
B_BAD_VALUE. *inSource*, *outInfo*, or *outNumInfo* is NULL.
Anything else. Error operating on *inSource*.

See also: Identify(), GetAllTranslators()

GetInputFormats(), GetOutputFormats()

virtual status_t **GetInputFormats**(translator_id *forTranslator*,
const char ***outFormats*, const char ***outNumFormats*)

virtual status_t **GetOutputFormats**(translator_id *forTranslator*,
const char ***outFormats*, const char ***outNumFormats*)

Returns an array of the published accepted input or output formats for translator *forTranslator*. *outNumFormats* is filled with the number of elements in the array.

Return values:

B_NO_ERROR. Success.
B_NO_TRANSLATOR. *forTranslator* not a valid translator_id.
B_NOT_INITIALIZED. Internal Translation Kit error.
B_BAD_VALUE. *outFormats* or *outNumFormats* is NULL.

See also: GetTranslatorInfo()

Identify()

> virtual status_t **Identify**(BPositionIO *inSource*, BMessage *ioExtension*,
>   translator_info *outInfo*, uint32 *inHintType* = 0,
>   const char *inHintMIME* = NULL, uint32 *inWantType* = 0)

Identifies the media in *inSource*, returning a best guess of the format and the translator best equipped to handle it in *outInfo*. If *inHintType* or *inHintMIME* is specified, only those translators that can accept data of the specified type are searched. If *inWantType* is specified, only those translators that can output data of that type are searched. *ioExtension* offers an opportunity for the application to specify additional configuration information to the add-ons.

If more than one translator can identify *inSource*, then the one with the highest *quality*capability* is returned.

Return values:

   B_NO_ERROR. Identification of *inSource* was successful.
   B_NO_TRANSLATOR. No suitable translator found.
   B_NOT_INITIALIZED. Internal Translation Kit error.
   B_BAD_VALUE. *inSource* or *outInfo* is NULL.
   Anything else. Error operating on *inSource*.

See also: GetTranslators(), GetAllTranslators()

MakeConfigurationView()

> virtual status_t **MakeConfigurationView**(translator_id *forTranslator*, BMessage
>   *ioExtension*, BView **outView*, BRect *outExtent*)

Returns, in *outView*, a BView containing controls to configure translator *forTranslator*. It is the application's responsibility to attach the BView to a BWindow. The initial size of the BView is given in *outExtent* but may be resized by the application.

Return values:

   B_NO_ERROR. Success.
   B_NO_TRANSLATOR. *forTranslator* not a valid translator_id.
   B_NOT_INITIALIZED. Internal Translation Kit error.
   B_BAD_VALUE. *outView* or *outExtent* is NULL.
   Anything else. Error passed on from add-on.

See also: GetConfigurationMessage(), Translate()

Translate()

virtual status_t **Translate**(BPositionIO *inSource*, const translator_info *inInfo*,
        BMessage *ioExtension*, BPositionIO *outDestination*,
        uint32 *inWantOutType*, uint32 *inHintType* = 0,
        const char *inHintMIME* = NULL)

virtual status_t **Translate**(translator_id *inTranslator*, BPositionIO *inSource*,
        BMessage *ioExtension*, BPositionIO *outDestination*,
        uint32 *inWantOutType*)

These two functions carry out data conversion, converting the data in *inSource* to type *inWantOutType* and placing the resulting output in *outDestination*. *inInfo* should always contain either the output of an `Identify()` call or NULL. The translation uses the translator identified by *inInfo->infoTranslator* or *inTranslator* as appropriate. If *inInfo* is NULL, `Translate()` will call first `Identify()` to discover the format of the input stream. *ioExtension*, if it is not NULL, provides a communication path between the translator and the application. *inHintType* and *inHintMIME*, if provided, are passed as hints to the translator.

Return values:
    B_NO_ERROR. Success.
    B_NO_TRANSLATOR. No suitable translators found.
    B_NOT_INITIALIZED. Internal Translation Kit error.
    B_BAD_VALUE. *inSource* or *outSource* is NULL.
    Anything else. Error passed on from add-on.

Archived Fields

The `Archive()` function adds the following field to its BMessage argument:

Field	Type code	Meaning
"be:translator_path" (array)	B_STRING_TYPE	The location of the Translation Kit add-on (one field per add-on).

BBitmapStream

Derived from: public BPositionIO

Declared in: be/translation/BitmapStream.h

Library: libtranslation.so

BBitmapStream allows for the easy conversion of a *translator bitmap*, the default Translation Kit bitmap format, to a BBitmap. It's a very limited subclass of

BPositionIO capable only of reading and writing translator bitmaps; performing I/O on the object with other types of data can yield strange results. The main attraction of the class is the `DetachBitmap()` method, which returns the contents of the object as a BBitmap.

Most of the time, you won't need to use BBitmapStream directly; BTranslationUtils contains the functionality required to load images from files, resources, or general BPositionIOs into BBitmaps.

The following snippet illustrates typical usage of BBitmapStream *sans* proper error checking:

```
BBitmap *FetchBitmap(char *filename)
{
   BFile file(filename, B_READ_ONLY);
   BTranslatorRoster *roster = BTranslatorRoster::Default();
   BBitmapStream stream;
   BBitmap *result = NULL;
   if (roster->Translate(&file, NULL, NULL, &stream,
         B_TRANSLATOR_BITMAP) < B_OK)
      return NULL;
   stream.DetachBitmap(&result);
   return result;
}
```

You can also initialize the class with a BBitmap and use it as input to `BTranslatorRoster::Translate()` to save it in a different format:

```
void StoreTranslatorBitmap(BBitmap *bitmap, char *filename, uint32 type)
{
   BTranslatorRoster *roster = BTranslatorRoster::Default();
   BBitmapStream stream(bitmap); // init with contents of bitmap
   BFile file(filename, B_CREATE_FILE | B_WRITE_ONLY);

   roster->Translate(&stream, NULL, NULL, &file, type);
}
```

Constructor and Destructor

BBitmapStream()

BBitmapStream(BBitmap *map* = NULL)

Creates a new instance of BBitmapStream. If *map* is NULL, the stream is initialized to be empty. Otherwise, the BBitmap is converted to a translator bitmap and placed in the stream. The application shares the BBitmap with the BBitmapStream object. It therefore shouldn't `delete` the BBitmap without first calling `DetachBitmap()`.

~BBitmapStream()

~BBitmapStream()

Frees all memory allocated by the BTranslatorRoster.

Member Functions

DetachBitmap()

status_t **DetachBitmap**(BBitmap **outMap*)

Returns, in *outMap*, a BBitmap representing the image contained in the BBitmapStream. Once `DetachBitmap()` has been called, no further operations should be performed on the BBitmapStream.

Return values:
- B_NO_ERROR. Success.
- B_BAD_VALUE. *outMap* is NULL.
- B_ERROR. There is no BBitmap available.

Position(), ReadAt(), Seek(), SetSize(), WriteAt()

off_t **Position**() const

ssize_t **ReadAt**(off_t *pos*, void **buffer*, size_t **size*)

off_t **Seek**(off_t *position*, uint32 *whence*)

status_t **SetSize**(off_t *size*) const

ssize_t **WriteAt**(off_t *pos*, const void **data*, size_t **size*)

These methods provide the implementation for the BPositionIO. The class functions identically to BPositionIO with the exception of `ReadAt()` and `WriteAt()`, which read and write only translator bitmaps as described in the class introduction.

See also: `BPositionIO`

Size()

off_t **Size**() const

Returns the number of bytes in the translator bitmap in the stream.

BTranslationUtils

Derived from: none

Declared in: be/translation/TranslationUtils.h

Library: libtranslation.so

BTranslationUtils contains a set of static functions that load bitmap images. The functions use the Translation Kit to convert the data from its native format to a `BBitmap` via a `BBitmapStream`, the upshot of which is that if you can convert the data to a translator bitmap, you can successfully use these functions. The image may come from a file, resource, or `BPositionIO`. The application is always responsible for deallocating the returned BBitmap.

Static Functions

GetBitmap()

static BBitmap **GetBitmap**(const char *name*, BTranslatorRoster *use* = NULL)
static BBitmap **GetBitmap**(uint32 *type*, int32 *id*, BTranslatorRoster *use* = NULL)
static BBitmap **GetBitmap**(uint32 *type*, const char *name*,
                            BTranslatorRoster *use* = NULL)
static BBitmap **GetBitmap**(BPositionIO *stream*, BTranslatorRoster *use* = NULL)

The first version of the function returns the image held in the file *name* if it exists. Otherwise, it returns the application resource of type `B_TRANSLATOR_BITMAP` named *name*.

The second and third versions of the function search for the specified resource and return the bitmap contained therein.

The final version returns the bitmap found in *stream*. This form of the function is particularly useful when used with `BMemoryIO`.

In all cases, *use* specifies the BTranslatorRoster to use in translating the image. If *use* is `NULL`, the default translator (as returned by BTranslatorRoster's `Default()`) is used.

If the file or stream doesn't contain a suitable bitmap, the functions return `NULL`.

See also: `BTranslatorRoster::Default()`

GetBitmapFile()

static BBitmap **GetBitmapFile**(const char *name*, BTranslatorRoster *use* = NULL)

Returns the image held in the file *name*. If the file doesn't contain a suitable image, the function returns NULL. *use* specifies the BTranslatorRoster used to translate the image. If *use* is NULL, the default translator (as returned by `BTranslatorRoster::Default()`) is used.

See also: `BTranslatorRoster::Default()`

Default Media Formats

This section describes the default media formats for each of the media groups defined by the Translation Kit.

Formats

B_TRANSLATOR_BITMAP

Declared in:		be/translation/TranslatorFormats.h

```
struct TranslatorBitmap {
    int32 magic;
    BRect bounds;
    uint32 rowBytes;
    color_space colors;
    uint32 dataSize;
}
```

`TranslatorBitmap` holds the header information for a translator bitmap. `magic` should always be set to `B_TRANSLATOR_BITMAP`. The uncompressed image data immediately follows the header in the stream. This image data should be precisely `dataSize` bytes long.

All data in this format is stored in big endian format. This requirement includes the header.

B_TRANSLATOR_PICTURE

Streams in this format are stored as `BPicture::Flatten()`.

B_TRANSLATOR_TEXT

This is a plain ASCII text file.

B_TRANSLATOR_SOUND

Declared in: be/translation/TranslatorFormats.h

```
struct TranslatorSound {
    int32 magic;
    uint32 channels;
    float sampleFreq;
    uint32 numFrames;
}
```

TranslatorSound holds the header information for the default sound format. `magic` should always be set to `B_TRANSLATOR_SOUND`. The raw sound data stored in 16-bit linear format, left channel first, immediately follows the header. As with TranslatorBitmap, all data in this stream is stored in big-endian format.

B_TRANSLATOR_MIDI

This is a standard type 1 MIDI file, as read by and written to the BMidiStore class.

B_TRANSLATOR_MEDIA

As of this writing, a standard for this format has not been finalized, although it will be in a future release.

B_TRANSLATOR_NONE

Obviously, there is no standard format for the no media type.

Creating a Translator Add-on

This section details the creation of a translator. If you only need to use the Translation Kit, you may safely skip this section. Otherwise, please read through the introduction to the BTranslatorRoster class before continuing here.

When an application requests the conversion of a stream from one format to another via BTranslatorRoster, the Translation Kit scans through its list of translators to determine the one best suited for translating the stream. Each translator is an add-on that exports several symbols to help BTranslatorRoster make its decision. The prototypes for these symbols may be found in *be/translation/TranslatorAddOn.h*. Once you have written the required functions and data, creating the add-on involves simply including *be/translation/TranslatorAddOn.h* and compiling with `-export pragma` to export the appropriate symbols. A summary of the exports follows:

Symbol	Required?	Description
GetConfigMessage()	no	save current configuration in a BMessage
Identify()	yes	identify data in a BPositionIO
inputFormats	no	list of supported input formats
MakeConfig()	no	create a view for user-configuration of translator
outputFormats	no	list of supported output formats
Translate()	yes	translate data from one format to another
translatorInfo	yes	long description of translator
translatorName	yes	short name of translator
translatorVersion	yes	translator version number

Functions and Structures

GetConfigMessage()

> status_t **GetConfigMessage**(BMessage *ioExtension*)

This function stores the current configuration in the *ioExtension* in such a manner that it may be flattened, unflattened, and then passed to `Translate()` as an *ioExtension*.

This is an optional function.

Identify()

> status_t **Identify**(BPositionIO *inSource*, const translation_format *inFormat*,
> BMessage *ioExtension*, translator_info *outInfo*, uint32 *outType*)

If the translator understands how to convert the data contained in *inSource* to media type *outType*, it fills *outInfo* with details about the input format and return B_OK. If it doesn't know how to translate the data, it returns B_NO_TRANSLATOR.

The *quality* and *capability* fields in *outInfo* are used by the Translation Kit in selecting the best suited translator for a given translation, so it is best to be conservative in choosing these values.

If the media format doesn't have a type code in *be/support/TypeConstants.h* (as will most likely be the case), choose a reasonable value. For example, the Targa handler included with the BeOS distribution uses the type code "TGA".

The translator need not fill in the *translator* field in *outInfo*; BTranslatorRoster fills in this value for you.

Remember that *inSource* may be arriving from any source, including a live network feed. It's therefore best to steer clear of calls such as `BPositionIO::Size()` which force all the data out of the stream. Similarly, it is good practice to read only as much of the stream as you need.

inFormat, if it is not `NULL`, is provided as a hint to the format of the data in *inSource*. Since it is only a hint, the data may very well be in some other format.

ioExtension, if it is not `NULL`, contains additional information for the add-on. It is described at length in the section in BTranslatorRoster titled "Configuration".

outType may be zero, in which case any output format is acceptable.

This is a required function.

inputFormats, outputFormats

> translation_format **inputFormats**[];

> translation_format **outputFormats**[];

These arrays tell BTranslatorRoster which formats the add-on supports. If they are not exported by the translator, the add-on's `Identify()` will be called each time an application requests a translation. Each array ends in an empty `translation_format` structure, so a typical *inputFormats* would look like:

```
translation_format inputFormats[] = {
    { 'TGA ', B_TRANSLATOR_BITMAP, 0.6, 0.5, "image/targa",
      "Targa bitmap format" },
    { B_TRANSLATOR_BITMAP, B_TRANSLATOR_BITMAP, 0.4, 0.6, "image/x-be-bitmap",
      "Be Bitmap format" },
    { 0, 0, 0, 0, 0, 0 }
};
```

and similarly for *outputFormats*.

These are optional data.

MakeConfig()

> status_t **MakeConfig**(BMessage *ioExtension*, BView **outView*, BRect *outExtent*)

This function creates a new BView through which the user configures the add-on. For example, it could be used to control the degree of image compression used or the video frame rate. The bounds of the view are returned in *outExtent*, although it can be resized at will by an external source. Changes to the configuration take effect immediately, although translations should be carried out with the same parameters throughout.

This is an optional function.

outputFormats   see inputFormats

Translate()

> status_t **Translate**(BPositionIO *inSource*, const translator_info **inInfo*,
>   BMessage **ioExtension*, uint32 *outType*,
>   BPositionIO **outDestination*)

The translator translates data from *inSource* to format *outType*, writing the output to *outDestination*. *outType* may be zero, in which case it is assumed to be the default format type for the media group. As in `Identify()`, *inInfo* serves as a hint to the format of the data in *inSource*. *ioExtension* fills its usual role as a container of configuration information. The function returns `B_OK` if it's able to convert the data successfully. If it's unable to do so, it returns either `B_NO_TRANSLATOR` or an error value as appropriate.

This is a required function.

translatorInfo, translatorName, translatorVersion

> char **translatorInfo**[];

> char **translatorName**[];

> int32 *translatorVersion*;

translatorName is a C string giving the short name of the translator, for example, "aiff translator". *translatorInfo* is a C string giving a long description of the translator, fpr example, "aiff translator by the Pie Man (pie@the.man)". *translatorVersion* gives a version number for the translator. For example, a translatorVersion of 314 is interpreted as version 3.14.

These are required data.

The Media Kit

The Media Kit

WARNING

The Media Kit is undergoing massive surgery. The current Kit (the one documented here) will be supported in future releases, but work on this Kit has stopped. Look for a new Media Kit in BeOS Release 4.

The Media Kit gives you tools that let you generate, examine, manipulate, and realize (or *render*) sound data in real-time. It's based on the notion of *subscribers* that receive buffers of data from one of two *audio streams* that are managed by the system wide *Audio Server*. The Kit provides three subscriber/stream classes:

- BSubscriber defines the basic rules to which all subscribers must adhere. If you want to bring sound data into your application, this is where you start to learn about it.

- BADCStream lets you read sound data coming in (the "sound-in stream") from an external source, such as a microphone or CD.

- BDACStream provides access to the "sound-out stream," which lets you access the sound being sent to the system speaker, headphones, or other sound output devices.

The Kit also provides a BSoundFile class that lets you read from and write to sound files, and global functions that let you play sound files.

Sound Hardware

The sound hardware consists of a number of physical devices (jacks, converters, and the like), a signal path that routes audio data between these devices, and "control points" along the signal path that let you adjust the format and flow of the audio data. These elements are depicted in the following illustration.

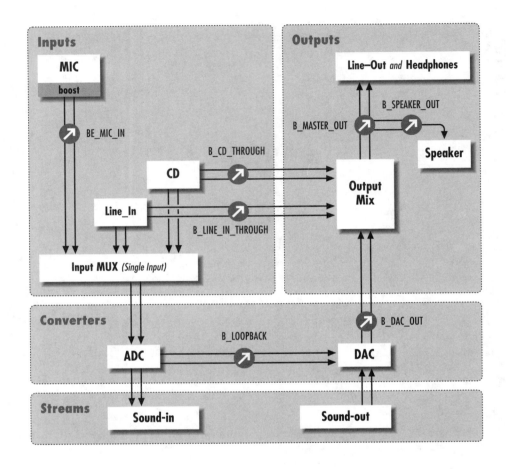

- The four large boxes ("inputs," "converters," "streams," and "outputs") divide the signal path into manageable territories; each territory is examined in separate sections, below.

- The smaller boxes ("MIC," "CD," and so on) are actual or virtual sound devices.

- The long-arrowed lines show how the devices are connected. A single line indicates a single channel, a double line means stereo. The arrowhead at the end of each line indicates the direction of the signal.

- The circled arrows show where the software can exhibit gain control over a device. Each control point is labelled as it's known to the Media Kit. Every control point has a volume control and can be individually enabled or disabled.

Not all hardware has all of these devices. Most Macintosh models, for example, do not have the line-in device.

Inputs

There are three analog audio input devices:

- *The microphone.* The microphone jack at the back of the computer accepts a stereo mini-phone (1/8") plug. The analog microphone signal has its own volume control and mute, and also allows a 20 dB boost. The microphone signal then feeds into the input MUX.

- *Line-in.* The stereo line-in jacks at the back of the computer bring a line-level analog signal into the computer. This signal can be routed directly to the audio output devices, and fed to the MUX. The direct-to-output, or "through," path has its own volume control and mute; this control point is called B_LINE_IN_THROUGH by the Kit. This input device is available on all BeBox models, but is not necessarily present on all Macintosh or PC systems.

- *CD input.* The CD (analog) input has the same features as line-in: The CD signal can be sent through to the output (B_CD_THROUGH), and it can be fed to the MUX.

Note that the microphone signal *doesn't* have a through path.

To bring an analog signal into your application (so you can record it, for example), the signal must pass through the input MUX:

- The MUX is a "mutually exclusive" device that lets you choose a single (analog) input from among the three sources listed above. In other words, you can bring in the microphone signal *or* the line-in signal *or* the CD signal, but you can't bring in any two or all of them at the same time. The MUX passes the input signal to its output without conversion to digital representation or other modification.

Converters

There are two sound data converters, the analog-to-digital converter (ADC) and the digital-to-analog converter (DAC):

- The ADC takes the analog signal that it reads from the MUX and converts it to digital representation. It does this by producing a series of *samples*, or instantaneous measurements of the signal's amplitude. The ADC control point is called B_ADC_IN.

- The DAC converts digital sound data into a continuous analog signal. The DAC control point is called B_DAC_OUT.

Acting as a sort of "short-circuit" between these two devices is the loopback:

- The loopback path takes the digital signal straight out of the ADC and sends it to the DAC. This path is intended, primarily, to simulate a "through" path for the microphone signal. There's little reason to send the line-in or CD signal down the loopback path since they have actual through paths built in.

Streams

The sound-in stream and sound-out stream are represented in the Media Kit by the BADCStream and BDACStream classes. By subscribing to the sound-in stream you receive the samples that are emitted by the ADC; and by subscribing to the sound-out stream, you can send buffers of digital sound data to the DAC.

The stream classes also furnish functions that let you set sound hardware parameters. For example, the BADCStream class has a `SetADCInput()` function that lets you set the input to the MUX.

Outputs

The output devices take analog signals and broadcast them to hardware that can turn the signals into sound.

- The output mixer mixes the signal from the DAC with the signals from the line-in and CD through paths. You can control the output of this mix at the `B_MASTER_OUT` control point.

- The mixed signal is presented at the stereo line-out jacks at the back of the computer. This is the same signal that's presented at the headphone jack.

- The stereo signal is mixed to mono (and attenuated by 6 dB) and sent to the abysmal internal speaker. The speaker has its own volume and mute control (`B_SPEAKER_OUT`).

Sound Data

The sound data that's brought into your application is *always* 16-bit linear stereo samples, with the left and right samples interleaved (left channel first). You can alter the sampling rate through functions provided by BADCStream and BDACStream.

BSubscriber

Derived from: *none*

Declared in: be/media/Subscriber.h

Library: libmedia.so

BSubscriber objects receive and process buffers of sound data that they receive from one of the Audio Server's sound streams (the sound-in and sound-out streams). A BSubscriber's tasks are (in this order):

- Subscribing to one of the streams (`Subscribe()`). This tells the server which stream the subscriber wants data from.

- Entering the stream (`EnterStream()`). Once a BSubscriber enters a stream, it begins receiving data buffers from the server.

- Processing the sound data it receives. It does this in its implementation of its "enter-stream hook." The Audio Server passes data to the BSubscriber by calling the BSubscriber's enter-stream hook (it calls the function once for each buffer of data).

A BSubscriber can receive buffers from (or "be subscribed to") only one stream at a time; however, more than one BSubscriber can subscribe to the same stream. The subscribers in a particular stream stand side by side, and buffers are passed from one to the next until they reach the end of the line (at which point they're "emptied" and recycled).

The BSubscribers in a given stream don't have to belong to the same application. This means that your BSubscriber may be examining, adding to, or filtering data that was generated by another application.

The Audio Server takes care of managing the data buffers in the sound-in and sound-out streams: It allocates new buffers, passes them from BSubscriber to BSubscriber, clears existing buffers for reuse, and so forth. A BSubscriber's job is to process the data that it receives as quickly as possible.

Subscribing

To subscribe to a stream, you need to instantiate an object that represents the stream, and then tell your BSubscriber to `Subscribe()` to that object. The Media Kit provides two stream classes: BADCStream for the sound-in stream, and BDACStream for the sound-out stream. For example, to subscribe to the sound-out stream you do this:

```
BDACStream*outStream = new BDACStream();
BSubscriber*outSubscriber = new BSubscriber();
outSubscriber->Subscribe(outStream);
```

Subscription to a stream doesn't cause the subscriber to immediately begin receiving buffers from that stream; it just means that the server has given the subscriber permission to enter the stream. In order to begin receiving buffers from the stream, the `EnterStream()` function has to be called.

Entering the Stream

Once the BSubscriber has successfully subscribed to a server's stream, it can enter the stream so it can start receiving data. You do this by calling the `EnterStream()` function:

> virtual status_t EnterStream(subscriber_id *neighbor*, bool *before*,
>   void **userData*, enter_stream_hook *enterHook*,
>   exit_stream_hook *exitHook*, bool *background*)

The specifics on how `EnterStream()` is used are described in the following sections.

Positioning Your BSubscriber

The first two arguments to the `EnterStream()` function let you position the subscriber in the stream relative to another subscriber that's already in the stream.

The *neighbor* argument identifies the BSubscriber (by ID number, as returned by the `ID()` function) that you want the entering BSubscriber to stand next to in the stream. The *before* argument is used to specify whether the entering BSubscriber will be placed before (`true`) or after (`false`) the *neighbor*. The neighbor doesn't have to belong to the same application as the entering object, but it must already have entered the stream.

If you want to put the BSubscriber at the beginning or the end of the stream (or to add the first BSubscriber to the stream, in which case there are no neighbors to stand next to), specify `NULL` as the *neighbor*. In this case, a *before* value of `true` indicates that the BSubscriber should be placed at the beginning of the stream, and a *before* value of `false` indicates that the BSubscriber should be placed at the end of the stream.

If your subscriber is at the front of the stream, it will be the first to receive buffers. If it's at the end of the stream, it will be the last to receive buffers before they're realized and recycled. Note, however, that a BSubscriber's position in the stream can't be locked. If you place your subscriber at the back of the stream, for example, another BSubscriber could be added to the end of the stream—possibly by another application—which would cause your BSubscriber to be bumped forward and no longer be the last subscriber in the stream.

Receiving and Processing Buffers

After your BSubscriber has entered the stream, it will begin receiving buffers of data. The *userData*, *enterHook*, and *background* arguments to `EnterStream()` tell the server how your BSubscriber will receive those buffers.

- *enterHook* is a pointer to the enter-stream hook (the complete protocol is given below) that will be invoked once for each buffer your object receives.

- *userData* is a pointer-sized value that will be passed as an argument to *enterHook*. You can use this to pass a reference to data your *enterHook* will need.

- The value of *background* is used to determine whether *enterHook* will be executed in a separate thread (`true`) or in the same thread (`false`) as that in which `EnterStream()` was called. If you run in the background, `EnterStream()` returns immediately; if not, the function doesn't return until the object has exited the stream.

Of key interest is the enter-stream hook that you must provide. This is a global C function or static C++ member function that's invoked once for each buffer received by the BSubscriber. The protocol for the function (which is `typedef`'d as `enter_stream_hook`) is:

bool `streamHook`(void *userData*, char *buffer*, size_t *count*, void *header*)

- *userData* is the same as the *userData* value passed to `EnterStream()`.

- *buffer* is a pointer to the buffer that has just arrived.

- *count* is the number of bytes of data in the buffer.

- *header* is a pointer to the header of the sound buffer. This value can usually be ignored.

You have to implement the enter-stream hook yourself; the Media Kit doesn't supply any default enter-stream hooks for you. From within your implementation of the function, you should process the data in the buffer in whatever way your program requires. As mentioned previously, keep in mind that your enter-stream hook should be as efficient as possible.

Above all else, remember the following rule:

- Never clear the buffer. If you're generating new data, add it to the data already in the buffer, but don't just overwrite it. Failure to follow this important rule will make other applications (and the people using them) very unhappy. An example of this is given in the description of the BDACStream class.

When your enter-stream hook is done processing the buffer, you simply return from the function. You don't have to do anything to cause the buffer to be sent to the next subscriber; that's handled for you by the Media Kit. The value your enter-stream hook returns is important, though. Return `true` if your BSubscriber wants to keep receiving buffers or `false` to be removed from the stream.

For an example of an enter-stream hook, see the description of the BDACStream class.

Exiting the Stream

There are two ways to remove a BSubscriber from a stream. The first was mentioned above: Return `false` from the enter-stream hook. The second method is to call `ExitStream()` directly. `ExitStream()` is particularly useful if you're running the enter-stream hook in the background and you want to stop it from another thread.

Whichever method is used, the BSubscriber's exit-stream hook is invoked upon exiting the stream. This is an optional callback function, similar to the enter-stream hook, that is supplied as the *exitHook* parameter to `EnterStream()`. You can specify `NULL` for this parameter if you don't want or need an exit-stream hook.

The protocol for the exit-stream hook is:

> status_t `exit_stream_hook`(void *_userData_, status_t _error_)

- The *userData* value is, again, taken from the `EnterStream()` call.

- *error* is a code that explains why the BSubscriber is exiting the stream.

Normally, *error* is `B_OK`. This means that the BSubscriber is exiting naturally—either because the enter-stream hook returned `false` or because `ExitStream()` was called. If *error* is `B_TIMED_OUT`, then the BSubscriber is exiting because of a delay in receiving the next buffer. You can set the timeout limit through BSubscriber's `SetTimeout()` function, specifying the time limit in microseconds. By default, the object will never time out. Any other error code will have been generated by a lower-level entity and can be loosely interpreted as "something went wrong."

The exit-stream hook is executed in the same thread as the enter-stream hook. If this isn't a background thread, the value returned by the exit-stream hook is then returned by `EnterStream()`. If you *are* using a background thread, the value returned by the exit-stream hook is lost.

You can perform whatever clean-up is necessary in your exit-stream hook. The only thing you must never do is delete the BSubscriber itself.

Constructor and Destructor

BSubscriber()

> BSubscriber(const char *_name_ = NULL)

Creates and returns a new BSubscriber object. The object can be given a name, which needn't be unique.

After creating a BSubscriber, you typically do the following (in this order):

- Subscribe the object to a buffer stream by calling `Subscribe()`.
- Allow the object to begin receiving buffers by calling `EnterStream()`.

The construction of a BSubscriber never fails.

~BSubscriber

> ~BSubscriber()

Destroys the BSubscriber object. You should never delete a BSubscriber from within an implementation of the object's enter-stream hook or exit-stream hook. It isn't necessary to tell the object to exit the buffer stream or to unsubscribe it before deleting; these actions will be taken automatically.

Member Functions

EnterStream()

> virtual status_t **EnterStream**(subscriber_id *neighbor*, bool *before*, void **userData*,
>   enter_stream_hook *enterHook*,
>   exit_stream_hook *exitHook*, bool *background*)

Causes the BSubscriber to begin receiving data buffers from its stream. The object must have successfully subscribed to the stream by calling `Subscribe()` before it can enter the stream. The arguments are:

- *neighbor* identifies the BSubscriber that this object will stand next to in the buffer stream. If neighbor is NULL, this BSubscriber will be positioned either at the front or the back of the buffer stream, depending on the value of the next argument.

- *before*, if `true`, causes the BSubscriber to be placed immediately before *neighbor* in the stream. If it's `false`, this object is placed after the *neighbor* in the stream. If neighbor was NULL, this object is placed at the front of the stream if *before* is `true` or the back of the stream if *before* is `false`.

- *userData* is a pointer-sized value that's forwarded as an argument to the enter- and exit-stream hooks, which are specified in the next two arguments to `EnterStream()`.

- *enterHook* is a global function that's called once for every buffer that's sent to the BSubscriber. The protocol for this function is:

  bool **enter_hook**(void **userData*, char **buffer*, size_t *count*, void **header*)

The *userData* argument taken here is the same value as was passed into the `EnterStream()` function. A pointer to the buffer itself is passed as *buffer*, and the size of the buffer, in bytes, is passed as *count*. *header* is a pointer to the buffer's header. If the enter-stream hook returns `true`, the object continues to receive buffers; if it returns `false`, the BSubscriber exits the stream.

- *exitHook* is a global function that's called after the BSubscriber has finished processing its last buffer. Its protocol is:

  status_t **exit_hook**(void **userData*, status_t *error*)

  Here, as before, *userData* is taken from the argument to `EnterStream()`. *error* is a code that describes why the object is exiting the stream: `B_OK` means that the object has received an `ExitStream()` call, or that the enter-stream hook returned `false`; an *error* of `B_TIMED_OUT` means the time limit between buffer receptions, as set through `SetTimeout()`, has expired.

  If the function isn't running in the background (as described in the next argument), the value returned by the exit-stream hook becomes the value that's returned by `EnterStream()`.

  The exit-stream hook is optional; a value of `NULL` is accepted.

- *background*, if `true`, causes the enter- and exit-stream hooks to be executed in a separate thread which is spawned for you by the Media Kit. In this case, `EnterStream()` returns immediately. If it's `false`, the functions are executed synchronously within the `EnterStream()` call.

Return values:
  B_OK. The subscriber successfully entered the stream. If *background* is `false`, indicates that the exit-stream hook returned `B_OK`.
  B_BAD_SUBSCRIBER. The BSubscriber is already in the stream.
  B_SUBSCRIBER_NOT_ENTERED. The *neighbor* isn't in the buffer stream.
  B_STREAM_NOT_FOUND. The subscriber's stream doesn't exist.
  Other errors, as returned by the exit-stream hook (if background is `false`).

See also: `ExitStream()`

ExitStream()

virtual status_t **ExitStream**(bool *andWait* = false)

Causes the BSubscriber to withdraw from the buffer stream after it completes the processing of its current buffer. If *andWait* is `true`, the function doesn't return until the object has completed processing this final buffer and has actually left the stream. If an exit-stream hook was supplied when `EnterStream()` was called, it will run to exit-stream before the `ExitStream()` function returns. If *andWait* is `false` (the default), `ExitStream()` returns immediately.

Return values:

B_OK. No error occurred.

B_BAD_SUBSCRIBER. The object doesn't have a valid subscriber ID.

B_SUBSCRIBER_NOT_ENTERED. The object isn't in the stream.

B_STREAM_NOT_FOUND. The subscriber's stream doesn't exist.

ID()

subscriber_id **ID**(void) const

Returns the `subscriber_id` value that uniquely identifies this BSubscriber. A subscriber ID is issued when the object subscribes to a stream, and is withdrawn when the object unsubscribes. ID values are used primarily to position a BSubscriber with respect to another BSubscriber within a buffer stream.

If the BSubscriber isn't currently subscribed to any stream, `B_NO_SUBSCRIBER_ID` is returned.

IsInStream()

bool **IsInStream**(void) const

Returns `true` if the object is currently in a stream; otherwise it returns `false`.

Name()

const char ***Name**(void) const

Returns a pointer to the name of the BSubscriber. The name is set when constructing the BSubscriber and cannot be changed.

- The pointer returned by `Name()` belongs to the BSubscriber object; do not alter or dispose of it.

SetTimeout(), Timeout()

void **SetTimeout**(bigtime_t *microseconds*)
bigtime_t **Timeout**(void) const

These functions set and return the amount of time, measured in microseconds, that a BSubscriber that has entered the buffer stream is willing to wait from the time that it finishes processing one buffer until the time that it gets the next buffer. If the time limit expires before the next buffer arrives, the BSubscriber exits the stream and the exit-stream hook is called with its error argument set to B_TIMED_OUT.

A time limit of 0 (the default) means no time limit—the BSubscriber will wait forever for its next buffer.

Timeout() see SetTimeout()

Subscribe()

> virtual status_t **Subscribe**(BAbstractBufferStream *stream*)

Asks for admission into the server's list of BSubscribers to which buffers of data will be sent by the server. Subscribing doesn't cause the BSubscriber to begin receiving buffers—it simply gives the object the *right* to do so. To begin receiving buffers, you must invoke EnterStream() on a BSubscriber that has been successfully subscribed.

The *stream* is a pointer to a buffer stream derived from the BAbstractBufferStream class. For instance, to subscribe to the sound-out stream, you would instantiate a BDACStream object, and pass a pointer to that stream object to the Subscribe() function. Likewise, a BADCStream object would be instantiated and passed as the *stream* argument if you wanted to subscribe to the audio input stream.

A successful subscription returns B_OK.

Return values:
> B_OK. The subscription request was successful.
> B_BAD_PORT_ID. The buffer stream's server is not initialized properly.
> B_TIMED_OUT. The buffer stream is locked and the request for access timed out.

Unsubscribe()

> status_t **Unsubscribe**(void)

Revokes the BSubscriber's access to its media server and sets its subscriber ID to B_NO_SUBSCRIBER_ID. If the object is currently in a stream, it is removed from the stream automatically and the object's exit-stream hook is called.

When you delete a BSubscriber, it's automatically unsubscribed from its stream.

Return values:
> B_OK. The BSubscriber successfully unsubscribed from the stream.
> B_BAD_SUBSCRIBER. The BSubscriber doesn't have a valid subscriber ID.
> B_STREAM_NOT_FOUND. The subscriber's stream does not exist.

BADCStream

Derived from:	BAbstractBufferStream
Declared in:	be/media/AudioStream.h
Library:	libmedia.so

The BADCStream class represents the sound-in stream. Subscribers to this stream receive buffers containing 16-bit linear stereo sample data that have been input from external sources (such as microphones or the CD audio player). This stream is available even in the absence of an input source (in which case the buffers your BSubscriber receives will have all zero samples).

Controlling the Hardware

The BADCStream class provides several functions that let you control the sound input hardware as well as determine the current state of the hardware. These functions can be used even if you haven't subscribed to the stream yet.

Selecting a Source

You can control which of the audio sources you wish to receive data from by using the `SetADCInput()` call. Likewise, you can determine which source is currently being used by calling `ADCInput()`:

```
BADCStream stream;
stream->SetADCInput(B_CD_IN);// Use CD-ROM audio input

int32 currentDevice;
stream->ADCInput(&currentDevice);// What device is input?
```

Valid devices are:

- `B_MIC_IN`. Microphone input.
- `B_CD_IN`. Compact disc input.
- `B_LINE_IN`. Line input.

The Microphone Boost

There's a 20 dB boost available for the microphone input. This can be turned on and off using the `BoostMic()` function. The current status of the boost can be determined using the `IsMicBoosted()` function.

```
if (!IsMicBoosted()) {
   stream->BoostMic(true);// Turn on the 20 dB boost
}
```

The above code turns on the boost if it's not already on (in reality, you don't need to check before turning the boost on—just turn it on if you need it, and turn it off if you don't). There is no guaranteed default value for whether or not the microphone is boosted; the Sound preference panel allows users to set the default for the 20 dB boost.

Sampling Rate

BADCStream provides two functions for controlling and determining the current sampling rate of the sound-in stream.

The `SetSamplingRate()` function is used to change the sampling rate currently in effect on the sound-in stream. If you want to sample CD-quality sound, for example, you would issue the following call, assuming that `stream` is a pointer to your BADCStream object:

```
stream->SetSamplingRate(44100.0);
```

You can specify any sampling rate you wish; if the rate you specify isn't supported by the sound hardware of the computer your application is running on, the closest available rate will automatically be selected.

To determine the current sampling rate, use the `SamplingRate()` function:

```
float currentRate;
stream->SamplingRate(&currentRate);
```

For more information on sampling rates and sample formats, see the BDACStream class.

Managing the Buffers

If you wish, you can refine the performance of your software by specifying the size and the number of audio buffers in the sound-in stream. The Audio Server provides acceptable defaults for both the size and number of buffers in the stream. However, you can change these settings using the `SetStreamBuffers()` function.

- By decreasing the size and/or number of buffers, you can decrease the maximum latency of the stream (the time it takes for a buffer to get from one end of the stream to the other). However, if you go too far in this direction, you run the risk of falling out of real time.

- By increasing the buffer size and count, you help ensure the real-time integrity of the stream, but you increase its maximum latency.

For instance, if your experiments have determined that your code will work most efficiently with six 4k buffers, you would use the following code to establish the new buffers:

```
outStream->SetStreamBuffers(4096, 6);
```

This specifies that each of the six buffers in the stream should be 4,096 bytes (4k) long. The change affects all applications using the sound-in stream. Since your application may not be alone using the stream, you should keep in mind that other applications may use this call as well, so be sure your code can handle buffers that change in size from one invocation of your enter-stream hook to the next.

Constructor and Destructor

BADCStream()

> BADCStream()

Creates and returns a new BADCStream object, which represents a sound-in stream.

After creating a BADCStream, you can use the resulting pointer as the stream parameter for your subscriber's `Subscribe()` call:

```
BSubscriber   *subscriber;
BADCStream    *stream;

subscriber = new BSubscriber();
stream = new BADCStream();
subscriber->Subscribe(stream);
```

Once you've subscribed to the output stream, you can proceed to enter the stream, at which point your enter-stream hook will begin receiving incoming audio buffers.

~BADCStream()

> ~BADCStream()

Destroys the BADCStream object. Don't do this if you have a BSubscriber currently subscribed to the stream.

Member Functions

ADCInput(), SetADCInput()

> status_t **ADCInput**(int32 *currentDevice*) const
> status_t **SetADCInput**(int32 *newDevice*)

These functions get and set the device that provides the sound input for this BADCStream object.

Valid values for *device* are:

- `B_MIC_IN`. Microphone input.
- `B_CD_IN`. Compact disc input.
- `B_LINE_IN`. Line input.

You don't have to be subscribed to the stream to use these functions. If an error occurs, `ADCInput()` does not alter the memory pointed to by *currentDevice*.

Return values:
> B_OK. The operation was a success.
> B_BAD_REPLY. Unable to determine or change the input device.
> B_SERVER_NOT_FOUND. The Audio Server is not running.

BoostMic(), IsMicBoosted()

> status_t **BoostMic**(bool *boost*)
> bool **IsMicBoosted**(void) const

`BoostMic()` enables (if *boost* is `true`) or disables (if *boost* is `false`) the 20 dB boost on the microphone signal. `IsMicBoosted()` returns the current state of the boost.

You don't have to already have subscribed to the stream to use these functions.

Return values:
> B_OK. The operation was a success.
> B_BAD_REPLY. Unable to determine or change the current boost setting.
> B_SERVER_NOT_FOUND. The Audio Server is not running.

SamplingRate(), SetSamplingRate()

> status_t **SamplingRate**(float **currentRate*)
> status_t **SetSamplingRate**(float *newRate*)

These functions allow you to get and set the current sampling rate of the stream.

When calling `SetSamplingRate()` to set the current sampling rate, the value you specify will automatically be rounded to the nearest value accepted by the hardware on which your application is running.

You don't have to already have subscribed to the stream to use these functions. If an error occurs, `SamplingRate()` does not alter the memory pointed to by *currentRate*.

Return values:
> B_OK. The operation was a success.
> B_BAD_REPLY. Unable to determine or change the current sampling rate.
> B_SERVER_NOT_FOUND. The Audio Server is not running.

SetADCInput()   see ADCInput()

SetSamplingRate()   see SamplingRate()

SetStreamBuffers()

> status_t **SetStreamBuffers**(size_t *bufferSize*, int32 *bufferCount*)

Sets the size in bytes and the number of buffers that are used to transport data through the stream. Although it's up to the server to provide reasonable default values, you can fine-tune the performance of the stream by adjusting these values:

- By decreasing the size and/or number of buffers, you can decrease the maximum latency of the stream (the time it takes for a buffer to get from one end of the stream to the other). However, if you go too far in this direction, you run the risk of falling out of real time.

- By increasing the buffer size and count, you help ensure the real-time integrity of the stream, but you increase its maximum latency.

Return values:

> B_OK. The operation was a success.

> B_BAD_REPLY. Unable to determine or change the buffer settings.

> B_SERVER_NOT_FOUND. The Audio Server is not running.

BDACStream

Derived from:	BAbstractBufferStream
Declared in:	be/media/AudioStream.h
Library:	libmedia.so

The BDACStream class represents the sound-out stream. It's used in tandem with the BSubscriber class to manipulate blocks of sound data flowing through the output stream.

The sound-out stream, which consists of buffers of sound data, flows from one BSubscriber to the next until finally it reaches the output device or devices (the speaker, headphone port, and line-out port).

Each subscriber can, if it wishes, change the data in the buffers it receives. These changes include, but aren't limited to:

- Mixing in additional sounds.

- Filtering the sound. Noise-removal, volume and pitch control, echo, and other effects can be added to sounds in the stream.

See the BSubscriber class for more information on how to enter the sound-out stream.

Controlling the Hardware

The BDACStream class defines several functions that control the sound output hardware and let you determine the current state of the hardware. These functions can be called even when you haven't subscribed to the stream.

Volume and Muting

To set the volume level of a particular sound device, use the `SetVolume()` function. This function accepts three parameters:

- A constant that identifies the device you want to control.
- A float representing the new volume for the left channel of the device.
- A float representing the new volume for the right channel of the device.

The possible device constants are:

Constant	Meaning
B_CD_THROUGH	CD throughput
B_LINE_IN_THROUGH	Line in throughput
B_ADC_IN	ADC input
B_LOOPBACK	Audio loopback
B_DAC_OUT	DAC output
B_MASTER_OUT	Master output
B_SPEAKER_OUT	Speaker output

All volume levels are floating-point numbers from 0.0 to 1.0, where 0.0 is silent and 1.0 is the loudest. If you're setting the volume of a single-channel device, such as the speaker, the left channel volume is used and the right channel volume is ignored. If you want to set the volume of one channel of a stereo device but leave the other channel's volume unchanged, specify the constant `B_NO_CHANGE` for the volume of the channel to leave alone.

For example, if you want to change the volume of the CD throughput signal, you could use the following code:

```
BDACStream    stream = BDACStream();

// Set the right channel's volume to 50% and
// leave the left channel's volume alone.

stream->SetVolume(B_CD_THROUGH, B_NO_CHANGE, 0.5);
```

Use the `GetVolume()` function to determine the current volume of a device's left and right channels:

```
float      left, right;
bool       enable;

stream->GetVolume(B_CD_THROUGH, &left, &right, &enable);
```

This code places the current left channel volume in the variable `left`, the right channel volume in the variable `right`, and sets the `enable` variable to `true` if the CD throughput device is currently enabled (not muted). You can specify `NULL` for any of these pointers (*left*, *right*, or *enable*) whose value you don't want to retrieve.

To mute a device, you must disable it using the `EnableDevice()` function. The first argument is the constant representing the device you want to control, and the second argument is a boolean specifying whether or not the device is currently active. This boolean should be `true` if the device should be enabled or `false` if it should be disabled.

To mute a sound (such as the built-in speaker), simply do the following:

```
stream->EnableDevice(B_SPEAKER_OUT, false);
```

To unmute the speaker, the following code can be used:

```
stream->EnableDevice(B_SPEAKER_OUT, true);
```

The `IsDeviceEnabled()` function can be used to determine if the device is enabled or not. It returns `true` if the device is enabled and `false` otherwise.

Sampling Rate

Sound is represented digitally by taking regular, periodic samples of a sound and storing those values in memory. The stream of samples comprises the complete sound. For instance, consider the following sound wave:

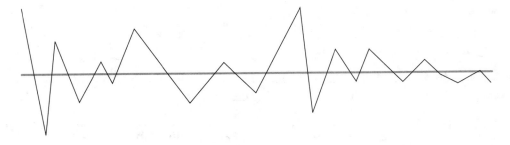

To represent this sound digitally, we break it up into a finite number of regular, periodic samples. Typically, these samples are represented by 8- or 16-bit integers (16-bit samples provide higher sample resolution, and thus higher sound quality, but double the size of the sound). The value 0 usually represents silence, and numbers increasingly far away specify the amplitude of the sound wave at the time increment represented by the individual sample.

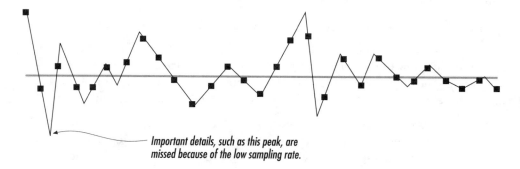

Important details, such as this peak, are
missed because of the low sampling rate.

In the diagram above, we've taken periodic samples of the sound. They're very far apart, and we miss some important details. That's because we used a low sampling rate—the samples we took of the sound are so far apart that we lose resolution in the sound. The more samples we use, the less risk there is of missing details in the sound.

Simply put: the higher the sampling rate used to record a sound, the less detail will be lost and the higher the quality of the recording. CD audio uses a sampling rate of 44.1kHz—44,100 samples per second.

However, the higher the sampling rate used, the more memory (and disk space) the sound will require. For instance, one minute of CD-quality audio (44.1kHz, 16-bit stereo) requires 10,584,000 bytes of memory:

• 44,100 bytes/sec * 2 bytes/sample * 2 channels * 60 sec/min = 10,584,000 bytes

If you use the 22,050 byte/sec sampling rate, you use half as much memory:

• 22,050 bytes/sec * 2 bytes/sample * 2 channels * 60 sec/min = 5,292,000 bytes

You can save even more memory by dropping to 8-bit audio:

• 22,050 bytes/sec * 1 byte/sample * 2 channels * 60 sec/min = 2,646,000 bytes

By carefully selecting the sampling rate and sample size (8 or 16 bits), you can compromise between your storage requirements and the quality of your audio.

When you create a sound, you specify the sampling rate at which the sound is sampled. Likewise, when you play back a sound, using the BDACStream class, you need to set the stream to play back the sound at the desired sampling rate (usually the same rate used when recording the sound, but you can get some interesting special effects by varying the output sampling rate).

BDACStream provides two functions for controlling and determining the current sampling rate of the sound-out stream.

The `SetSamplingRate()` function is used to change the sampling rate currently in effect on the sound-out stream. If you want to play back sound sampled at 44.1kHz, you would issue the following call, assuming that *outStream* is a pointer to your BDACStream object:

```
outStream->SetSamplingRate(44100.0);
```

You can specify any sampling rate you wish; if the rate you specify isn't supported by the sound hardware of the computer you're running the BeOS on, the closest possible rate will automatically be selected.

To determine the current sampling rate, use the `SamplingRate()` function:

```
float  currentRate;
outStream->SamplingRate(&currentRate);
```

If the above code were run with the stream set to 44.1kHz, the *currentRate* variable would contain the value 44100.0 after `SamplingRate()` returns.

Wading Into the Stream

Your application can subscribe to the audio stream and add to or alter the sound flowing through the stream. To do so, you first have to instantiate a BDACStream object to represent the stream itself. Then you have to establish a subscriber, which represents an inlet into the stream:

```
BDACStream*outStream;
BSubscriber*outSubscriber;

// Create the output stream and the subscriber.

outStream = new BDACStream();
outSubscriber = new BSubscriber("Output_Stream_Name");

// Subscribe to the output stream.

outSubscriber->Subscribe(outStream);
```

This doesn't actually give the subscriber access to the stream, though. When you're ready to begin altering the output stream, you have to enter the stream by calling the BSubscriber's `EnterStream()` function. When you enter the audio stream, you establish a pointer to a function which receives blocks of audio data as they flow down the stream. That function can insert new data into the stream or alter the data already present in the stream. `EnterStream()` is described in great detail in the BSubscriber section. An example of how to use the BDACStream class in tandem with BSubscriber is provided in a later section.

Managing the Buffers

If you wish, you can refine the performance of your software by specifying the size and the number of audio buffers in the sound-out stream. The Audio Server provides acceptable defaults for both the size and number of buffers in the stream. However, you can change these settings using the `SetStreamBuffers()` function.

- By decreasing the size and/or number of buffers, you can decrease the maximum latency of the stream (the time it takes for a buffer to get from one end of the stream to the other). However, if you go too far in this direction, you run the risk of falling out of real time.

- By increasing the buffer size and count, you help ensure the real-time integrity of the stream, but you increase its maximum latency.

For instance, if your experiments have determined that your code will work most efficiently with six 4k buffers, you would use the following code to establish the new buffers:

```
outStream->SetStreamBuffers(4096, 6);
```

This specifies that each of the six buffers in the stream should be 4,096 bytes (4k) long. The change affects all applications using the sound-out stream. Since your application may not be alone using the stream, you should keep in mind that other applications may use this call as well, so be sure your code can handle buffers that change in size from one invocation of your enter-stream hook to the next.

An Example

In this example, we'll create a class that makes sounds played by other programs play quieter than normal (at a third normal volume). This is a fairly trivial example, but it covers all the basics. First, the class definition:

```
class DimSound : public BDACStream {
   public:
      void Start(void);// Start dimming sound
      void Stop(void);// Cut it out!

   private:
      static bool_dim_sound(void *userData,
                char *buffer,
                size_t count,
                void *header);
      bool DimIt(char *buffer, size_t count);

      BSubscriber  subscriber;
};
```

This class, derived from BDACStream, has public functions to start and stop the sound dimming effect (creatively named `Start()` and `Stop()`), as well as the private `_dim_sound()` function (which is the enter-stream hook we'll pass to `EnterStream()`, and the `DimIt()` function, which is called by `_dim_sound()`. In addition, this class has a BSubscriber that will be used to subscribe to the sound-out stream.

Since the audio received by the subscriber is always in 16-bit stereo format, we'll define a special structure called a `standard_frame` that will represent a single frame of audio in this format. Also, we create the `STANDARD_FRAME_SIZE` constant to represent the size of one of these frames in bytes.

```
struct standard_frame {
   int16  left; // Left channel's sample
   int16  right;// Right channel's sample
};
typedef struct standard_frame standard_frame;

#define STANDARD_FRAME_SIZE 4
```

The `Start()` function, below, simply subscribes to the audio stream and, if successful, enters the stream. Since the DimSound class is derived from BDACStream, we pass a reference to the DimSound object to `Subscribe()`. Also, we pass a pointer to the DimSound object to `EnterStream()` as the *userData* parameter, so that the enter-stream hook can access the object. This function would be called when you want to start dimming the volume of sounds.

```
void DimSound::Start(void) {
   if (subscriber.Subscribe(this) == B_OK) {
      subscriber.EnterStream(NULL, false, this, _dim_sound,
             NULL, true);
   }
}
```

The `Stop()` function does the opposite. It exits and unsubscribes from the sound-out stream.

```
void DimSound::Stop(void) {
   subscriber.ExitStream(false);// Leave the stream
   subscriber.Unsubscribe();// And unsubscribe from it
}
```

Now we get to the meat of things. The `_dim_sound()` function is the static function we passed to `EnterStream()` as the *enterStreamHook* parameter. This function is called once for each block of audio data so we can process the data. In our case, we pass through to the `DimIt()` function, which does the actual processing. We do this using *userData*, which is a pointer to the DimSound object itself.

```
bool DimSound::_dim_sound(void *userData, char *buffer,
             size_t count, void *header) {
   return (((DimSound *) userData)->DimIt(buffer, count));
}
```

DimIt() is where the actual bit-twiddling is done. We begin by establishing a local pointer of type `standard_frame *` to the audio buffer. Since the count parameter specifies the size of the buffer in bytes, we have to compute the number of frames by dividing by STANDARD_FRAME_SIZE.

Once we've done that, we can loop through each of the frames in the buffer and divide the left and right samples of each frame by three. When we're finished, we return true; if we returned false, we would be automatically exited from the stream.

```
bool DimSound::DimIt(char *buffer, size_t count) {
   standard_frame *soundData;// Pointer to the frame to alter
   int32       frameCount;// Number of frames to manage

   soundData = (standard_frame *) buffer;

   frameCount = count/STANDARD_FRAME_SIZE;

   while (frameCount-- > 0) {
      soundData->left /= 3;
      soundData->right /= 3;
      soundData++;// Move on to the next frame
   }

   return true;
}
```

We wrap things up by providing a tiny little `main()` function for demonstration purposes. It simply starts the dimmer, waits for the user to press the return key, and stops the dimmer. If you want to play with this sample, try launching another program that plays sound (such as CDPlayer) and then run dimmer from a Terminal window.

```
void main(void) {
   DimSound dimmer;

   dimmer.Start();// Start dimming the sound

   printf("Now dimming sounds. Hit return to stop.\n");
   getchar();

   dimmer.Stop();// Stop diming the sound
}
```

This is a pretty simple example. You can get more ambitious; you can alter the sound in the buffer in any way you desire, including adding new sound data to the stream. There's one important thing to remember, though:

WARNING

Never clear the data already in the buffers you receive! Other programs are counting on you to be polite and leave their sounds alone. If you want to play a sound, add your sound data to the data already in the stream.

To properly play a sound, add your sample data to the stream like this:

```
soundData->left += myNewSample->left;
soundData->right += myNewSample->right;
```

Also, keep in mind before adding samples to the stream that you'll have to convert your data into 16-bit stereo format. If your sound is in 8-bit mono format, for example, you might do something like this:

```
char   *mysoundbuffer;
int32  i;

mysoundbuffer = read_sound_buffer(count);
while (i < frameCount) {
    soundData->left += ((int16) mysoundbuffer[i++]) << 8;
}
```

The `read_sound_buffer()` function's implementation is left as an exercise, but its purpose is to return a pointer to a buffer of *count* bytes of 8-bit mono sound data. Then, we loop through each frame, taking a byte from the sound data, shifting it up 8 bits (thereby converting it into a 16-bit sample) and adding it to the stream buffer.

You should check for possible clipping problems; this can occur if the sum of the existing sample and your new sample is greater than (or less than) can be represented in a 16-bit signed integer.

Constructor and Destructor

BDACStream()

BDACStream()

Creates and returns a new BDACStream object, which represents a sound output stream.

After creating a BDACStream, you can use the resulting pointer as the stream parameter for your subscriber's `Subscribe()` call.

~BDACStream()

~BDACStream()

Destroys the BDACStream object. Don't do this if a BSubscriber is currently subscribed to the stream.

Member Functions

EnableDevice(), IsDeviceEnabled()

> status_t **EnableDevice**(int32 *device*, bool *enable*)
> bool **IsDeviceEnabled**(int32 *device*) const

`EnableDevice()` lets you turn on and off sound output devices, and `IsDeviceEnabled()` returns the current state of a given output device.

For instance, to mute the internal speaker, you would use `EnableDevice()` as follows:

```
EnableDevice(B_SPEAKER_OUT, false);
```

Valid values for *device* are:

Constant	Meaning
B_CD_THROUGH	CD throughput
B_LINE_IN_THROUGH	Line in throughput
B_ADC_IN	ADC input
B_LOOPBACK	Audio loopback
B_DAC_OUT	DAC output
B_MASTER_OUT	Master output
B_SPEAKER_OUT	Speaker output

You don't have to be subscribed to the stream to use these functions.

Return values:
> B_OK. The operation was a success.
> B_BAD_REPLY. Unable to determine or change the output device.
> B_BAD_VALUE. Invalid *device* specified.
> B_SERVER_NOT_FOUND. The Audio Server is not running.

GetVolume(), SetVolume()

> status_t **GetVolume**(int32 *device*, float **leftVolume*, float **rightVolume*,
>   bool **enable*)

> status_t **SetVolume**(int32 *device*, float *leftVolume*, float *rightVolume*)

This pair of functions lets you get and set the volumes of the left and right channels of a given sound output device.

`GetVolume()` stores the left and right volumes in the floating-point variables pointed to by *leftVolume* and *rightVolume*, and also stores a boolean value in *enable* signifying whether or not the device is enabled (`true` if the device is active, `false` otherwise). You may pass a `NULL` pointer for any combination of these arguments for any information you don't need reported.

`SetVolume()` sets the current volumes of the left and right channels for the *device* to the values specified by *leftVolume* and *rightVolume*.

The volume ranges from 0.0 to 1.0, where 0.0 is silent and 1.0 is the maximum volume. If you're setting the volume of a single-channel device (such as the speaker), the left channel is used—the value you pass as the right channel volume is ignored. If you want to set the volume of one channel of a stereo device without changing the value of the other channel, pass the `B_NO_CHANGE` constant for the no-change channel.

You don't have to be subscribed to the stream to use these functions. If an error occurs, `GetVolume()` doesn't change the memory pointed to by *leftVolume*, *rightVolume*, and *enable*.

Return values:
  B_OK. The operation was a success.
  B_BAD_REPLY. Unable to determine or change the volume.
  B_BAD_VALUE. Invalid *device* specified.
  B_SERVER_NOT_FOUND. The Audio Server is not running.

IsDeviceEnabled() see EnableDevice()

SamplingRate(), SetSamplingRate()

  status_t **SamplingRate**(float **currentRate*)
  status_t **SetSamplingRate**(float *newRate*)

These functions allow you to get and set the current sampling rate of the stream.

When calling `SetSamplingRate()` to set the current sampling rate, the value you specify will automatically be rounded to the nearest value accepted by the hardware on which your application is running.

You don't have to be subscribed to the stream to use these functions. If an error occurs, `SamplingRate()` does not alter the memory at pointed to by *currentRate*.

Return values:
  B_OK. The operation was a success.
  B_BAD_REPLY. Unable to determine or change the current sampling rate.
  B_SERVER_NOT_FOUND. The Audio Server is not running.

SetStreamBuffers()

> status_t **SetStreamBuffers**(size_t *bufferSize*, int32 *bufferCount*)

Sets the size in bytes and the number of buffers that are used to transport data through the stream. Although it's up to the server to provide reasonable default values, you can fine-tune the performance of the stream by adjusting these values:

- By decreasing the size and/or number of buffers, you can decrease the maximum latency of the stream (the time it takes for a buffer to get from one end of the stream to the other). However, if you go too far in this direction, you run the risk of falling out of real time.

- By increasing the buffer size and count, you help ensure the real-time integrity of the stream, but you increase its maximum latency.

Return values:
 B_OK. The operation was a success.
 B_BAD_REPLY. Unable to change the buffer settings.
 B_SERVER_NOT_FOUND. The Audio Server is not running.

SetVolume() see GetVolume()

BSoundFile

Derived from: *none*

Declared in: be/media/SoundFile.h

Library: libmedia.so

BSoundFile objects give you access to files that contain sound data. The BSoundFile functions let you examine the format of the data in the sound file, read and write the data, and position a "frame pointer" in the file. BSoundFile does not, however, include functions for playing from a sound file. You can play a BSoundFile's data, but you'll have to set up code to do this yourself, using a BSubscriber object and a BDACStream object.

WARNING

At this time, BSoundFile does not allow writing to AIFF files. All other supported file formats can be written to.

To use a BSoundFile, you set its entry_ref, and then you open the file using the SetTo() call (there's also a version of the BSoundFile constructor that does this when the object is constructed). If you want to read the sound file (to play it, for example), open the file with B_READ_ONLY access. To write into the sound file (while recording, perhaps), use B_WRITE_ONLY access. B_READ_WRITE access is not allowed.

Sound File Formats

The BSoundFile class understands AIFF, WAVE, and "standard" UNIX sound files (*.snd* and *.au*). When you give BSoundFile a reference to a file, it opens the file and determines the format of the data it contains—you can't force it to assume a particular format. If the file is not in a format it understands ("unknown" format), it assumes that the file contains 44.1kHz, 16-bit stereo data, and that the file doesn't have a header (it assumes that the entire file is sound data). The admission of the unknown format means that *any* file can act as sound data. BSoundFile doesn't know the meaning of "inappropriate data."

The file formats are represented by the constants B_AIFF_FILE, B_WAVE_FILE, B_UNIX_FILE, and B_UNKNOWN_FILE. You can determine the format of the file represented by a BSoundFile object by using its FileFormat() function.

WARNING

Eight-bit WAVE data is, by definition, unsigned. When you use the Read-Frames() function to read data in this format, you must be sure to convert each sample into signed format before manipulating it further, since all other sound formats supported by BeOS are signed (including both the sound-in and sound-out streams).

WARNING

To convert an 8-bit WAVE sample into a signed 8-bit sample, just subtract 128 from the sample.

Sound Data Parameters

Once you've opened your BSoundFile, you can ask for information about the format of the data by calling the various format-retrieving functions (SamplingRate(), CountChannels(), SampleSize(), and so forth). There are also functions for setting these parameters (SetSamplingRate(), SetChannelCount(), SetSampleSize(), and so on). Note that these functions don't actually modify the data in the file (or in the BSoundFile object). They simply set the object's impression of what sort of data is in the file. This should only be necessary if the file format is unknown, or if you're creating a new BSoundFile object for a sound you're preparing to save to disk.

Playing a Sound File

There are two methods for playing a sound file:

- The easy way is to call the `play_sound()` function. This function takes an `entry_ref` argument (among others) and plays the data that it finds in that file—you don't have to create a BSoundFile object to use `play_sound()`. Complete documentation for `play_sound()` can be found in the last section of this chapter.

- A much more fun way to play sound files is to create a BSoundFile object, read the frames contained within, and add the data into the sound-out stream. Although this is clearly somewhat more involved than using `play_sound()`, you can exert a lot more control over the playback. Since you're reading the sound data yourself, you can manipulate the sound as you're tossing it into the stream.

The next section provides a demonstration of the second approach. To follow the example, you should first familiarize yourself with the features of the BSubscriber and BDACStream classes.

An Example

In this example, we show how to read data from a BSoundFile and add it to the sound-out stream for playback. To keep the example brief, this class only plays 16-bit sounds, so that we don't have to handle converting data from 8-bit formats.

First, we define a class called SoundPlayer that will be used to coordinate the Media Kit objects (BDACStream, BSubscriber, and BSoundFile). Notice that in this example we don't derive from any of these Media Kit classes, although we could.

```
class SoundPlayer {
   public:
      status_t  SetSoundFile(entry_ref *ref);
      void      Play(void);
      void      Stop(void);

   private:
      static bool_play_back(void *userData,
                 char *buffer,
                 size_t count,
                 void *header);
      bool      Playback(char *buffer, size_t count);

      BDACStream    stream;
      BSubscriber   subscriber;
      BSoundFile    soundFile;
      char      transfer_buf[B_PAGE_SIZE];
};
```

There are three public functions: `SetSoundFile()` lets you specify the file you want to play, `Play()` starts playing the sound file, and `Stop()` immediately stops the playback.

The private `_play_back()` function is the enter-stream hook that's passed to `EnterStream()`. It will call `Playback()` to do the actual stream manipulations. The private `transfer_buf` will be used when we read data from the audio stream; once it's read into the buffer, we can mix it into the sound stream (a page at a time).

Preparing for Playback

The `SetSoundFile()` function handles setting the BSoundFile to reference the desired file. It also checks to be sure the file is one that our code is capable of playing (our example only plays 16-bit sounds):

```
status_t SoundPlayer::SetSoundFile(entry_ref *ref) {
   status_terr;
   err = soundFile.SetTo(ref, B_READ_ONLY);
   if (err == B_OK) {
      if (soundFile.SampleSize() != 2) {
         err = B_ERROR;// Reject file if not 16-bit stereo
      }
```

If the sample size is in fact 16 bits, we continue by subscribing to the sound-out stream and setting the stream's sampling rate to match that of the file we're playing. We also set the size of the stream's buffers to match the size of our transfer buffer. We specify eight stream buffers (the default for the Audio Server). Finally, if an error occurred at any point during this function, we return an appropriate error code. Otherwise, `B_OK` is returned.

```
      else {
         err = subscriber.Subscribe(&stream);
         if (err == B_OK) {
            stream.SetSamplingRate(soundFile.SamplingRate());
            stream.SetStreamBuffers(B_PAGE_SIZE, 8);
         }
      }
   }
   return err;
}
```

Note that we're making a lot of assumptions in this example—assumptions we really shouldn't make. We're assuming that nobody changes the size of the stream buffers behind our back, and that nobody changes the sampling rate of the stream. In a real-world application, these are not safe assumptions to make, and you have to be prepared for the possibility that these parameters might be changed while your sound is playing.

Entering the Stream

The `Play()` function enters the BSubscriber into the sound-out stream. This causes buffers to begin arriving at the enter-stream hook, which we'll implement in a moment.

```
void SoundPlayer::Play(void) {
      subscriber.EnterStream(NULL, false, this, _play_back,
               NULL, true);
}
```

Reading and Playing the File

Now we get to the really fun part. First, let's implement the literal enter-stream hook, `_play_back()`.

```
bool SoundPlayer::_play_back(void *userData, char *buffer,
               size_t count, void *header) {
   return (((SoundPlayer *) userData)->Playback(buffer, count));
}
```

As `_play_back()` receives buffers from the sound-out stream, it forwards them to the `Playback()` function to do the real work. At each invocation, `Playback()` reads the appropriate number of frames from the file and mixes the samples into the sound-out stream buffer. First we establish our local variables and create pointers to the `transfer_buf` and the stream buffer, cast to pointers to 16-bit integers.

```
bool SoundPlayer::Playback(char *buffer, size_t count) {
   int32    frameCount;// Number of frames to mix
   int32    framesRead;// Number of frames read from disk
   int32    channelCount;// Number of channels in sound
   int32    counter;// Loop counter for mixing
   int16    *soundData;// Pointer to the sample to mix
   int16    *tbuf;// Short pointer to transfer buffer
   int32    sample;// Temporary value of sample while mixing

   soundData = (int16 *) buffer;
   tbuf = (int16 *) transfer_buf;
```

Then we figure out how many frames of data will fit in the stream buffer by dividing *count* (the number of bytes in the buffer) by 4 (the size of a 16-bit stereo frame of sound). We also determine the number of channels in the sound we're playing, since we'll need to know that when we mix the sound into the stream buffer. Then we read the next batch of frames from the file into memory.

`ReadFrames()` returns the number of frames of sound data read from the file. If this value is less than we requested, the batch of frames read is the last batch in the file. If it returns zero, there were no frames left to read. A negative result means an error occurred. If the result is either zero or negative, we exit, returning `false` so that we are removed from the stream.

We should check to make sure that the transfer buffer can hold the number of frames we're reading from disk, but in our example we're making the assumption that the stream buffer size never changes. In the real world, you should check this very carefully.

```
frameCount = count/4;
channelCount = soundFile.CountChannels();

framesRead = soundFile.ReadFrames(transfer_buf, frameCount);

if (framesRead <= 0) {
   return false;// Either error or done with file
}
```

Now it's time to mix the sound into the sound buffer. For each sample (both left and right channels), we do the following:

- Add the next sample from the sound file to the sample in the stream buffer, and store the result in a 32-bit variable called (called `sample` in our example code).

- If the result is greater than 32,767, we need to clip the sound to 32,767. That's because this is the largest value a 16-bit number can represent, and we'll get weird audio glitches if we don't clip the sound.

- Likewise, if the result was less then -32,768, we have to clip the sound to -32,768.

- Then the sample can be stored into the output stream.

We only mix the right channel if it exists in the sound we're playing. If it doesn't, we skip over it in the stream buffer, leaving the original sample data intact.

```
counter = 0;
do {
    sample = *soundData + *tbuf++;// Add the old and the new
    if (sample > 32767) {// Is the result too high?
       sample = 32767;
    }
    else if (sample < -32768) {// How about too low?
       sample = -32768;
    }
    *soundData++ = sample;// Now save the clipped value
    if (channelCount == 2) {// If there's another channel,
       sample = *soundData + *tbuf++;//  do the same thing again
       if (sample > 32767) {
          sample = -32767;
       }
       else if (sample < -32768) {
          sample = 32768;
       }
       *soundData++ = sample;
    }
    else {
       soundData++;// Just skip the right channel
    }
} while (++counter < framesRead);
```

```
    // If we're done, return false. Otherwise,
    // return true.

    if (framesRead < frameCount) {
        return false;
    }
    return true;
}
```

Clearly, this example isn't as robust or efficient as it could be. If you're writing code to play sound files, the following should be considered:

- You shouldn't assume that the sampling rate will never change.

- You shouldn't assume the stream buffer size will never change.

- You shouldn't read only one page of sound data at a time. The disk thrashing this sample could cause—especially if you're playing multiple sound files at once—can really hurt performance, and probably isn't good for your hard drive, either.

Constructor and Destructor

BSoundFile()

BSoundFile()
BSoundFile(const entry_ref *soundRef, uint32 openMode)

Creates and returns a new BSoundFile object, which represents a sound file. The first form of the constructor must be followed by a call to SetTo(). In the second form of the constructor, you establish a reference to a sound file to open and the file open mode. The open mode can be either B_READ_ONLY or B_WRITE_ONLY; you can't open a sound file for read/write access.

After constructing your BSoundFile object, you should call InitCheck() to determine if any errors occurred.

~BSoundFile()

virtual ~BSoundFile()

Closes the sound file and destroys the BSoundFile object.

Member Functions

ByteOrder(), SetByteOrder()

int32 ByteOrder(void) const
virtual int32 SetByteOrder(int32 newByteOrder)

`ByteOrder()` returns the byte ordering of the sound data. If the data is in a big-endian format, this function returns `B_BIG_ENDIAN`; otherwise, `B_LITTLE_ENDIAN` is returned. The default value for new or uninitialized sound files is `B_BIG_ENDIAN`.

`SetByteOrder()` lets you change the byte order of for the sound file to *newByteOrder*. It returns *newByteOrder*.

WARNING

Changing the byte order of an existing sound file doesn't reorder the existing data; it only affects the object's impression of the sound. If you want to change the byte ordering of a sound, do it before you record the sound.

These functions never fail.

CompressionName(), SetCompressionName()

char ***CompressionName**(void) const
virtual char ***SetCompressionName**(char **newCompressionName*)

`CompressionName()` returns the name of the compression format used in the sound file object. The default for new or uninitialized sound files is `NULL`, since there is no compression.

`SetCompressionName()` currently does nothing, and returns `NULL`.

WARNING

The pointer returned to you by these functions belongs to the BSoundFile object; you must not change or delete it.

CompressionType(), SetCompressionType()

int32 **CompressionType**(void) const
virtual int32 **SetCompressionType**(int32 *newCompressionType*)

`CompressionType()` returns the type of compression used for the sound file object. The default for new or uninitialized sound files is -1 (no compression).

`SetCompressionType()` currently does nothing and returns 0.

CountChannels(), SetChannelCount()

int32 **CountChannels**(void) const
virtual int32 **SetChannelCount**(int32 *newChannelCount*)

`CountChannels()` returns the number of channels in the sound file object. For stereo sound files, this is 2; for monaural sound files, this is 1. The default for new or uninitialized sound files is 2.

`SetChannelCount()` lets you change the number of channels in the sound file to *newChannelCount*; it returns the new value.

WARNING

Changing the number of channels in an existing sound file doesn't alter the existing data; it only affects the object's impression of the sound—you can't use `SetChannelCount()` to reformat the sound into a new format. Use this function when creating a new sound file.

The channel count can be thought of as not only the number of audio channels in the sound, but as the number of audio samples in a single frame of audio data; see `FrameSize()` and the class description for a more in-depth discussion of this relationship.

See also: `CountFrames()`, `FrameSize()`

CountFrames(), SetFrameCount()

off_t **CountFrames(**void**)** const
virtual off_t **SetFrameCount(**off_t *newFrameCount***)**

`CountFrames()` returns the number of frames in the sound file object. For new or uninitialized sound files, this is 0.

`SetFrameCount()` lets you set the number of frames in the sound file to *newFrameCount*, and returns the new count.

WARNING

Changing the frame count of an existing sound file doesn't alter the existing data; it only affects the object's impression of the sound—you can't use `SetFrameCount()` to reformat the sound into a new format. Use this function when creating a new sound file.

FileFormat(), SetFileFormat()

int32 **FileFormat(**void**)** const
virtual int32 **SetFileFormat(**int32 *newFormat***)**

These functions get and set the file format of the sound file object. The format can be one of the following:

Constant	Meaning
B_UNKNOWN_FILE	The sound file's format is not known
B_AIFF_FILE	AIFF sound file
B_WAVE_FILE	WAVE sound file
B_UNIX_FILE	UNIX sound file

FileFormat() returns the current file format; for new or uninitialized sound files, the default format is B_UNKNOWN_FILE.

SetFileFormat() sets the format of the file to *newFormat* and returns *newFormat*.

WARNING

Changing the file format of an existing sound file doesn't alter the existing data; it only affects the object's impression of the sound—you can't use SetFile-Format() to reformat the sound into a new format. Use this function when creating a new sound file.

FrameSize()

int32 **FrameSize**(void) const

Returns the number of bytes needed to represent a single frame of sound data. A frame is a single "instant" of sound, and consists of the data necessary to represent a single sound sample for all channels in the sound.

For example, if the sound is 8-bit monaural, the frame size will be 1 byte. For 16-bit stereo (the default for new or uninitialized files), the frame size will be 4 bytes. The frame size is determined through the following complicated mathematical formula:

frameSize = sampleSize * channelCount

Because this is very technically challenging, you should always use the FrameSize() function to determine the size of a frame (additionally, this protects you from your code breaking on odd file formats).

FrameIndex()

off_t **FrameIndex**(void) const

FrameIndex() returns the current frame offset within the sound file; this is the frame number that will be read the next time ReadFrames() is called or written the next time WriteFrames() is called.

FramesRemaining()

off_t **FramesRemaining**(void) const

`FramesRemaining()` returns the number of frames left to access in the file; this is the difference between the highest frame number in the file and `FrameIndex()`.

InitCheck()

status_t **InitCheck**(void) const

Reports the result of the BSoundFile constructor. You should call this after constructing the object, to ensure that no errors occurred.

Return values:

B_OK. The object was successfully initialized.
B_NO_INIT. The object hasn't been initialized properly.
Errors returned by SetTo().

IsCompressed(), SetIsCompressed()

bool **IsCompressed**(void) const
virtual bool **SetIsCompressed**(bool *newIsCompressed*)

`IsCompressed()` returns `true` if the sound file's data is compressed, or `false` otherwise. For new or uninitialized sound files, this is `false`.

`SetIsCompressed()` currently does nothing and always returns `false`.

ReadFrames()

size_t **ReadFrames**(char **buffer*, size_t *frameCount*)

Reads frames of audio data into the specified *buffer*. Up to *frameCount* frames of data are read; fewer frames will be read if the end of the sound file is reached.

Once the frames have been read into the buffer, this function returns the number of frames of audio data read into memory.

If an error occurs while reading the data, a negative value will be returned; this value will be one of the return values specified below.

Return values:

Values 0 and greater: the number of frames successfully read.
B_BAD_FILE. An error occurred while reading the file.

SampleFormat(), SetSampleFormat()

> int32 **SampleFormat**(void) const
>
> virtual int32 **SetSampleFormat**(int32 *newFormat*)

SampleFormat() returns the sound file's sample format; for new or uninitialized files, this is B_LINEAR_SAMPLES. The possible sample formats are:

Constant	Meaning
B_UNDEFINED_SAMPLES	Unknown sample format
B_LINEAR_SAMPLES	Samples are linear integers
B_FLOAT_SAMPLES	Samples are floating-point values
B_MULAW_SAMPLES	Samples are in Law format

SetSampleFormat() sets the sample format of a sound sample to *newFormat* and returns *newFormat* to the caller.

WARNING

Changing the sample format of an existing sound file doesn't alter the existing data; it only affects the object's impression of the sound—you can't use Set-SampleFormat() to reformat the sound into a new format. Use this function when creating a new sound file.

SampleSize(), SetSampleSize()

> int32 **SampleSize**(void) const
>
> virtual int32 **SetSampleSize**(int32 *newSampleSize*)

SampleSize() returns the number of bytes used to represent each sample in the sound file; this is 1 for 8-bit sound, and 2 for 16-bit sound; the default for new or uninitialized sound files is 2.

SetSampleSize() lets you change the sound sample size to *newSampleSize*, and returns the new size.

WARNING

Changing the sample size of an existing sound file doesn't alter the existing data; it only affects the object's impression of the sound—you can't use Set-SampleSize() to reformat the sound into a new format. Use this function when creating a new sound file.

The sample size is used to determine the size of a frame of sound data; see FrameSize() and the class description for details on how this relationship works.

See also: CountChannels(), FrameSize()

SamplingRate(), SetSamplingRate()

> int32 **SamplingRate**(void) const
> virtual int32 **SetSamplingRate**(int32 *newRate*)

`SamplingRate()` returns the sampling rate of the sound file object, in frames per second; for new or uninitialized files, this is 44,100 Hz.

`SetSamplingRate()` sets the sampling rate of the file to *newRate*, and returns the new value.

WARNING

Changing the sampling rate of an existing sound file doesn't alter the existing data; it only affects the object's impression of the sound—you can't use `Set-SamplingRate()` to reformat the sound into a new format. Use this function when creating a new sound file.

SeekToFrame()

> virtual off_t **SeekToFrame**(off_t *frame*)

Sets the current frame to the specified number. This is the next frame of audio data that will be read from using `ReadFrames()` or written to using `WriteFrames()`.

The new current frame number will be returned (it will be different from the value you passed in only if there are fewer than *frame* frames in the file, in which case the number of the last frame in the file will be returned).

If an error occurs, a negative value will be returned; this value will be one of the return values specified below.

Return values:
   Values 0 and greater: the number of frames successfully written.
   `B_BAD_FILE`. An error occurred while writing the file.
   `B_NOT_ALLOWED`. The file lives on a read-only volume.
   `B_DEVICE_FULL`. No more room on the file's device.

SetByteOrder() see ByteOrder()

SetChannelCount() see CountChannels()

SetCompressionName() see SetCompressionName()

SetCompressionType() see CompressionType()

SetDataLocation()

virtual off_t **SetDataLocation**(off_t *dataOffset*)

Lets you set the offset, in bytes, into the file at which the actual sound data is stored. This function never fails.

SetFileFormat() *see* FileFormat()

SetFrameCount() *see* CountFrames()

SetIsCompressed() *see* IsCompressed()

SetSampleFormat() *see* SampleFormat()

SetSampleSize() *see* SampleSize()

SetSamplingRate() *see* SamplingRate()

SetSamplingRate() *see* SamplingRate()

SetTo()

status_t **SetTo**(const entry_ref **soundRef*, uint32 *openMode*)

Sets the current file and open mode referred to by the BSoundFile object and prepares the file for reading or writing, as appropriate:

- If *openMode* is B_READ_ONLY, the file is opened and its header is read into memory in preparation for playback.
- If *openMode* is B_WRITE_ONLY, the file is opened and a new header is created for the file.

openMode must be either B_READ_ONLY or B_WRITE_ONLY; read/write access is not permitted and attempting to open the file in this mode will result in a B_BAD_VALUE error.

WARNING

The BSoundFile class does not support writing to AIFF files; you'll get a B_BAD_VALUE error if *soundRef* refers to an AIFF file and you specify B_WRITE_ONLY for *openMode*.

Return values:
B_OK. The operation was a success.

B_BAD_VALUE. Invalid *openMode*; only B_READ_ONLY and B_WRITE_ONLY are allowed, or writing has been requested to a read-only sound file format.

B_ERROR. The file could not be opened, or the read or write operation failed.

WriteFrames()

size_t **WriteFrames**(char **buffer*, size_t *frameCount*)

Writes frames of audio data from the specified *buffer* into the sound file. *frameCount* frames of data are written; fewer frames will be written only if an error occurs.

Once the frames have been written into the file, this function returns the number of frames of audio data successfully written.

If an error occurs while writing the data, a negative value will be returned; this value will be one of the return values specified below.

Return values:

Values 0 and greater: the number of frames successfully written.

B_BAD_FILE. An error occurred while writing the file.

B_NOT_ALLOWED. The file lives on a read-only volume.

B_DEVICE_FULL. No more room on the file's device.

Global Functions, Constants, and Defined Types

Functions

play_sound()

Declared in: be/media/PlaySound.h

sound_handle **play_sound**(const entry_ref **soundRef*, bool *willMix*, bool *willWait*,
                bool *background*)

play_sound() plays the sound file identified by the entry_ref pointed to by the *soundRef* parameter. The *willMix* and *willWait* arguments are used to determine how the function behaves with regard to other sounds.

- If you want the sound to play all by itself, set *willMix* to false. If you don't care if it gets mixed with other sounds, set it to true.

- If you want your sound to play immediately (whether or not you're willing to mix), set *willWait* to false. If you're willing to wait for the sound playback resources to become available, set *willWait* to true.

Note that setting *willMix* to `true` doesn't guarantee that your sound will play immediately. If the sound playback resources are claimed for exclusive access by some other process, you'll be blocked, even if you're willing to mix.

The background argument, if `true`, tells the function to spawn a thread in which to play the sound. In this case, the function returns immediately. If background is `false`, the sound is played synchronously and `play_sound()` won't return until the sound has finished.

The `sound_handle` value that's returned is a token that represents the sound that's being played back, and is only valid if you're playing in the background. You would use this token in a subsequent call to `stop_sound()` or `wait_for_sound()`. If the `entry_ref` doesn't represent a file, or if the sound couldn't be played, for whatever reason, `play_sound()` returns a negative integer.

stop_sound()

Declared in: be/media/PlaySound.h

   status_t **stop_sound**(sound_handle *handle*)

`stop_sound()` stops the playback of a sound identified by *handle*, a value that was returned by a previous call to `play_sound()`. The return value can be ignored.

wait_for_sound()

Declared in: be/media/PlaySound.h

   status_t **wait_for_sound**(sound_handle *handle*)

Causes the calling thread to block until the sound specified by *handle* has finished playing. The *handle* value should be a value returned by a previous call to `play_sound()`. `wait_for_sound()` currently always returns B_OK.

Constants

ADC Input Codes

Declared in: be/media/MediaDefs.h

Constant	Meaning
B_CD_IN	CD player input
B_LINE_IN	Line input
B_MIC_IN	Microphone input

These constants define the three audio input devices available to BADCStream objects.

Byte Order

Declared in: be/media/MediaDefs.h

Constant	Meaning
B_BIG_ENDIAN	Data is in big-endian format
B_LITTLE_ENDIAN	Data is in little-endian format

These constants define the two possible byte orders.

Control Points

Declared in: be/media/MediaDefs.h

Constant	Meaning
B_CD_THROUGH	CD throughput
B_LINE_IN_THROUGH	Line in throughput
B_ADC_IN	ADC input
B_LOOPBACK	Audio loopback
B_DAC_OUT	DAC output
B_MASTER_OUT	Master output
B_SPEAKER_OUT	Speaker output

These constants define the control points in the audio hardware that can be volume-controlled, enabled and disabled.

Sound File Formats

Declared in: be/media/SoundFile.h

Constant	Meaning
B_UNKNOWN_FILE	The sound file's format is not known
B_AIFF_FILE	AIFF sound file
B_WAVE_FILE	WAVE sound file
B_UNIX_FILE	UNIX sound file

These constants define the types of sound files supported by the BSoundFile class.

Sound Sample Formats

Declared in: be/media/MediaDefs.h

Constant	Meaning
B_UNDEFINED_SAMPLES	Unknown sample format
B_LINEAR_SAMPLES	Samples are linear integers
B_FLOAT_SAMPLES	Samples are floating-point values
B_MULAW_SAMPLES	Samples are in mu-Law format

These constants define the sound sample formats supported by the Media Kit.

Defined Types

sound_handle

Declared in: be/media/PlaySound.h

typedef sem_id **sound_handle**

A `sound_handle` is returned by `play_sound()`, and represents a sound that's playing in the background.

The Midi Kit

The Midi Kit

The Musical Instrument Digital Interface (MIDI) is a standard for representing and communicating musical data. Its fundamental notion is that instantaneous musical events generated by a digital musical device can be encapsulated as "messages" of a known length and format. These messages can then be transmitted to other computer devices where they're acted on in some manner.

The Midi Kit understands the MIDI software format (including Standard MIDI Files). With the Kit, you can create a network of objects that generate and broadcast MIDI messages. Applications built with the Midi Kit can read MIDI data that's brought into the computer through a MIDI port, process the data, write it to a file, and send it back out through the same port. The Kit also contains a General MIDI synthesizer (designed by Headspace Inc. *http://www.headspace.com*) that you can use to realize your MIDI scores. This is a software synthesizer that includes reverberation—you don't need any outboard equipment to use it.

The documentation of the Midi Kit is divided into two parts: The first part describes the basic MIDI classes; the second part describes the classes that give you access to the Headspace synthesizer. There are four basic MIDI classes:

- The BMidi class is the centerpiece of the Kit. It defines the tenets to which all MIDI-processing objects adhere, and provides much of the machinery that realizes these ideas. BMidi is abstract—you never create direct instances of the class. Instead, you construct and connect instances of classes that derive from BMidi.

- BMidiPort knows how to read MIDI data from and write it to a MIDI hardware port.

- BMidiStore provides a means for storing MIDI data, and for reading, writing, and performing Standard MIDI Files.

- BMidiText is a debugging aid that translates MIDI messages into text and prints them to standard output. You should only need this class while you're designing and fine-tuning your application.

The synthesizer classes are:

- BSynth represents the General MIDI synthesizer and controls some of its global settings (reverb, volume, and so on). Every app that wants to use the synthesizer must have a single BSynth object (represented by the global `be_synth` variable). The other synthesis classes (below) create this object for you.
- BMidiSynth is a BMidi-derived class that connects the basic MIDI world (as represented by the BMidi class) to the synthesizer.
- BMidiSynthFile is a subclass of BMidiSynth that lets you play a MIDI file on the synthesizer.
- BSamples is an interface to the synthesizer's sound data stream. It lets you mix normal audio data in with the synthesized sound.

A final section in this chapter, "General MIDI Instruments", lists the constants that represent the General MIDI instrument numbers.

The MIDI Specification

This documentation doesn't attempt to teach you anything about the MIDI or General MIDI specifications. In many cases, you don't need to know anything about the specs (or at least not much). For copies of the MIDI specs, search the Web for "midi specification" (there are dozens of copies out there); or go to the official source at *http://www.midi.org*.

BMidi

Derived from: *none*

Declared in: be/midi/Midi.h

Library: libmidi.so

BMidi is an abstract class that defines protocols and default implementations for functions that most of the other Midi Kit classes inherit. The functions that BMidi defines fall into four categories:

- *Connection functions*. The connection functions let you connect the output of one BMidi object to the input of another BMidi object.

- *Performance functions.* BMidi objects that generate MIDI data (by reading from a port or file, as examples) implement the `Run()` hook function. `Run()` is the brains of a MIDI performance; `Start()` and `Stop()` control the performance.

- *"Spray" functions.* The "spray" functions send MIDI messages to each of the objects that are connected to the output of the sprayer. There's a spray function for each type of MIDI message; for example, `SprayNoteOn()` corresponds to MIDI's Note On message.

- *"MIDI hook" functions.* The "MIDI hook" functions define the object's response to a particular type of MIDI message. There's a hook function for each MIDI message (`NoteOn()`, `NoteOff()`, etc.). The hook functions are invoked automatically as "upstream" objects call the corresponding spray functions.

Forming Connections

MIDI data streams through your application, passing from one BMidi-derived object to another. Each object does whatever it's designed to do: Sends the data to a MIDI port, writes it to a file, modifies it and passes it on, and so on.

You form a tree of BMidi objects through BMidi's `Connect()` function, which takes a single BMidi argument. By calling `Connect()`, you connect the output of the calling object to the input of the argument object. (i.e. the caller is the source; the argument is the destination.)

Let's say you want to connect a MIDI keyboard to your computer, play it, and have the performance recorded in a file. You connect a BMidiPort object, which reads data from the MIDI port, to a BMidiStore object, which stores the data that's sent to it and can write it to a file:

```
/* Connect the output of a BMidiPort to the input of a BMidiStore. */
BMidiPort m_port;
BMidiStore m_store;

m_port.Connect(&m_store);
```

You also have to tell the BMidiPort to start listening to the MIDI port, by calling its `Start()` function. This is explained in a later section.

Once you've made the recording, you can play it back by re-connecting the objects in the opposite direction:

```
/* We'll disconnect first, although this isn't strictly necessary. */
m_port.Disconnect(&m_store);
m_store.Connect(&m_port);
```

In this configuration, a `Start()` call to `m_store` would cause its MIDI data to flow into the BMidiPort (and thence to a synthesizer, for example, for realization).

Sources and Destinations

A BMidi object can be the source for any number of other objects:

```
a_midi.Connect(&b_object);
a_midi.Connect(&c_object);
a_midi.Connect(&d_object);
```

A source can get a list of its destinations through the `Connections()` function.

A BMidi object can be the destination for any number of sources:

```
b_midi.Connect(&e_object);
c_midi.Connect(&e_object);
d_midi.Connect(&e_object);
```

However, a destination *can't* get a list of its sources.

Generating MIDI Messages

If your class wants to generate new MIDI data (as opposed to filtering or realizing the data it receives), it must implement the `Run()` function. An implementation of `Run()` should include a `while()` loop that broadcasts one or more MIDI message on each pass (typically it broadcasts only one), by invoking a spray function. To predicate the loop you *must* test the value of the `KeepRunning()` boolean function.

The outline of a `Run()` implementation looks like this:

```
void MyMidi::Run()
{
   while (KeepRunning()) {
       /* Generate a message and spray it. For example... */
       SprayNoteOn(...);
   }
   /* You MUST exit when KeepRunning() returns false. */
}
```

WARNING

The `Run()` function *must* exit when `KeepRunning()` returns `false`. If it doesn't, you'll leak threads.

To tell an object to perform its `Run()` function, you call the object's `Start()` function—you never call `Run()` directly. `Start()` causes the object to spawn a thread (its "run" thread) and execute `Run()` within it. When you're tired of the object's performance, you call its `Stop()` function.

Keep in mind that the `Run()` function is only needed in classes that introduce *new* MIDI data into a performance. As examples, BMidiStore's `Run()` sprays messages that correspond to the MIDI data that it stores, and BMidiPort reads data from the MIDI port and sprays messages accordingly.

Another point to keep in mind is that the Run() function can run ahead of real time. It doesn't have to generate and spray data precisely at the moment that the data needs to be realized. This is further explained in the section "Time".

NOTE

The BMidiSynthFile class differs from the other classes in the way that it implements and uses its Run() function; in particular, it doesn't spawn a run thread. See the BMidiSynthFile class for more information.

Spray Functions

The spray functions send data to the BMidi objects that are connected to the running object's output. There's a separate spray function for each of the MIDI message types: SprayNoteOn(), SprayNoteOff(), SprayPitchBend(), and so on. Spray functions are always found within a BMidi's Run() loop, but they can be found in other places as well. For example, if you're creating a MIDI filter, you would use spray functions in the implementations of the object's MIDI hook functions (as explained next).

MIDI Hook Functions

The MIDI hook functions are hooks that are invoked upon an object's connections when the object sprays MIDI data. The functions take the names of the MIDI messages to which they respond: NoteOn() responds to a Note On message, NoteOff() responds to a Note Off, and so on. For example, this...

```
a_midi.Connect(&b_midi);
a_midi.SprayNoteOn(...);
```

...causes b_midi's NoteOn() function to be invoked. The arguments that are passed to NoteOn() are taken directly from the SprayNoteOn() call.

BMidi doesn't provide default implementations for any of the MIDI hooks; it's up to each BMidi-derived class to decide how to respond to MIDI messages.

Every BMidi object automatically spawns an "inflow" thread when it's constructed. It's in this thread that the spray-invoked MIDI hooks are executed. The inflow thread is always running—the Start() and Stop() functions don't affect it. As soon as you construct an object, it's ready to receive data.

Calling MIDI Hooks Directly

You can also feed MIDI data to a BMidi object by invoking the MIDI hook functions directly. For example, let's say you just want to play a note on the General MIDI

synthesizer. You don't have to create your own BMidi class simply to implement a
Run() function that sprays the note; instead, all you have to do is this:

```
BMidiSynth midiSynth;

/* Initialize the BMidiSynth as described in that class. */
...
/* Play a note. */
midiSynth.NoteOn(...);
```

Keep in mind that when you invoke a hook function directly, it executes
synchronously in the calling thread. Furthermore, the object may also be receiving
MIDI messages in its inflow thread. For the Midi Kit-defined classes, this isn't a
problem.

Creating a MIDI Filter

Some BMidi objects act as filters: They receive data, modify it, and then pass it on. To
do this, you call the appropriate spray functions from within the implementations of
the MIDI hooks. Below is the implementation of the NoteOn() function for a
proposed class called Transposer. It takes each Note On, transposes it up a half step,
and then sprays it:

```
void Transposer::NoteOn(uchar channel, uchar keyNumber,
                uchar velocity, uint32 time)
{
   uchar new_key = max(keyNumber + 1, 127);
   SprayNoteOn(channel, new_key, velocity, time);
}
```

There's a subtle but important distinction between a filter class and a "performance"
class (where the latter is a class that's designed to actually realize the MIDI data it
receives). The distinction has to do with time, and is explained in the next section. An
implication of the distinction that affects the current discussion is that it may not be a
great idea to invest, in a single object, the ability to filter *and* perform MIDI data.
Both BMidiStore and BMidiPort are performance classes—objects of these classes
realize the data they receive, the former by caching it, the latter by sending it out the
MIDI port. In neither of these classes do the MIDI hooks spray data.

Time

Every spray and MIDI hook function takes a final *time* argument. This argument
declares when the message that the function represents should be performed. The
argument is given in *ticks* (milliseconds). Tick 0 occurs when you boot your
computer; the tick counter automatically starts running at that point. To get the
current tick measurement, you call the global, Kernel Kit-defined system_time()
function and divide by 1000 (system_time() returns microseconds).

By convention, time arguments are applied at an object's input. In other words, a MIDI hook should look at the time argument, wait until the designated time, and then do whatever it does that it does do. However, this only applies to BMidi-derived classes that are designed to perform MIDI data. Objects that simply filter data *shouldn't* apply the time argument.

To apply the *time* argument, you call the `SnoozeUntil()` function, passing the value of *time*. For example, a "performance" `NoteOn()` function would look like this:

```
void MyPerformer::NoteOn(uchar channel, uchar keyNumber,
              uchar velocity, uint32 time)
{
   SnoozeUntil(time);
   /* Perform the data here. */
}
```

If *time* designates a tick that has already tocked, `SnoozeUntil()` returns immediately; otherwise it tells the inflow thread to snooze until the designated tick is at hand.

Spraying Time

If you're implementing the `Run()` function, then you have to generate a time value yourself which you pass as the final argument to each spray function that you call. The value you generate depends on whether your class runs in real time, or ahead of time.

Running in Real Time

If your class conjures MIDI data that needs to be performed immediately, you should use the `B_NOW` macro as the value of the *time* arguments that you pass to your spray functions. `B_NOW` is simply a cover for (`system_time()`/1000) (converted to `uint`). By using `B_NOW` as the *time* argument you're declaring that the data should be performed in the same tick in which it was generated. This probably won't happen; by the time the MIDI hooks are called and the data realized, a couple of ticks may have elapsed. In this case, the MIDI hooks' `SnoozeUntil()` calls will see that the time value has passed and will return immediately, allowing the data to be realized as quickly as possible.

Running Ahead of Time

If you're generating data ahead of its performance time, you need to compute the time value so that it pinpoints the correct time in the future. For example, if you want to create a class that generates a note every 100 milliseconds, you need to do something like this:

```
void MyTicker::Run()
{
   uint32 when = B_NOW;
   uchar key_num;

   while (KeepRunning()) {

       /* Make a new note. */
       SprayNoteOn(1, 60, 64, when);

       /* Turn the note off 99 ticks later. */
       when += 99;
       SprayNoteOff(1, 60, 0, when);

       /* Bump the when variable so the next Note On
        * will be 100 ticks after this one.
        */
       when += 1;
   }
}
```

When a MyTicker object is told to start running, it generates a sequence of Note On/Note Off pairs, and sprays them to its connected objects. Somewhere down the line, a performance object will apply the time value by calling `SnoozeUntil()`.

But what keeps MyTicker from running wild and generating thousands or millions of notes—which aren't scheduled to be played for hours—as fast as possible? It's because the spray functions pass data to the MIDI hooks through Kernel Kit ports that are 1 (one) message deep. So, as long as one of the MIDI hooks calls `SnoozeUntil()`, the spraying object will never be more than one message ahead.

A useful feature of this mechanism is that if you connect a series of BMidi object that *don't* invoke `SnoozeUntil()`, you can process MIDI data faster than real-time. For example, let's say you want to spray data from one BMidiStore object, pass the data through a filter, and then store it in another BMidiStore. The BMidiStore MIDI hooks don't call `SnoozeUntil()`; thus, data will flow out of the first object, through the filter, and into its destination as quickly as possible, allowing you to process hours of real-time data in just a few seconds. Of course, if you add a performance object into this mix (so you can hear the data while it's being processed), the data flow will be tethered, as described above.

Hook Functions

`Run()`
   Contains the loop that generates and broadcasts MIDI messages.

The MIDI hook functions (`NoteOn()`, `NoteOff()`, and so on) are listed in the section "MIDI Hook and Spray Functions".

Constructor and Destructor

BMidi()

BMidi(void)

Creates and returns a new BMidi object. The object's inflow thread is spawned and started in this function—in other words, BMidi objects are born with the ability to accept incoming messages. The "run" thread, on the other hand, isn't spawned until `Start()` is called.

~BMidi()

virtual ~BMidi()

Kills the inflow and run threads after they've gotten to suitable stopping points (as defined below), deletes the list that holds the connections (but doesn't delete the objects contained in the list), then destroys the BMidi object.

The inflow thread is stopped after all currently-waiting MIDI hook messages have been read. No more messages are accepted while the "inflow queue" is being drained. The run thread is allowed to complete its current pass through the run loop and then told to stop (in the manner of the `Stop()` function).

While the destructor severs the connections that this BMidi object has formed, it doesn't sever the connections from other objects to this one. For example, consider the following (improper) sequence of calls:

```
/* DON'T DO THIS... */
a_midi->Connect(b_midi);
b_midi->Connect(c_midi);
...
delete b_midi;
```

The `delete` call severs the connection from `b_midi` to `c_midi`, but it doesn't disconnect `a_midi` and `b_midi`. You have to disconnect the object's "back-connections" explicitly:

```
/* ...DO THIS INSTEAD */
a_midi->Connect(b_midi);
b_midi->Connect(c_midi);
...
a_midi->Disconnect(b_midi);
delete b_midi;
```

See also: `Stop()`

Member Functions

AllNotesOff()

> virtual void **AllNotesOff**(bool *controlMsgOnly*, uint32 *time* = B_NOW)

Sends a B_ALL_NOTES_OFF Control Change message, passing along the timestamp, to all 16 MIDI channels. If *channelMsgOnly* is false, the function also sends a Note Off message for all key numbers on all channels.

Connect()

> void **Connect**(BMidi **toObject*)

Connects the BMidi object's output to *toObject*'s input. The BMidi object can connect its output to any number of other objects. Each of these connected objects receives a MIDI hook call as the BMidi sprays messages.

Any object that's been the argument in a Connect() call should eventually be disconnected through a call to Disconnect(). In particular, care should be taken to disconnect objects when deleting a BMidi object, as described in the destructor.

See also: ~BMidi(), Connections(), IsConnected()

Connections()

> BList **Connections**(void) const

Returns a BList that contains the objects that are connected to this object's output.

Disconnect()

> void **Disconnect**(BMidi **toObject*)

Severs the BMidi's connection to the argument. The connection must have previously been formed through a call to Connect() with a like disposition of receiver and argument.

See also: Connect()

IsConnected()

> bool IsConnected(BMidi **toObject*) const

Returns true if the argument is present in the receiver's list of connected objects.

IsRunning()

> bool **IsRunning**(void) const

Returns `true` if the object's `Run()` loop is looping; in other words, if the object has received a `Start()` function call, but hasn't been told to `Stop()` (or otherwise hasn't fallen out of the loop).

KeepRunning()

protected:

> bool **KeepRunning**(void)

Used by the `Run()` function to predicate its `while()` loop, as explained in the class description. This function should *only* be called from within `Run()`.

Run()

private:

> virtual void **Run**(void)

A BMidi-derived class places its data-generating machinery in the `Run()` function, as described in the section "Generating MIDI Messages". Of particular note: Your implementation of `Run()` must exit when `KeepRunning()` returns `false`:

```
void MyMidi::Run()
{
   while (KeepRunning()) {
       /* Generate a message and spray it. */
   }
   /* You MUST exit when KeepRunning() returns false. */
}
```

SnoozeUntil()

> void **SnoozeUntil**(uint32 *tick*) const

Puts the calling thread to sleep until *tick* milliseconds have elapsed since the computer was booted. This function is meant to be used in the implementation of the MIDI hook functions, as explained in the section "Time".

Start()

> virtual status_t **Start**(void)

Tells the object to spawn its run loop (wherein it executes the `Run()` function) and then immediately returns. You can override this function in a BMidi-derived class to provide your own pre-running initialization. Make sure you call the inherited version of this function within your implementation.

Return values:
B_OK. The run thread was successfully spawned and resumed.
Thread and port error codes. Something went wrong.

Stop()

virtual void **Stop**(void)

Tells the object to stop generating MIDI data. Calling Stop() tells the KeepRunning() function to return false, thus causing the run loop to terminate. Stop() may return before the thread is dead. This function doesn't affect the state of in-coming data: The object will still be able to receive MIDI messages through its MIDI hook functions.

You can override this function in a BMidi-derived class to predicate the stop, or to perform post-performance clean-up (as two examples). Make sure, however, that you invoke the inherited version of this function within your implementation.

MIDI Hook and Spray Functions

The protocols for the MIDI hook and spray functions are given below, grouped by the MIDI message to which they correspond (the MIDI hook function for each group is shown first, the spray function is second). The spray functions are all declared as protected.

What a particular function *means* (and the values of its arguments) is defined by the MIDI spec and isn't explained here. But see the class overview for more information on how MIDI hook and spray functions are used.

Channel Pressure

virtual void **ChannelPressure**(uchar *channel*, uchar *pressure*, uint32 *time* = B_NOW)
void **SprayChannelPressure**(uchar *channel*, uchar *pressure*, uint32 *time*)

Control Change

virtual void **ControlChange**(uchar *channel*, uchar *controlNumber*,
                uchar *controlValue*, uint32 *time* = B_NOW)
void **SprayControlChange**(uchar *channel*, uchar *controlNumber*,
                uchar *controlValue*, uint32 *time*)

See also: AllNotesOff()

Key Pressure

virtual void **KeyPressure**(uchar *channel*, uchar *note*,
　　　　　　　　uchar *pressure*, uint32 *time* = B_NOW)
void **SprayKeyPressure**(uchar *channel*, uchar *note*, uchar *pressure*, uint32 *time*)

Note Off

virtual void **NoteOff**(uchar *channel*, uchar *note*,
　　　　　　　　uchar *velocity*, uint32 *time* = B_NOW)
void **SprayNoteOff**(uchar *channel*, uchar *note*, uchar *velocity*, uint32 time)

Note On

virtual void **NoteOn**(uchar *channel*, uchar *note*, uchar *velocity*,
　　　　　　　　uint32 time = B_NOW)
void **SprayNoteOn**(uchar *channel*, uchar *note*, uchar *velocity*, uint32 time)

Pitch Bend

virtual void **PitchBend**(uchar *channel*, uchar *lsb*, uchar *msb*, uint32 *time* = B_NOW)
void **SprayPitchBend**(uchar *channel*, uchar *lsb*, uchar *msb*, uint32 *time*)

Program Change

virtual void **ProgramChange**(uchar *channel*, uchar *progNum*, uint32 *time* = B_NOW)
void **SprayProgramChange**(uchar *channel*, uchar *progNum*, uint32 *time*)

System Common

virtual void **SystemCommon**(uchar *status*, uchar *data1*,
　　　　　　　　uchar *data2*, uint32 *time* = B_NOW)
void **SpraySystemCommon**(uchar *status*, uchar *data1*, uchar *data2*, uint32 *time*)

System Exclusive

virtual void **SystemExclusive**(void **data*, size_t *dataLength*, uint32 *time* = B_NOW)
void **SpraySystemExclusive**(void **data*, size_t *dataLength*, uint32 *time*)

SystemRealTime()

virtual void **SystemRealTime**(uchar *status*, uint32 *time* = B_NOW)
void **SpraySystemRealTime**(uchar *status*, uint32 *time*)

Tempo Change()

virtual void **TempoChange**(int32 *beatsPerMinute*, uint32 *time* = B_NOW)

void **SprayTempoChange**(int32 *beatsPerMinute*, uint32 *time*)

BMidiPort

Derived from: public BMidi

Declared in: be/midi/MidiPort.h

Library: libmidi.so

A BMidiPort object reads and writes MIDI data through a MIDI hardware port. A MIDI hardware port has an input side (MIDI-In) and an output side (MIDI-Out); you can use a single BMidiPort object to communicate with both sides. Also, you can create and use any number of BMidiPort objects in your application—multiple BMidiPort objects can open and use the same hardware port at the same time.

You identify a MIDI port by name, passing it to the BMidiPort constructor or `Open()` function. Use the `GetDeviceName()` function to retrieve the names of the MIDI ports. The ports are closed through `Close()`; they're automatically closed when the BMidiPort object is destroyed.

On a Macintosh, there are two MIDI ports:

• "midi1" is the modem port.
• "midi2" is the printer port.

On Intel hardware the MIDI ports are brought out on the sound card that you're using.

The BeBox has two built-in MIDI ports. The top port is "midi1"; the bottom port is "midi2".

A BMidiPort object can only open one port at a time.

Running and the MIDI Hook Functions

Running a BMidiPort corresponds to MIDI-In: When you tell a BMidiPort to run (through the `Start()` function) the object begins reading from MIDI-In and spraying the MIDI messages to its connected objects.

On the other side, the MIDI hook functions (`NoteOn()`, `NoteOff()`, etc.) send MIDI messages to MIDI-Out.

It's possible to use the same BMidiPort object to accept data from MIDI-In and broadcast different data to MIDI-Out. You can even connect a BMidiPort object to itself to create a "MIDI through" effect: Anything that shows up at the MIDI-In port will automatically be sent out the MIDI-Out port.

Constructor and Destructor

BMidiPort()

> BMidiPort(const char *name = NULL)

Creates a new BMidiPort object and opens it on the named port. If no name is given, the object remains unopened until Open() is called.

~BMidiPort()

> virtual ~BMidiPort()

Closes the connections to the MIDI ports.

Member Functions

AllNotesOff()

> bool AllNotesOff(bool controlOnly, uint32 time = B_NOW)

Commands the BMidiPort object to issue an All Notes Off MIDI message to the MIDI-Out port. If controlOnly is true, only the All Notes Off message is sent. If it's false, a Note Off message is also sent for every key number on every channel.

Close()

> void Close(void)

Closes the object's MIDI port. The port should have been previously opened through a call to Open().

CountDevices(), GetDeviceName()

> int32 CountDevices(void)
> status_t GetDeviceName(int32 n, char *name,
>   size_t bufSize = B_OS_NAME_LENGTH)

These two function work together to let you retrieve the names of all MIDI ports. CountDevices() returns the number of MIDI ports that are supported by the machine. GetDeviceName() returns, in *name*, the name of the *n*'th MIDI port. *bufSize* is the length of the *name* buffer, in bytes. It needn't be longer than B_OS_NAME_LENGTH (defined in OS.h).

Return values:
> GetDeviceName() returns...
> B_OK. Success.
> B_BAD_VALUE. *n* is out of range.
> B_NAME_TOO_LONG. The device name length is greater than *bufSize*.

InitCheck()

> status_t **InitCheck**() const

Returns the status of the previous port-opening call. This function is provided primarily so you can get the status after opening the port through the constructor.

Return values:
> B_OK. The port was successfully opened.
> *POSIX errors*. The open was thwarted.

Open()

> status_t **Open**(const char **name*)

Opens the MIDI port identified by *name*, so the object can read and write MIDI data. Use the GetDeviceName() function to get the names of the MIDI ports. The object isn't given exclusive access to the ports that it has opened—other BMidiPort objects, potentially from other applications, can open the same MIDI ports. When you're finished with the ports, you should close them through a (single) call to Close().

The MIDI-Out connection is active from the moment the object is opened: Messages that arrive through the MIDI hook functions are automatically sent to the MIDI-Out port. To begin reading from the MIDI-In port, you have to invoke the object's Start() function.

The function returns B_OK if the port was successfully opened.

Start(), Stop()

> virtual status_t **Start**(void)
> virtual void **Stop**(void)

Start() tells the object to begin listening to MIDI-In. For each MIDI message that it hears, the object calls the appropriate spray function.

Stop() tells the object to stop listening to MIDI-In.

Neither of these functions affects the MIDI-Out side of the port.

MIDI Hook Functions

The BMidiPort class implements the MIDI hook functions to send MIDI data to the MIDI-Out side of the port. For the syntax of the MIDI hook functions, see the BMidi class.

BMidiStore

Derived from:	public BMidi
Declared in:	be/midi/MidiStore.h
Library:	libmidi.so

The BMidiStore class defines a MIDI recording and playback mechanism. The MIDI messages that a BMidiStore object receives (at its input) are stored as *events* in an *event list*, allowing a captured performance to be played back later. The object can also read and write—or *import* and *export*—standard MIDI files.

Recording

The ability to record a MIDI performance is vested in BMidiStore's MIDI hook functions (`NoteOn()`, `NoteOff()`, etc.). When a MIDI hook is invoked, the function fabricates a discrete event based on the data it has received in its arguments, and adds the event to its event list. You don't need to tell a BMidiStore to start recording; it can record from the moment it's constructed.

For example, to record a performance from an external MIDI keyboard, you connect a BMidiStore to a BMidiPort object and then tell the BMidiPort to start:

```
/* Record a keyboard performance. */
BMidiStore MyStore;
BMidiPort MyPort;

MyPort.Open(...);
MyPort.Connect(MyStore);
MyPort.Start();
/* Start playing... */
```

At the end of the performance, you tell the BMidiPort to stop:

```
MyPort.Stop();
```

Timestamps

Events are added to a BMidiStore's event list immediately upon arrival. Each event is given a timestamp as it arrives; the value of the timestamp is the value of the *time* argument that was passed to the MIDI hook function by the "upstream" object's spray function. There's no guarantee that the time arguments of successive MIDI events will be in chronological order. To ensure that the events are properly ordered, you should call `Sort()` before you read from the list (note that writing to a MIDI file automatically sorts the list).

BMidiStore's input functions don't call `SnoozeUntil()`: A BMidiStore writes to its event list as soon as it gets a new message, it doesn't wait until the time indicated by the *time* argument.

Erasing and Editing a Recording

You can't. If you make a mistake while you're recording (for example) and want to try again, you can simulate emptying the object by disconnecting the input to the BMidiStore, destroying the object, making a new one, and reconnecting.

Editing the events in the event list is less than impossible (were such a state possible). You can't do it, and you can't simulate it, at least not with the default implementation of BMidiStore. If you want to edit MIDI data, you have to provide your own BMidi-derived class.

Playback

To "play" a BMidiStore's list of events, you call the object's `Start()` function. As described in the BMidi class specification, `Start()` invokes `Run()`. BMidiStore's `Run()` reads events in the order that they appear in the event list, and sprays the appropriate messages to the connected objects. You can interrupt a BMidiStore playback by calling `Stop()`; uninterrupted, the object will stop by itself after it has sprayed the last event in the list.

The events' timestamps are used as the *time* arguments in the spray functions that are called from within `Run()`. But with a twist: The *time* argument that's passed in the first spray call (for a given performance) is always `B_NOW`; subsequent *time* arguments are re-computed to maintain the correct timing in relation to the first event. In other words, when you tell a BMidiStore to start playing, the first event is performed immediately regardless of the actual value of its timestamp.

Setting the Current Event

You can tell the BMidiStore to begin playing from somewhere in the middle of the list by calling `SetCurrentEvent()` before starting the playback. The function takes an index into the list.

If you want to start playing from a particular time offset into the event list, you first have to figure out which event lies at that time. To do this, you ask for the event that occurs at or after the time offset (in milliseconds) through the `EventAtDelta()` function. The value that's returned by this function is suitable as the argument to `SetCurrentEvent()`.

Keep in mind that `EventAtDelta()` returns the index of the first event at *or after* the desired offset. If you need to know the actual offset of the winning event, you can pass its index to `DeltaOfEvent()`:

```
long firstEvent = MyStore->EventAtDelta(3000);
long actualDelta = MyStore->DeltaOfEvent(firstEvent);
```

Reading and Writing MIDI Files

You add events to a BMidiStore's event list by reading, or *importing*, a Standard MIDI File through the `Import()` function. You can import any number of files into the same BMidiStore object. After you import a file, the event list is automatically sorted.

One thing you shouldn't do is import a MIDI file into a BMidiStore that contains events that were previously recorded from a BMidiPort (in an attempt to mix the file and the recording). Nor does the reverse work: You can't import a file and *then* record from a BMidiPort. The file's timestamps are incompatible with those that are generated for events that are received from the BMidiPort; the result certainly won't be satisfactory.

To write the event list as a MIDI file, you call BMidiStore's `Export()` function.

Constructor and Destructor

BMidiStore(), ~BMidiStore()

> BMidiStore(void)
> virtual ~BMidiStore()

The constructor creates a new, empty BMidiStore object. The destructor destroys the object and its storage.

Member Functions

BeginTime()

```
uint32 BeginTime(void) const
```

Returns the time, in ticks, at which the most recent performance started. This function is only valid if the object has actually performed.

CountEvents(), SortEvents(), DeltaOfEvent(), EventAtDelta()

```
uint32 CountEvents(void) const
void SortEvents(bool force = false)
uint32 DeltaOfEvent(uint32 index) const
uint32 EventAtDelta(uint32 delta) const
```

CountEvents() returns the number of events in the object's event list.

SortEvents() time-sorts the events in the event list. The object maintains a (conservative) notion of whether the events are already sorted; if *force* is `false` and the object doesn't think the operation is necessary, the sorting isn't performed. If force is `true`, the operation is always performed, regardless of its necessity.

DeltaOfEvent() returns the "delta time" of the *index*'th event in the object's list of events. An event's delta time is the time span, in ticks, between the first event in the event list and itself.

EventAtDelta() Returns the index of the event that occurs on or after *delta* ticks from the beginning of the event list.

CurrentEvent() see SetCurrentEvent()

DeltaOfEvent() see CountEvents()

EventAtDelta() see ChrisEvert()

Export(), Import()

```
status_t Export(const entry_ref *to_file, int32 format)
status_t Import(const entry_ref *from_file)
```

Export() time-sorts the object's event list, and then writes the list as a standard MIDI file in the designated format; the *format* argument should be either 0 or 1. The file that *to_file* refers to must already exist, and is *not* cleared before it's written.

`Import()` reads the standard MIDI file from the designated file and adds its events to the object's event list.

Return values:

B_OK. The file was successfully written or read.

B_NO_MEMORY (`Import()` only). Couldn't allocate enough memory to accommodate the file.

POSIX errors. Some other file error prevented the operation.

SetCurrentEvent(), CurrentEvent()

> void `SetCurrentEvent`(uint32 *index*)
> uint32 `CurrentEvent`(void)

Sets the object's "current event"—the event that it will perform next—to the event at *index* in the event list.

Returns the index of the event that will be performed next.

SetTempo(), Tempo()

> void **SetTempo**(int32 *beatsPerMinute*)
> int32 **Tempo**(void) const

Sets and returns the object's tempo—the speed at which it performs events—in beats per minute. The default tempo is 60 bpm.

SortEvents *see* CountEvents()

BMidiText

Derived from:	public BMidi
Declared in:	be/midi/MidiText.h
Library:	libmidi.so

A BMidiText object prints, on standard output, a text description of each MIDI message it receives. You use BMidiText objects to debug and monitor your application; it has no other purpose.

To use a BMidiText object, you construct it and connect it to some other BMidi object as shown below:

```
BMidiText midiText;

otherMidiObj.Connect(midiText);
otherMidiObj.Start();
```

BMidiText's output (the text it displays) is timed: When it receives a MIDI message that's timestamped for the future, the object waits until that time has come before it displays its message. While it's waiting, the object won't process any other in-coming messages. Because of this, you shouldn't connect the same BMidiText object to more than one BMidi object. To monitor two or more MIDI-producing objects, you should connect a separate BMidiText object to each.

The text that's displayed by a BMidiText follows this general format:

timestamp: MESSAGE TYPE; message data

(Message-specific formats are given in the section "Output Text".) Of particular note is the *timestamp* field. Its value is the number of milliseconds that have elapsed since the object received its first message. The time value is computed through the use of an internal timer; to reset this timer—a useful thing to do between performances, for example—you call the `ResetTimer()` function.

The BMidiText class doesn't generate or spray MIDI messages, so the performance and connection functions that it inherits from BMidi have no effect.

Constructor and Destructor

BMidiText(), ~BMidiText()

BMidiText(void)
virtual ~BMidiText()

The constructor creates a new BMidiText object. The object's timer is set to zero and doesn't start ticking until the first message is received. To force the timer to start, call `ResetTimer(true)`.

The destructor destroys the object.

Member Functions

ResetTimer()

void **ResetTimer**(bool *start* = false)

Sets the object's internal timer to zero. If *start* is `false` the timer doesn't start ticking until the next MIDI message is received. If *start* is `true`, the timer begins immediately.

The timer value is used to compute the timestamp that's displayed at the beginning of each message description.

Output Text

The text strings that a BMidiText object displays are shown below, listed by MIDI event.

Channel Pressure

timestamp: CHANNEL PRESSURE; channel = *channel*, pressure = *pressure*

Control Change

timestamp: CONTROL CHANGE; channel = *channel*, control = *ctrl_num*,
    value = *ctrl_value*

Key Pressure

timestamp: KEY PRESSURE; channel = *channel*, note = *note*, pressure = *pressure*

Note Off

timestamp: NOTE OFF; channel = *channel*, note = *note*, velocity = *velocity*

Note On

timestamp: NOTE ON; channel = *channel*, note = *note*, velocity = *velocity*

Pitch Bend

timestamp: PITCH BEND; channel = *channel*, lsb = *lsb*, msb = *msb*

Program Change

timestamp: PROGRAM CHANGE; channel = *channel*, program = *program_num*

System Common

timestamp: SYSTEM COMMON; status = *status*, data1 = *data1*, data2= *data2*

System Exclusive

timestamp: SYSTEM EXCLUSIVE;

Followed by the data itself (in hex, byte-by-byte), starting on the next line.

SystemRealTime()

timestamp: SYSTEM REAL TIME; status = *status*

BSynth

Derived from:	*none*
Declared in:	be/midi/Synth.h
Library:	libmidi.so

The BeOS includes a 16-channel General MIDI software synthesizer designed by HeadSpace Inc. The BSynth class is the interface to the synthesizer itself. Any application that wants to use the synthesizer must include a BSynth object; however, most applications won't need to create the object directly: The BMidiSynth, BMidiSynthFile, and BSamples classes create a BSynth object for you. Furthermore, since BSynth doesn't inherit from BMidi, it doesn't have any API for actually playing MIDI data. To play MIDI data, you need an instance of BMidiSynth or BMidiSynthFile.

An application can have only one BSynth object at a time. The object is represented globally (within your app) as **be_synth**. The classes that create a BSynth for you (BMidiSynth and so on) won't clobber an existing **be_synth**, but the BSynth constructor will.

When it's created, the **be_synth** object tries to find an instrument definition (or "synth") file. This is a file that contains the data (samples and instructions) for creating General MIDI instruments. The BeOS provides two such files (both designed by HeadSpace, and both stored in **B_SYNTH_DIRECTORY**):

- **B_BIG_SYNTH_FILE** (*/boot/beos/etc/synth/big_synth.sy*) contains 16-bit, 22 kHz data. It takes about 5 Mb of memory when fully loaded.

- **B_LITTLE_SYNTH_FILE** (*/boot/beos/etc/synth/little_synth.sy*) is 8-bit, 11 kHz data. It's a quarter the size of the big synth, but lacks the big file's fidelity.

The instrument data is read from the file as it's needed. To "pre-load" the entire synth file, use the **BMidiSynth::EnableInput()** function.

BSynth and the Audio Server

The synthesizer produces sound by taking over the Audio Server's DAC stream. It resets the size and number of buffers in the stream, sets the sampling rate, and adds a BSubscriber to the front of the stream. If you want to mix sound files into the MIDI synthesis, you should use the BSamples object rather than add your own DAC stream subscribers. However, if you really want to add your own sample-generating subscribers, *don't* add them to the front of the DAC stream after the `be_synth` subscriber has been added—your subscriber's samples will be clobbered.

The interaction between the synthesizer and the Media Kit will be cleaned up in a subsequent release.

The DAC stream's previous settings are restored when `be_synth` is destroyed.

Synthesis Capacity

The synthesizer can generate up to 32 voices at a time, where a "voice" is either an individual (synthesized) note, or a stream of samples from a BSamples object. By default, it apportions 28 voice "slots" for synthesis and 4 for samples. You can change the settings through the `SetVoiceLimits()` function.

If you ask for more voices than there are voice slots (for example, if you ask for a 29'th note when there are already 28 singing), the synthesizer will try to kill an old note in order to make room for the new note.

There's no guarantee that the synthesizer and DAC stream will have enough time to generate and process everything you ask for, even if you're running below the 32 voice limit. On a lightly loaded, reasonably fast machine, you shouldn't hear any glitches, but a heavy MIDI command stream (for example) could bog it down.

Recording a Performance

There's no API for automatically writing the synthesizer's output to a file. To record a synthesizer performance you have to create your own BSubscriber, add it to the DAC stream (downstream of the synthesizer), and write out the samples that it receives. (See the Media Kit for more information.)

In some cases, the act of recording can be enough of a CPU drag that the synthesizer falls behind realtime (actually, it's the synthesizer's BSubscriber that's getting behind). It may not sound great while you're monitoring the recording, but the data that's written to the file probably won't be affected—the glitches won't be written to the file.

Constructor and Destructor

BSynth()

BSynth(void)
BSynth(synth_mode *mode*)

Creates and initializes a new BSynth object and sets be_synth to point to it. The BSynth that be_synth currently points to (if any) is deleted. You can only construct one BSynth object per application. Every application that wants to use the synthesizer must have its own BSynth—you can't "share" another application's be_synth object. The constructors for the other synthesis classes (BMidiSynth, BMidiSynthFile, and BSamples) create a BSynth for you if one doesn't already exist.

The default constructor sets the following synthesis parameters, shown here with the functions that you can use to reset the values—and that you should refer to for further explanation:

Parameter	Value	Function
Output sampling rate	22 kHz	SetSamplingRate()
Sample interpolation	B_LINEAR_INTERPOLATION	SetInterpolation()
Max synth voices	28	SetVoiceLimits()
Max sample voices	4	SetVoiceLimits()
Limiter threshhold	7	SetVoiceLimits()
Reverb enabled	true	EnableReverb()
Reverb	B_REVERB_BALLROOM	SetReverb()
Synth mode	B_SYNTH_NONE	LoadSynthData()

You must call LoadSynthData() after calling the default constructor to set the synth mode.

The synth_mode constructor sets the synthesis parameters (as above) and then sets the synth mode to the argument, one of B_BIG_SYNTH, B_LITTLE_SYNTH, or B_SAMPLES_ONLY. See LoadSynthData() for synth_mode definitions.

~BSynth()

> virtual ~BSynth()

The destructor stops the synthesizer if it's currently playing anything, frees all synthesis-related storage that the BSynth object allocated, and sets be_synth to point to NULL.

Member Functions

CountClients()

> int32 CountClients(void) const

Returns the number of synthesis objects (BMidiSynth and BMidiSynthFile) that are actively feeding data to the synthesizer. Note that this count does *not* include BSamples objects.

EnableReverb(), IsReverbEnabled(), SetReverb(), Reverb(), reverb_mode

> status_t **EnableReverb**(bool *reverbEnabled*)
> bool **IsReverbEnabled**(void) const
>
> void **SetReverb**(reverb_mode *reverb*)
> reverb_mode **Reverb**(void) const
> typedef enum { **B_REVERB_NONE, B_REVERB_CLOSET, B_REVERB_GARAGE,**
>   **B_REVERB_BALLROOM, B_REVERB_CAVERN,**
>   **B_REVERB_DUNGEON** } reverb_mode

`EnableReverb()` turns on and off be_synth's reverberator. `IsReverbEnabled()` returns the current reverberator-enabled state. Reverb is enabled by default.

`SetReverb()` sets the reverberator's strength. The constants, shown above, are listed in order of increasing "wetness." `Reverb()` returns the current setting. Setting the reverb mode *doesn't* enable the reverberator.

To turn off the reverberator, do this:

`EnableReverb(false); /* Good *.`

...rather than:

`SetReverb(B_REVERB_NONE); /* Bad */`

Return values:
> `EnableReverb()` returns...
> B_OK. The reverberator was successfully enabled/disabled.
> B_NO_MEMORY. Not enough memory to setup the reverberator.

GetAudio()

> int32 **GetAudio**(int16 **left*, int16 **right*, int32 *sampleCount*) const

Returns, in *left* and *right*, the last *sampleCount*'th sample frames (split into left and right channels) generated by the synthesizer. Storage for the samples must be allocated by the caller. The function may return fewer samples than requested. The function returns the number of samples that were written into (each of) *left* and *right*.

This function is designed to feed waveform displays (and the like); it isn't intended to be used as a "sound spigot" that you can pipe to a file (for example).

Interpolation() *see* SetSamplingRate()

interpolation_mode *see* SetSamplingRate()

IsLoaded() *see* LoadSynthData()

IsReverbEnabled() *see* EnableReverb()

LimiterThreshhold() *see* SetVoiceLimits()

LoadSynthData(), Unload(), SynthMode(), IsLoaded()

```
status_t LoadSynthData(synth_mode mode)
status_t LoadSynthData(entry_ref *instrumentFile)
void Unload(void)
synth_mode SynthMode(void) const
bool IsLoaded(void) const
```

LoadSynthData() tells be_synth which synth file to use (and unloads the one currently in use, if any). The first version lets you specify the synth file through a synth_mode constant:

- B_BIG_SYNTH. Use the big synth file.

- B_LITTLE_SYNTH. Use the little synth file.

- B_SAMPLES_ONLY. Don't use a synth file, but prepare the object so it can play sampled sounds. You only use this mode if you're only going to use the BSamples object (in other words, if you're not using BMidiSynth or BMidiSynthFile).

If the synthesizer is initialized with a synth file, it will automatically know how to play BSample data.

WARNING

Currently, B_SAMPLES_ONLY doesn't work. You must use one of the other two constants (B_BIG_SYNTH or B_LITTLE_SYNTH).

The second version lets you set the synth file as an entry_ref, thus providing the opportunity to specify a custom synth file. Unfortunately, the synth file format isn't currently public, so you can't create your own synth files (yet).

LoadSynthData() doesn't actually read the instrument definitions from the synth file—in other words, it doesn't really "load" anything. The instruments are loaded as needed during a performance (as specified by a BMidiSynth[File] object). To force instruments to be read, use BMidiSynth's EnableInput() or LoadInstrument() function.

`Unload()` stops the synthesizer (if it's currently playing), forgets the instrument file that was used to initialize the synthesizer, and steps out of the audio output mechanism. After you call `Unload()`, the be_synth object is good for nothing until `LoadSynthData()` is called (whether directly or through a constructor).

`SynthMode()` returns be_synth's current synth mode, one of the three modes listed above or `B_NO_SYNTH` if the mode hasn't been set.

`IsLoaded()` returns `true` if be_synth has been initialized and is ready to go. Otherwise, it returns `false`.

Return values:
    `LoadSynthData()` returns...
    `B_OK`. be_synth was successfully initialized.
    `B_BAD_VALUE`. Invalid argument.
    `B_NO_MEMORY`. Not enough memory to initialize the synthesizer.
    POSIX errors. The synth file wasn't found or couldn't be opened.

MaxSampleVoices() *see* SetVoiceLimits()

MaxSynthVoices() *see* SetVoiceLimits()

Pause(), Resume()

> void **Pause**(void)
> void **Resume**(void)

`Pause()` tells the synthesizer to stop producing sound. It doesn't suspend non-synthesis BMidi objects—in other words, `Pause()` doesn't suspend BMidiPort or BMidiStore objects.

`Resume()` tells the synthesizer to resume producing sound. BMidiSynthFile objects continue reading from where they were paused; BSamples objects start playing from the beginning of their sample data (they *don't* continue from where they were paused).

Reverb() *see* EnableReverb()

reverb_mode *see* EnableReverb()

SampleVolume() *see* SetSynthVolume()

SamplingRate() *see* SetSamplingRate()

SetControllerHook(), synth_controller_hook

> void **SetControllerHook**(int16 *controller*, synth_controller_hook *controlHook*)

> typedef void (***synth_controller_hook**)(int16 *channel*, int16 *controller*, int16 *value*)

Registers a hook function (*controlHook*) that's invoked whenever a MIDI control message is applied to *controller*. The hook function is invoked just after the control message is processed by the synthesizer. The function is passed the channel, controller number, and controller value as taken from the control message.

SetInterpolation() *see* SetSamplingRate()

SetReverb() *see* EnableReverb()

SetSampleVolume() *see* SetSynthVolume()

SetSamplingRate(), SamplingRate(), SetInterpolation(), Interpolation(), interpolation_mode

> status_t **SetSamplingRate**(int32 *rate*)
> int32 **SamplingRate**(void) const

> status_t **SetInterpolation**(interpolation_mode *interp*)
> interpolation_mode **Interpolation**(void) const
> typedef enum { **B_DROP_SAMPLE**,
>   **B_2_POINT_INTERPOLATION**,
>   **B_LINEAR_INTERPOLATION** } interpolation_mode

`SetSamplingRate()` sets the frequency at which `be_synth` produces data, in frames (of audio data) per second. Acceptable rates are 44100, 22050, and 11025; *rate* is rounded to the nearest acceptable value. The default is 22050.

`SamplingRate()` returns the sampling rate as previously set by `SetSamplingRate()`.

`be_synth`'s sampling rate is independent of the DAC stream's sampling rate. For example, while the default `be_synth` rate is 22050, the default DAC stream rate is 44100. If the two rates don't match, `be_synth`'s BSubscriber object "interpolates" the `be_synth` data before dumping it into the DAC stream. There are three interpolation schemes, which you set through `SetInterpolation()`:

Constant	Meaning
B_DROP_SAMPLE	Samples are repeated or dropped. It sounds cheap because it *is* cheap.
B_2_POINT_INTERPOLATION	Linear interpolation between adjacent samples. Much better quality, and more expensive, than drop-sample.

Constant	Meaning
B_LINEAR_INTERPOLATION	"Wide" linear interpolation. The best quality, but the most expensive.

Interpolation() returns the current interpolation mode setting. The default is B_LINEAR_INTERPOLATION.

Return values:
> SetSamplingRate() and SetInterpolation() return...
> B_OK. The function was successful.
> B_BAD_VALUE. Invalid argument.

SetSynthVolume(), SetSampleVolume(), SynthVolume(), SampleVolume()

> void **SetSynthVolume**(double *scale*)
> void **SetSampleVolume**(double *scale*)

> double **SynthVolume**(void) const
> double **SampleVolume**(void) const

These functions get and set the master volume scalars for MIDI synthesis and BSamples playback. The scalar is linear: A *scale* of 1.0 (the default) has no affect; a scale of 2.0 multiplies the output by 2.0, and so on. The *scale* value must be at least 0.0 (no gain).

SetVoiceLimits(), MaxSynthVoices(), MaxSampleVoices(), LimiterThreshhold()

> status_t **SetVoiceLimits**(int16 *maxSynthVoices*, int16 *maxSampleVoices*, int16 *limiter Threshhold*)

> int16 **MaxSynthVoices**(void) const
> int16 **MaxSampleVoices**(void) const
> int16 **LimiterThreshhold**(void) const

The synthesizer can generate as many as 32 "voices" simultaneously, where a voice is a MIDI note or a stream of BSamples. The first two arguments tell the synthesizer to set aside some number of voice slots for MIDI synthesis and for samples, respectively; combined, the two arguments mustn't exceed 32. If you ask for too many voices during a performance, the synthesizer will (try to) kill old voices first. By default, the voices are allocated 28 for MIDI synthesis and 4 for samples.

You use the *limiterThreshhold* to estimate the typical voice density (number of simultaneous voices) for a performance. It must be at least 1; the default is 7. The synthesizer uses the value as an amplitude scalar:

- When the voice density during a performance is less than (or equal to) the threshhold (n), the dynamic range is "divided" into n parts, where each voice gets one part.

- When the voice density (m) exceeds the threshhold, the dynamic range is divided into m parts.

If you set the value too high (if there are typically fewer simultaneous voices than you estimated) the signal-to-noise ratio will suffer—you'll be dividing the dynamic range into too many (small) parts. If you set it too low and the voice density changes a lot, the balance between voices may become hard to predict and control. A change to the *limiterTreshhold* doesn't affect notes/samples that are currently being produced.

The other three functions return the values that you passed to `SetVoiceLimits()`. Note that these functions don't actually consult the synthesizer—if you pass illegal values to `SetVoiceLimits()`, the querying functions will return those values without complaint.

Return values:
> `SetVoiceLimits()` returns...
> B_OK. The limits were successfully set.
> B_BAD_VALUE. Bad argument value; the previous settings are left unchanged.

synth_controller_hook see SetControllerHook()

SynthMode() see LoadSynthData()

SynthVolume() see SetSynthVolume()

Unload() see LoadSynthData()

BMidiSynth

Derived from: BMidi

Declared in: be/midi/MidiSynth.h

Library: libmidi.so

The BMidiSynth class is the MIDI interface to the General MIDI synthesizer. If you want to send MIDI data to the synthesizer, you have to create an instance of BMidiSynth. You can send MIDI messages to the object directly:

```
/* Create and initialize a BMidiSynth. */
BMidiSynth midiSynth;
midiSynth.EnableInput(true, true);
```

```
/* Choose an instrument and play a note. */
midiSynth.ProgramChange(1, B_ACOUSTIC_GRAND);
midiSynth.NoteOn(1, 40, 100, B_NOW);
snooze(1000000);
midiSynth.NoteOff(1, 40, 100, B_NOW);
```

Or you can connect the BMidiSynth to the output of some other BMidi object, such as a BMidiPort:

```
/* Connect the synth to a MIDI port. */
BMidiPort midiPort;
char buf[B_OS_NAME_LENGTH];

/* Initialize the BMidiPort. */
if (midiPort.GetDeviceName(0, buf) == B_OK) {
   midiPort.Open(buf);

   /* midiSynth from above -- already created and initialized. */
   midiPort.Connect(&midiSynth);
   midiPort.Start();
   ...
}
```

The one thing you shouldn't do is connect a BMidiFile to a BMidiSynth. If you want to realize the contents of a MIDI file, you should use an instance of BMidiSynthFile instead (BMidiSynthFile is derived from BMidiSynth).

BMidiSynth doesn't spray MIDI messages, so it doesn't do any good to connect other BMidi objects to its output. In other words, don't do this:

```
/* --- DON'T DO THIS ---   It's meaningless. */
midiSynth.Connect(someOtherMidiObject);
```

Initializing Your BMidiSynth

When you create a BMidiSynth object, it creates an instance of BSynth for you (if the object doesn't already exist). The BSynth object, which its represented globally in your application as be_synth, provides control over some of the synthesizer's global parameters, such as volume and reverberation.

Before you send messages to your BMidiSynth, you have to call EnableInput(). The function enables the object's input and tells the synthesizer whether it should load the synth file. If you tell EnableInput() not to load the file, you'll have to load the instruments that you want yourself. For example, here we load a single instrument, then play a note. We also have to send a ProgramChange() message to tell the BMidiSynth object use our loaded instrument on the proper channel (i.e. the channel that we're playing the note on):

```
/* Enable input, but don't load the synth file. */
midiSynth.EnableInput(true, false);
```

```
/* Load a couple of instruments. */
midiSynth.LoadInstrument(B_TINKLE_BELL);
midiSynth.LoadInstrument(B_VIOLIN);

/* Associate the instrument with a MIDI channel. */
midiSynth.ProgramChange(1, B_TINKLE_BELL);
midiSynth.ProgramChange(2, B_VIOLIN);

/* Play. */
midiSynth.NoteOn(1, 84, 100);
snooze(10);
midiSynth.NoteOn(2, 60, 100);
snooze(1000000);
midiSynth.NoteOff(1, 84, 100);
snooze(10);
midiSynth.NoteOff(2, 60, 100);
```

The order and number of instruments follow the General MIDI specification, but begin with instrument 0 (some synthesizers and sequencers expect instrument numbers to start at 1). The handy `midi_axe` constants, defined in *be/midi/MidiDefs.h*, provide the descriptive instrument names used here.

Instrument Scope

All of the instrument loading functions (`EnableInput()` and the functions described under `LoadInstrument()`) affect all `be_synth` clients (i.e. all BMidiSynth objects in your application). This can be beneficial: Loading an instrument from one BMidiSynth object means it doesn't have to be loaded again when, for example, a BMidiSynthFile needs it (the synthesizer is smart about reloading: If an instrument is already loaded, it won't try to load it again). As another example, if you have more than one BMidiSynth object, they can each load all instruments (through `EnableInput()`) without suffering a performance penalty.

However, there's a dark side: If a BMidiSynth unloads an instrument (through `UnloadInstrument()` or `FlushInstrumentCache(false)`), that instrument disappears for all other BMidiSynth objects as well. You can prevent unwanted instrument unloading by calling `FlushInstrumentCache(true)` (see the function description for more information).

Percussion Instruments

To use the MIDI Channel 10 percussion instruments, you *must* load all instruments:

```
/* I want percussion, therefore... */
midiSynth.EnableInput(true, true);
```

Constructor and Destructor

BMidiSynth()

> BMidiSynth(void)

Creates a new BMidiSynth object. Also constructs a BSynth object and assigns the object to the app-wide **be_synth** variable (if the object doesn't already exist). To turn on your BMidiSynth object, you must call **SetEnabled()** after construction.

~BMidiSynth()

> virtual **~BMidiSynth()**

Disconnects the object from the synthesizer, and destroys the object.

Member Functions

EnableInput(), IsInputEnabled()

> status_t **EnableInput**(bool *enable*, bool *loadSynthFile*)
> bool **IsInputEnabled**(void) const

EnableInput() tells the object to connect and disconnect itself to the synthesizer, as *enable* is **true** or **false**. A disabled BMidiSynth doesn't pass on any MIDI messages to the synthesizer.

If *enable* is **true** and *loadSynthFile* is **true**, any instruments in the synth file (as designated by **be_synth**) that haven't already been loaded are immediately loaded. Loading the entire synth file can take a long time (more than a second, less than a minute), and this isn't your last shot at loading instruments, so you may not want to load all at once. If you want to defer loading, you can call **LoadInstrument()** after calling **EnableInput()**.

IsInputEnabled() tells you if the BMidiSynth is currently enabled.

See "Initializing Your BMidiSynth" for more on instrument loading, instrument scope, and the use of Channel 10 percussion.

NOTE

BMidiSynthFile objects do not have to call **EnableInput()**. Input is automatically enabled when the object loads a file.

Return values:
Currently, **EnableInput()** always return B_OK.

FlushInstrumentCache() see LoadInstrument()

GetMuteMap() see MuteChannel()

GetSoloMap() see MuteChannel()

IsInputEnabled() see EnableInput()

LoadInstrument(), RemapInstrument(), UnloadInstrument(), FlushInstrumentCache()

status_t **LoadInstrument**(int16 *instrument*)
status_t **RemapInstrument**(int16 *from*, int16 *to*)
status_t **UnloadInstrument**(int16 *instrument*)
void **FlushInstrumentCache**(bool *flush*)

NOTE

See "Initializing Your BMidiSynth" for more on instrument loading, instrument scope, and the use of Channel 10 percussion.

Return values:

Currently, `UnloadInstrument()` always returns `B_OK`. The other two `status_t` functions return...

`B_OK`. Instrument successfully loaded or remapped.

`B_BAD_INSTRUMENT`. Illegal instrument specification.

`B_NO_MEMORY`. Not enough memory to load instrument.

MuteChannel(), GetMuteMap(), SoloChannel(), GetSoloMap()

WARNING

These functions are broken; don't use them.

RemapInstrument() see LoadInstrument()

SetTransposition(), Transposition()

void **SetTransposition**(int16 *transpose*)
int16 **Transposition**(void) const

`SetTransposition()` sets the amount, in halfsteps, by which subsequently generated notes will be transposed (shifted in pitch). Notes that are already sounding are not transposed. The transposition affects all channels of the invoked-upon object.

`Transposition()` returns the current transposition amount (in halfsteps); the default is 0.

SetVolume(), Volume()

> void **SetVolume**(double *volume*)
> double **Volume**(void) const

`SetVolume()` scales the object's amplitude (on all channels) by *volume*. In addition to affecting subsequently-generated notes, the new volume scale affects notes that are currently being generated by this object.

`Volume()` returns the current amplitude scalar value; the default is 1.0.

SoloChannel() *see* MuteChannel()

Tick()

> uint32 **Tick**(void) const

Returns the number of microseconds since the object was created. You should use this measurement for relative values only (for measuring the time between notes, for example). Also, note that the *time* argument to the MIDI hook functions measures time in milliseconds.

Transposition() *see* SetTransposition()

UnloadInstrument() *see* LoadInstrument()

Volume() *see* SetVolume()

BMidiSynthFile

Derived from:	public BMidiSynth
Declared in:	be/midi/MidiSynthFile.h
Library:	libmidi.so

The BMidiSynthFile class reads a standard MIDI file and plays it on the General MIDI synthesizer. Each BMidiSynthFile object can read (and play) only one file at a time. To use a BMidiSynthFile, you create the object, load a MIDI file, and tell the object to `Start()`:

```
/* Create and initialize a BMidiSynthFile. */
BMidiSynthFile midiSynthFile;
entry_ref midiRef;
```

```
get_ref_for_path("/boot/optional/midi/QuickBrownFox.mid", &midiRef);
midiSynthFile.LoadFile(&midiRef);

/* Play the file. */
midiSynthFile.Start();
```

You should create a different BMidiSynthFile object for each MIDI file that you want to mix together into a single performance.

WARNING

In certain circumstances, a single BMidiSynthFile object can load and play more than one MIDI file at the same time, but you shouldn't rely on this feature.

Loading and Playing

When you call `LoadFile()`, the BMidiSynthFile object automatically calls...

```
EnableInput(true, false)
```

It then loads the file's MIDI data into the synthesizer, which loads all the instruments that are needed by the file. If the file uses a lot of different instruments, loading the file can take some time.

When the file is finished playing (either because it's reached the end, or because you called `Stop()`) the instruments are *not* unloaded. This cuts the overhead if you play the file a second time.

The Run Thread and Function

BMidiSynthFile is different from other `Start()`-able BMidi objects in that it doesn't have a run loop. The MIDI data is parsed and realized in the synthesizer's subscriber thread (the thread that dumps data into the DAC stream). The lack of a run loop shouldn't affect the way you write your code, but you should be aware that the thread isn't there so you won't go looking for it while you're developing your app.

Furthermore, BMidiSynthFile doesn't implement the `Run()` function. Starting and stopping the object's performance (activities that are normally handled in the `Run()` function) are handled by the synthesizer in its subscriber thread. If you create a BMidiSynthFile subclass, *don't* try to resurrect the `Run()` function—leave it as a no-op.

As with the BMidiSynth class, the BMidiSynthFile MIDI hook implementations don't call the spray functions. This means that you can't, for example, connect a BMidiSynthFile to a BMidiPort. If you want to play a MIDI file out a MIDI port, use BMidiStore to represent and play the file.

Constructor and Destructor

BMidiSynthFile()

BMidiSynthFile(void)

Creates a new, empty BMidiSynthFile object. Also constructs a BSynth object and assigns the object to the app-wide **be_synth** variable (if the object doesn't already exist). To load a MIDI file into the BMidiSynthFile object, you must call `LoadFile()` after construction. Unlike plain BMidiSynth instances, however, you *don't* have to call `EnableInput()` (`LoadFile()` calls it for you).

~BMidiSynthFile()

virtual ~BMidiSynthFile()

Disconnects the object from the synthesizer, unloads the object's file (and all its instruments) and destroys the object.

Member Functions

Duration(), Position(), Seek()

int32 **Duration**(void) const
status_t **Position**(int32 *ticks*)
int32 **Seek**(void)

`Duration()` returns the length of the object's loaded data, measured in tempo independent ticks.

`Position()` sets the object's current position within the data.

`Seek()` returns the object's current position.

The actual quanta used by these functions is a bit odd. If you want to reposition the "song pointer," you should do it as a percentage of the `Duration()` measurement.

Return values:
Currently `Position()` always returns B_OK.

EnableLooping() see Start()

GetMuteMap() see MuteTrack()

GetPatches()

> status_t **GetPatches**(int16 *instruments*, int16 *count*)

Returns an array of the instruments numbers that are needed by the loaded MIDI file. The *instruments* array should be 128 elements long (to be on the safe side), and must be allocated before it's passed in. Upon return, function sets *count* to the number of instrument numbers that it placed in the array. For example:

```
int16 insts[128];
int16 count;
midiSynthFile.GetPatches(insts, &count);
for (int n = 0; n < count; n++)
   printf("The file uses instrument #%d\n", array[n]);
```

GetSoloMap() see MuteTrack()

IsFinished() see Start()

LoadFile(), UnloadFile()

> status_t **LoadFile**(const entry_ref *midiFileRef*)
> void **UnloadFile**(void) const

LoadFile() tells the object to load, into the synthesizer, the MIDI data from the *midiFileRef*. The synthesizer caches the data for subsequent playback (which you initiate through Start()). All instruments that are needed to play the file are loaded into the synthesizer, if they're aren't loaded already.

UnloadFile() stops playback of the data that was loaded through this object (if it's playing), and flushes the data (removes it from the synthesizer).

WARNING

In certain circumstances, a single BMidiSynthFile object can load and play more than one MIDI file at the same time, but you shouldn't rely on this feature.

Return values:
   B_OK. The file was found and loaded.
   B_BAD_MIDI_DATA. *midiFileRef* isn't a MIDI file, or contains corrupt data.
   B_NO_MEMORY. Not enough memory to load the file.
   Other POSIX errors. The file couldn't be opened or read.

MuteTrack(), GetMuteMap(), SoloTrack(), GetSoloMap()

WARNING

These functions are broken; don't use them.

Pause() see Start()

Position() see Duration()

Resume() see Start()

ScaleTempoBy() see Tempo()

Seek() see Duration()

SetFileHook() see Start()

SetTempo() see Tempo()

SoloTrack() see MuteTrack()

Start(), Stop(), Fade(), Pause(), Resume(), IsFinished(), EnableLooping(), SetFileHook(), synth_file_hook

```
virtual status_t Start(void)
virtual void Stop(void)
void Fade(void)
void Pause(void)
void Resume(void)
bool IsFinished(void) const
void EnableLooping(bool loop)
void SetFileHook(synth_file_hook fileDone, int32 arg)
typedef void (*synth_file_hook)(int32 arg)
```

These functions control the object's performance.

`Start()` tells the synthesizer to start playing the object's loaded MIDI data beginning at the beginning. Note that `Start()` does *not* halt a performance in progress; in other words, if the object is already playing its data, you'll get a second performance while the first continues.

`Stop()` immediately halts the currently playing data. `Fade()` also stops playback, but is a bit more graceful: It fades out the sound before killing it.

WARNING

BMidiSynthFile's `Start()` and `Stop()` replace the functions defined by BMidi.

`Pause()` and `Resume()` do as they say. Note that when you resume playback, "old" notes are not regenerated, but exact timing is respected. For example, lets say you have a MIDI file that contains two notes, one that starts at time 1.0 (seconds) and lasts for 10.0 seconds, and the other starts at time 9.0. You start the file, then `Pause()` at time 3.0; as expected, the first note stops. After awhile, you `Resume()`; there's a six second silence and then the second note plays.

`IsFinished()` returns `false` if the object is currently playing (or paused during play). Note that the function returns `false` before you load a file, and returns `true` after you've loaded a file but before you begin playing it.

`EnableLooping(true)` tells the object to replay the file when it reaches the end of the data. If the argument is `false`, the file isn't replayed. `Stop()` always shuts up playback, even if looping is enabled.

`SetFileHook()` registers a function that's called when the object is finished playing (either because it ran out of data or `Stop()` was called. *arg* is passed to the hook function as its sole argument. Note that the hook function is called when the object is *completely* finished—it isn't called at the end of each pass through the data while looping is enabled.

Return values:
    `Start()` returns...
    B_OK. The data was successfully started.
    B_TOO_MANY_SONGS_PLAYING. The synthesizer is too busy with other data streams.

Stop() see Start()

synth_file_hook see Start()

Tempo(), SetTempo(), ScaleTempoBy()

    int32 **Tempo**(void) const
    void **SetTempo**(int32 *beatsPerMinute*)
    void **ScaleTempoBy**(double *scalar*)

`Tempo()` returns the tempo of the data, as read from the MIDI file (or as set by the other functions), in beats-per-minute. The other two functions set the tempo: `SetTempo()` sets it absolutely in beats-per-minute, and `ScaleTempoBy()` scales the current tempo by the argument (*scalar* == 2.0 means the data is played twice as fast, *scalar* == .5 is twice as slow, and so on).

UnloadFile() see LoadFile()

BSamples

Derived from: *none*

Declared in: be/midi/Samples.h

Library: libmidi.so

The BSamples class lets you add a stream of audio samples into the General MIDI mix. The main functionality of the class (such as how you define the sound you want to play, whether it should repeat, what speed it should play at, and so on) is embedded in the `Start()` function; the class' other functions control and fine-tune the sound as it's playing. To learn how to use a BSamples object, go to the `Start()` function.

Theoretically, you can create and play (at the same time) as many BSamples as you want. In practice, you are limited to the sample voice limit set through BSynth's `SetVoiceLimits()` function; by default the limit is set to four.

Constructor and Destructor

BSamples()

BSamples(void)

Creates a new, empty BSamples object. Also constructs a BSynth object and assigns the object to the app-wide **be_synth** variable (if the object doesn't already exist). To initialize and use the BSamples object, invoke its `Start()` function.

WARNING

Currently, the "samples only" synth mode (`B_SAMPLES_ONLY`) is broken. Unfortunately, this is the mode used by the BSamples constructor if it has to create a **be_synth** object. The easiest way around this bug is to construct a BMidiSynth or BMidiSynthFile object. If you don't need the object, you can immediately destroy it; the fix is effected by the object's construction.

~BSamples()

virtual **~BSamples**()

Stops the object's playback, calls the "exit hook" function (as set by `Start()`), and destroys the object.

Member Functions

EnableReverb()

> void **EnableReverb**(bool *reverb*)

If *reverb* is true, the object's sound data is sent through the synthesizer's reverberator. To set the reverberation depth (for all reverberated sound), use BSynth::SetReverb().

IsPlaying() see Stop()

Pause() see Stop()

Placement() see SetSamplingRate()

Resume() see Stop()

SamplingRate() see SetSamplingRate()

SetPlacement() see SetSamplingRate()

SetSamplingRate(), SamplingRate(), SetPlacement(), Placement(), SetVolume(), Volume()

> void **SetSamplingRate**(double *samplingRate*)
> double **SamplingRate**(void) const

> void **SetPlacement**(double *stereoPan*)
> double **Placement**(void) const

> void **SetVolume**(double *volume*)
> double **Volume**(void) const

These functions set parameters of the sound data. They can be called while the sound is playing. For details of what these parameters mean, and the values that they accept, see the descriptions of the *samplingRate*, *stereoPan*, and *volume* arguments of the Start() function.

SetVolume() see SetSamplingRate()

Start(), sample_loop_hook, sample_exit_hook

void **Start**(void *samples*, int32 *frameCount*, int16 *sampleSize,* int16 *channelCount,*
double *samplingRate,* int32 *loopStart,* int32 *loopEnd,*
double *volume,* double *stereoPan,* int32 *hookArg,*
sample_loop_hook *loopHook,* sample_exit_hook *exitHook*)

typedef bool (***sample_loop_hook**)(int32 *arg*)
typedef void (***sample_exit_hook**)(int32 *arg*)

`Start()` passes in a buffer of audio samples that are immediately played. The playback is performed by the synthesizer in its BSubscriber thread; the `Start()` function itself returns immediately.

The audio data is assumed to be little-endian linear; other parameters of the data (sample size, channel count, etc.) are variable and are declared in the function's arguments. The arguments are:

- *samples* is a pointer to the data itself.

- *frameCount* is the number of frames of audio data in the buffer.

- *sampleSize* is the size of a single sample, in bytes. Currently, the synthesizer only accepts 1- and 2-byte samples.

- *channelCount* is the number of channels of data (1 or 2).

- *samplingRate* is the rate at which you want to the data played back, expressed as frames-per-second; for example, if your sound data was sampled at 44.1kHz and you want to play it back at its "native" pitch, you would set *samplingRate* to 44100.0. The range of valid sampling rate values is [0, ~65 kHz]. The sampling rate is independent of the data's channel count and sample size, and is independent of `be_synth`'s sampling rate. You can change the object's sampling rate on the fly through `SetSamplingRate()`.

- *loopStart* and *loopEnd* specify the first and last frames that are in the "loop section." The loop section can be any valid section of frames within the sound data (i.e. [0, *frameCount* - 1] inclusive). Everything up to the beginning of the loop section is the "attack section"; everything after the loop section is the "release section." When the sound is played, the attack section is heard, then the loop section is repeated until the object is told to `Stop()`, or until the "loop hook" function (defined below) returns `false`, at which point the release section is played. If you don't want the sound to loop, set these *loop...* arguments to 0.

WARNING

Currently, the release section is automatically faded out over a brief period of time. If your release section is designed to do a slow fade (for example) you probably won't hear it.

- *volume* is an amplitude scalar for this sound. The volume can also be set through `SetVolume()`.

- *stereoPan* locates the sound stereophonically, where -1.0 is hard left, 0.0 is center, and 1.0 is hard right. Notice that if this is a stereo sound, a *stereoPan* value of (say) -1.0 completely attenuates the right channel—it doesn't "move" the right channel into the left channel.

- *hookArg* is an arbitrary value that's passed to the *loopHook* and *exitHook* functions.

- *loopHook* is a hook function that's called each time the loop section is about to repeat. If the function returns `true`, the loop is, indeed, repeated. If it returns `false`, the release section is played and the sound stops. If you don't supply a *loopHook*, the loop is automatically repeated.

- *exitHook* is called when the sound is all done playing, regardless of how it stopped (whether through `Stop()`, a *hookFunc* return of `false`, or because the BSamples object was deleted).

Stop(), Pause(), Resume(), IsPaused(), IsPlaying()

virtual void **Stop**(void)
void **Pause**(void)
void **Resume**(void)
bool **IsPlaying**(void) const
bool **IsPaused**(void) const

`Stop()` tells the object to stop playing its sound data, and invokes the exit function, as set through `Start()`.

`Pause()` suspends playback and `Resume()` resumes it from where it was paused.

WARNING

`Pause()` and `Resume()` are backwards. To pause a sound, call `Resume()`. To resume it, call `Pause()`. Sorry about that.

`IsPlaying()` returns `true` if the object is currently playing (paused or not).

`IsPaused()` returns `true` if the sound is currently paused.

WARNING

`IsPaused()` returns `true` if you've called `Pause()`. Thus, since `Pause()` and `Resume()` are backwards, the sense of `IsPaused()` is also backwards.

Volume() see SetSamplingRate()

General MIDI Instruments

Declared in: be/midi/MidiDefs.h

The General MIDI Specification declares a set of 128 instruments, numbered 0-127. The Midi Kit provides a set of handy `midi_axe` constants that you can use to identify a MIDI instrument in functions such as `BMidiSynth::LoadInstrument()` and `BMidi::ProgramChange()`.

Instrument Constants

#	Pianos
0	B_ACOUSTIC_GRAND
1	B_BRIGHT_GRAND
2	B_ELECTRIC_GRAND
3	B_HONKY_TONK
4	B_ELECTRIC_PIANO_1
5	B_ELECTRIC_PIANO_2
6	B_HARPSICHORD
7	B_CLAVICHORD

#	Tuned Idiophones
8	B_CELESTA
9	B_GLOCKENSPIEL
10	B_MUSIC_BOX
11	B_VIBRAPHONE
12	B_MARIMBA
13	B_XYLOPHONE
14	B_TUBULAR_BELLS
15	B_DULCIMER

#	Organs
16	B_DRAWBAR_ORGAN
17	B_PERCUSSIVE_ORGAN
18	B_ROCK_ORGAN
19	B_CHURCH_ORGAN
20	B_REED_ORGAN
21	B_ACCORDION

#	Organs
22	B_HARMONICA
23	B_TANGO_ACCORDION

#	Guitars
24	B_ACOUSTIC_GUITAR_NYLON
25	B_ACOUSTIC_GUITAR_STEEL
26	B_ELECTRIC_GUITAR_JAZZ
27	B_ELECTRIC_GUITAR_CLEAN
28	B_ELECTRIC_GUITAR_MUTED
29	B_OVERDRIVEN_GUITAR
30	B_DISTORTION_GUITAR
31	B_GUITAR_HARMONICS

#	Basses
32	B_ACOUSTIC_BASS
33	B_ELECTRIC_BASS_FINGER
34	B_ELECTRIC_BASS_PICK
35	B_FRETLESS_BASS
36	B_SLAP_BASS_1
37	B_SLAP_BASS_2
38	B_SYNTH_BASS_1
39	B_SYNTH_BASS_2

#	Strings and Timpani
40	B_VIOLIN
41	B_VIOLA
42	B_CELLO
43	B_CONTRABASS
44	B_TREMOLO_STRINGS
45	B_PIZZICATO_STRINGS
46	B_ORCHESTRAL_STRINGS
47	B_TIMPANI

#	Ensemble Strings and Voices
48	B_STRING_ENSEMBLE_1
49	B_STRING_ENSEMBLE_2
50	B_SYNTH_STRINGS_1

#	Ensemble Strings and Voices
51	B_SYNTH_STRINGS_2
52	B_VOICE_AAH
53	B_VOICE_OOH
54	B_SYNTH_VOICE
55	B_ORCHESTRA_HIT

#	Brass
56	B_TRUMPET
57	B_TROMBONE
58	B_TUBA
59	B_MUTED_TRUMPET
60	B_FRENCH_HORN
61	B_BRASS_SECTION
62	B_SYNTH_BRASS_1
63	B_SYNTH_BRASS_2

#	Reeds
64	B_SOPRANO_SAX
65	B_ALTO_SAX
66	B_TENOR_SAX
67	B_BARITONE_SAX
68	B_OBOE
69	B_ENGLISH_HORN
70	B_BASSOON
71	B_CLARINET

#	Pipes
72	B_PICCOLO
73	B_FLUTE
74	B_RECORDER
75	B_PAN_FLUTE
76	B_BLOWN_BOTTLE
77	B_SHAKUHACHI
78	B_WHISTLE
79	B_OCARINA

#	Synth Leads	(Synonyms)
80	B_LEAD_1	B_SQUARE_WAVE
81	B_LEAD_2	B_SAWTOOTH_WAVE
82	B_LEAD_3	B_CALLIOPE
83	B_LEAD_4	B_CHIFF
84	B_LEAD_5	B_CHARANG
85	B_LEAD_6	B_VOICE
86	B_LEAD_7	B_FIFTHS
87	B_LEAD_8	B_BASS_LEAD

#	Synth Pads	(Synonyms)
88	B_PAD_1	B_NEW_AGE
89	B_PAD_2	B_WARM
90	B_PAD_3	B_POLYSYNTH
91	B_PAD_4	B_CHOIR
92	B_PAD_5	B_BOWED
93	B_PAD_6	B_METALLIC
94	B_PAD_7	B_HALO
95	B_PAD_8	B_SWEEP

#	Musical Effects
96	B_FX_1
97	B_FX_2
98	B_FX_3
99	B_FX_4
100	B_FX_5
101	B_FX_6
102	B_FX_7
103	B_FX_8

#	Ethnic
104	B_SITAR
105	B_BANJO
106	B_SHAMISEN
107	B_KOTO
108	B_KALIMBA
109	B_BAGPIPE

#	Ethnic
110	B_FIDDLE
111	B_SHANAI

#	Percussion
112	B_TINKLE_BELL
113	B_AGOGO
114	B_STEEL_DRUMS
115	B_WOODBLOCK
116	B_TAIKO_DRUMS
117	B_MELODIC_TOM
118	B_SYNTH_DRUM
119	B_REVERSE_CYMBAL

#	Sound Effects
120	B_FRET_NOISE
121	B_BREATH_NOISE
122	B_SEASHORE
123	B_BIRD_TWEET
124	B_TELEPHONE
125	B_HELICOPTER
126	B_APPLAUSE
127	B_GUNSHOT

CHAPTER SEVEN

The Game Kit

The Game Kit

The Game Kit is built for speed and direct access to underlying hardware, the sort of thing game developers crave. It consists of two classes, BWindowScreen and BDirectWindow, and one global function, set_mouse_position(). The two classes give you direct access to the graphics card frame buffer; the difference between them is that BWindowScreen always takes over the entire screen (and bypasses the App Server), while BDirectWindow can draw in a window. Also, while BDirectWindow can do everything a BWindowScreen can, BWindowScreen is often easier to use.

Although designed with games in mind, nothing in the Game Kit is restricted to game applications, except that the user will have to deposit another 50 cents every three minutes.

BDirectWindow

Derived from: public BWindow

Declared in: be/kit/game/DirectWindow.h

Library: libgame.so

The BDirectWindow class gives your code direct access to the graphics frame buffer on the video card. BDirectWindow can be used in both "full-screen" (exclusive) and "window" modes. In the latter mode, the BDirectWindow looks just like a normal window, but lets your code draw into it by directly accessing the frame buffer. BDirectWindow lets you switch between modes without breaking down and rebuilding the object. A call to the SetFullScreen() function does the job.

WARNING

Not all video cards support window mode; use the `SupportsWindowMode()` function if you need to know whether or not window mode is available.

BDirectWindow lets you access all the BWindow functions; you can literally treat your BDirectWindow just like another BWindow object. However, there are two important caveats:

- Don't draw into the direct window from its own thread; you should spawn another thread for drawing into the window, and use the `DirectConnected()` function to synchronize the interaction between BDirectWindow and your drawing thread.

- If you choose to use BWindow or BView API inside a BDirectWindow, be sure you don't block the `DirectConnected()` function.

Getting Connected (and Staying That Way)

The key to the BDirectWindow class is the `DirectConnected()` function, which your code must implement. This function is called whenever a change that your drawing code may need to be aware of occurs.

When your `DirectConnected()` function is called, it's passed a pointer to a `direct_buffer_info` structure, as follows:

```
typedef struct {
    direct_buffer_state    buffer_state;
    direct_driver_state    driver_state;
    void                   *bits;
    void                   *pci_bits;
    int32                  bytes_per_row;
    uint32                 bits_per_pixel;
    color_space            pixel_format;
    buffer_layout          layout;
    buffer_orientation     orientation;
    uint32                 _reserved[9];
    uint32                 _dd_type_;
    uint32                 _dd_token_;
    uint32                 clip_list_count;
    clipping_rect          window_bounds;
    clipping_rect          clip_bounds;
    clipping_rect          clip_list[1];
} direct_buffer_info;
```

`buffer_state`, when masked by `B_DIRECT_MODE_MASK`, indicates what change is occurring in the direct buffer access privileges. The mask will reveal one of the following values:

Constant	Description
B_DIRECT_START	Your BDirectWindow has just received direct screen access to the part of the screen described by the `direct_buffer_info` structure.
B_DIRECT_STOP	Your direct screen access privileges have been suspended. None of the other fields in the `direct_buffer_info` structure are valid.
B_DIRECT_MODIFY	A change has occurred to the direct screen access buffer; your drawing code needs to take whatever action is necessary to adjust to the new state.

You will always receive a `B_DIRECT_START` notification when your BDirectWindow is first connected to the screen, followed by any number of `B_DIRECT_MODIFY` notifications (it's possible you won't receive any at all). After handling `B_DIRECT_START` or `B_DIRECT_MODIFY`, your application must abide by the frame buffer configuration specified by the `direct_buffer_info` structure until another `B_DIRECT_MODIFY` notification is received (or `B_DIRECT_STOP` occurs).

You'll receive a `B_DIRECT_STOP` notification when the window is closed, hidden, moved, or if a screen resolution or color depth change occurs. Once your `DirectConnected()` function returns from handling this notification, you mustn't touch the frame buffer (until you receive another `B_DIRECT_START`).

In a `B_DIRECT_START` or `B_DIRECT_MODIFY` notification, the `buffer_state` field will contain other flags that tell you what has changed since the last notification:

Constant	Description
B_BUFFER_MOVED	The content of your window has been moved, either by a call to `MoveTo()` or `MoveBy()` or by the user manually dragging the window. The contents of the window are always moved relative to the top-left corner of the window.
B_BUFFER_RESET	The entire direct access buffer has been reset. This can happen if the user changes the depth or resolution of the screen, or if the window had previously been hidden and has been made visible again.
B_BUFFER_RESIZED	The content area of your window has been resized.
B_CLIPPING_MODIFIED	The visible region of the content area of your window changed. This doesn't imply anything about the position of the window or the size of the content area of the window—it simply means that the part of the window that's visible has changed shape.

The **driver_state** field indicates changes in the state of the graphics card on which your direct window is displayed. There are two possible values:

Constant	Description
B_MODE_CHANGED	The resolution or depth of the graphics card has changed.
B_DRIVER_CHANGED	The window was moved onto another monitor.

The **bits** field is a pointer to the frame buffer in your own team's memory space.

The **pci_bits** field is a pointer to the frame buffer in the PCI memory space; this value is typically needed to control DMA.

bytes_per_row is the number of bytes used to represent a single row of pixels in the frame buffer.

bits_per_pixel is the number of bits actually used to store a single pixel, including reserved, unused, or alpha channel bits. This value is usually a multiple of eight.

pixel_format is the format used to encode a pixel, as defined in the `color_space` type in *be/interface/GraphicsDefs.h*.

The **layout**, **orientation**, **_reserved**, **_dd_type_**, and **_dd_token_** fields are all reserved for future use and must not be used.

window_bounds is a rectangle that defines the full content area of the window, in screen coordinates. You can convert these coordinates into frame buffer addresses using the values in the **bits**, **bytes_per_row**, and **bits_per_pixel** fields. The `clipping_rect` structure is:

```
typedef struct {
    int32   left;
    int32   top;
    int32   right;
    int32   bottom;
} clipping_rect;
```

Note that, as always, these edges are inclusive; for example, if left is 5 and top is 3, the pixel at (5,3) is included in the rectangle's contents.

clip_bounds is the bounding rectangle of the visible part of the content area of the window, in screen coordinates. This rectangle is the smallest rectangle that contains all the rectangles in the **clip_list**, described below.

clip_list_count is the number of rectangles in the **clip_list**. The **clip_list** is a list of rectangles that together define the visible region of the content area of the window, in screen coordinates.

The data in the `direct_buffer_info` structure is only valid until `DirectConnected()` returns, so if you need to reference any of the information later, you should make a copy of the fields you need.

Window Mode vs. Full Screen Mode

There are some differences in how BDirectWindow behaves depending on whether it's in window mode or full-screen exclusive mode.

In window mode, the BDirectWindow behaves almost exactly like a BWindow—so much so that you can use a BDirectWindow in any situation you'd normally use a BWindow. The `window_bounds` rectangle is the same size and shape as the window itself, as you'd expect. If window mode is available (`SupportsWindowMode()` returns true), `DirectConnected()` will be called as described above, thereby providing the means to directly access the frame buffer. If the graphics card doesn't support access to the frame buffer while in window mode, `DirectConnected()` will never be called, and you can only use BWindow and BView functions as you work in the window.

In full-screen exclusive mode, the `window_bounds` is actually the size and shape of the entire screen, even if the screen isn't the same size as the direct window you created. You have to handle the difference yourself.

Full-screen exclusive mode also guarantees that your window will always be the focus, always be in front, and will always stay full-screen (the Application Server will resize the window for you if the screen resolution changes). Since no other windows can come in front of a full-screen exclusive direct window, any Interface Kit objects that use a window to display their contents won't work; this includes any type of menu.

If you want your BDirectWindow to be full-screen, but still compatible with menus or other windows, create it as a non-exclusive window, then use the following code:

```
BScreen screen(this);
MoveTo(0,0);
ResizeTo(screen.width, screen.height);
```

This will make the non-exclusive direct window fill the entire screen. Keep in mind that in this case, other windows may appear in front of yours, and if the screen resolution changes, you will have to resize the window yourself if you want to continue to fill the entire screen.

Using a Direct Window

Let's put together a simple class, derived from BDirectWindow, that demonstrates the basics of drawing into a direct window.

```
class DirectSample : public BDirectWindow {
  public:
                    DirectSample(BRect frame);
                    ~DirectSample();
    virtual bool  QuitRequested();
    virtual void  DirectConnected(direct_buffer_info *info);

    uint8       *fBits;
    int32        fRowBytes;
    color_space  fFormat;
    clipping_rect fBounds;

    uint32       fNumClipRects;
    clipping_rect *fClipList;

    bool    fDirty;// needs refresh?
    bool    fConnected;
    bool    fConnectionDisabled;
    BLocker  *locker;
    thread_id    fDrawThreadID;
};
```

The DirectSample class implements a constructor as well as the `QuitRequested()` and `DirectConnected()` functions.

Some variables are added to the class for caching information about the frame buffer.

- **fBits** will contain a pointer to the frame buffer's bitmap.

- **fRowBytes** will contain the number of bytes per row of screen data.

- **fFormat** will contain the pixel format (such as **B_CMAP8** for 8-bit indexed color graphics mode). Our sample program will only work in this mode.

- **fBounds** will contain the bounds rectangle for the window.

- **fNumClipRects** will contain the number of rectangles in the clip rectangle list.

- **fClipList** is the actual list of clip rectangles, and will be allocated on-the-fly as needed.

- **fDirty** will be `true` if the window needs to be redrawn.

- **fConnected** is `true` if the window is connected to the frame buffer.

- **fConnectionDisabled** is `true` if the window is in the process of being closed.

- **locker** is a BLocker that will be used to ensure mutual exclusion when the frame buffer or buffer information data we've cached is being manipulated.

- **fDrawThreadID** contains the `thread_id` of the drawing thread, which is responsible for drawing the contents of the window.

The specifics of what these variables are and why the information contained in them is maintained will be discussed when we get to the `DirectConnected()` and `DrawingThread()` functions.

The constructor for the DirectSample class looks like this:

```
DirectSample::DirectSample(BRect frame)
        : BDirectWindow(frame, "DirectWindow Sample",
              B_TITLED_WINDOW,
              B_NOT_RESIZABLE|B_NOT_ZOOMABLE) {

    fConnected = false;
    fConnectionDisabled = false;
    locker = new BLocker();
    fClipList = NULL;
    fNumClipRects = 0;

    AddChild(new SampleView(Bounds()));

    if (!SupportsWindowMode()) {
        SetFullScreen(true);
    }

    fDirty = true;
    fDrawThreadID = spawn_thread(DrawingThread, "drawing_thread",
                B_NORMAL_PRIORITY, (void *) this);
    resume_thread(fDrawThreadID);
    Show();
}
```

This code establishes the direct window by deferring to BDirectWindow. Then the `fConnected` and `fConnectionDisabled` flags are initialized to indicate that the window isn't connected yet, and the connection isn't in the process of being torn down by the DirectSample destructor. The `locker` is created, and the clip rectangle list is initialized to a `NULL` pointer, with a count of 0.

Then it adds a child view that occupies the entire window. The primary purpose of this view in this sample is to set the view color to `B_TRANSPARENT_32_BIT`, to prevent the Application Server from erasing the window with a default color.

If the video card doesn't support window mode, we call `SetFullScreen()` to switch the direct window into full-screen exclusive mode. This guarantees that you'll get connected with direct screen access (in a window if possible, otherwise in full-screen exclusive mode). If you don't use `SetFullScreen()`, and window mode isn't supported, `DirectConnected()` will never be called, and you won't have direct screen access.

Then the `fDirty` flag is set to true, which indicates that the window needs to be updated, and the drawing thread is started; the drawing thread will handle all actual drawing into the window. The argument passed to the drawing thread is a pointer to the DirectSample window itself. You should always use a separate thread for drawing into a BDirectWindow.

Finally, `Show()` is called to make the direct window visible.

The destructor needs to make sure there's no chance someone will try to draw while the window is being destructed:

```
DirectSample::~DirectSample() {
   int32 result;

   fConnectionDisabled = true;// Connection is dying
   Hide();
   Sync();
   wait_for_thread(fDrawThreadID, &result);
   free(fClipList);
   delete locker;
}
```

The first thing the destructor does is set the **fConnectionDisabled** flag to `true`, which indicates that the window is in the process of being destroyed, and that future calls to `DirectConnected()` or the drawing thread should be ignored. The window is then hidden by calling `Hide()`. Finally, `Sync()` is called to block until the window is actually hidden.

`wait_for_thread()` waits until the drawing thread terminates. The drawing thread (as we'll see shortly) is designed to terminate when the `fConnectionDisabled` flag is `true`.

Then the clip rectangle list is freed and the locker deleted.

The `QuitRequested()` function is implemented as usual.

The `DirectConnected()` function is called whenever a change occurs that affects how your code should access the frame buffer:

```
void DirectSample::DirectConnected(direct_buffer_info *info) {
   if (!fConnected && fConnectionDisabled) {
      return;
   }
   locker->Lock();

   switch(info->buffer_state & B_DIRECT_MODE_MASK) {
      case B_DIRECT_START:
         fConnected = true;
      case B_DIRECT_MODIFY:
         fBits = (uint8 *) info->bits;
         fRowBytes = info->bytes_per_row;
         fFormat = info->pixel_format;
         fBounds = info->window_bounds;
         fDirty = true;
```

```
               // Get clipping information

               if (fClipList) {
                   free(fClipList);
                   fClipList = NULL;
               }
               fNumClipRects = info->clip_list_count;
               fClipList = (clipping_rect *)
                       malloc(fNumClipRects*sizeof(clipping_rect));
               memcpy(fClipList, info->clip_list,
                       fNumClipRects*sizeof(clipping_rect));
               break;
           case B_DIRECT_STOP:
               fConnected = false;
               break;
       }
       locker->Unlock();
   }
```

DirectConnected() begins by checking the fConnected and fConnectionDisabled flags; the code in DirectConnected() is only run if the connection is opened (fConnected is true) or if we want to start it again (fConnectionDisabled is false). This arrangement prevents the DirectConnected() function from trying to reconnect if the destructor has started running. Otherwise, the locker is locked, to prevent DirectConnected() and the drawing thread from colliding.

If the buffer state is B_DIRECT_START, the fConnected flag is set to true. This keeps track of the fact that the Application Server has given permission to draw directly into the region of the frame buffer controlled by the direct window.

If the buffer state is B_DIRECT_START or B_DIRECT_MODIFY (in which case the direct_buffer_info structure describes changes to the frame buffer), any previously-existing clip rectangle list is deleted, then we cache the information that interests us and set the fDirty flag to true (to indicate that the display needs to be redrawn to reflect the changed graphics settings).

The clip list is also cached by saving the number of rectangles in the list in the fNumClipRects field and by making a copy of the clip list into a newly malloc()d block of memory.

If the state is B_DIRECT_STOP, the fConnected flag is set to false, to indicate that we shouldn't draw into the frame buffer anymore.

Finally, the locker is unlocked, which lets the drawing thread start running again.

Now let's have a look at DrawingThread(); this function serves as the drawing thread, and is a global function:

```
int32 DrawingThread(void *data) {
   DirectSample *w;
```

```
    w = (DirectSample *) data;
    while (!w->fConnectionDisabled) {
        w->locker->Lock();
        if (w->fConnected) {
            if (w->fFormat == B_CMAP8 && w->fDirty) {
                int32 y;
                int32 width;
                int32 height;
                int32 adder;
                uint8 *p;
                clipping_rect *clip;
                int32 i;

                adder = w->fRowBytes;// Stash locally for this pass
                for (i=0; i<w->fNumClipRects; i++) {
                    clip = &(w->fClipList[i]);
                    width = (clip->right - clip->left)+1;
                    height = (clip->bottom - clip->top)+1;
                    p = w->fBits+(clip->top*w->fRowBytes)+clip->left;
                    y = 0;
                    while (y < height) {
                    memset(p, 0x00, width);
                    y++;
                    p+=adder;
                    }
                }
            }
            w->fDirty = false;
        }
        w->locker->Unlock();
        // Use BWindow or BView APIs here if you want
        snooze(16000);
    }
    return B_OK;
}
```

DrawingThread() starts by casting the argument, *data*, into a pointer to the DirectSample window into which it will be drawing.

The while loop that follows will continue to run as long as the fConnectionDisabled flag is false—in other words, it will keep looping as long as the connection is enabled.

The drawing loop itself begins by locking the locker to ensure that DirectConnected() doesn't change anything while we're working, then checking to be sure the connection is opened (fConnected is true). If the connection is open, we verify that format of the window is still 8-bit color and that the display needs to be updated. If the display needs updating and the pixel format is still B_CMAP8, the drawing code begins.

The fRowBytes field of the DirectSample window is cached in a local variable called adder. Then each rectangle in the clip list is drawn, one at a time, using a for loop.

A pointer to the clip rectangle to be drawn is stored in `clip`, and the `width` and `height` of the rectangle are computed. Then `p` is set to be a pointer to the first pixel in the frame buffer that's contained by the clip rectangle. Since 8-bit color pixels each occupy exactly one byte of video memory, this pixel's address can be computed by taking the base `fBits` pointer, adding the number of bytes per row times the number of rows between the top of the screen and the first row in the clip rectangle, then adding the number of bytes between the left edge of the screen and the left edge of the clip rectangle, as seen in the line:

```
p = w->fBits+(clip->top*w->fRowBytes)+clip->left;
```

Then a while loop is used to iterate over each line in the clip rectangle, by ranging the variable `y` from 0 to the `height` of the clip rectangle. `memset()` is used to clear the row to black, which is represented by the byte value 0x00. `y` is incremented by one for each pass through the loop, to count the rows being drawn for each iteration, and the pointer `p` is incremented by `adder` to move down to the beginning of the next row in the clip rectangle.

Once each clip rectangle has been drawn, the for loop exits, and the `fDirty` flag is set to false to indicate that the screen is up-to-date. Once that's done, the locker is unlocked, which lets `DirectConnected()` do its thing if it's called. To avoid using an unreasonable amount of processing time, `snooze()` is called to give up CPU time to other threads.

If you want to use calls to BWindow or BView API in your drawing thread, you should do so just after unlocking the window.

When the thread terminates (which will only happen when the connection is disabled), the drawing thread returns `B_OK`.

This drawing function is designed to draw nothing unless it's necessary; `DirectConnected()` will set the `fDirty` flag when something happens to cause the screen to need a refresh, and other code elsewhere in the application could also set the `fDirty` flag to indicate that the screen should be redrawn.

Since we're taking over drawing the contents of the window, we need to tell the Application Server not to draw anything. This is done by adding the following line to the constructor for the SampleView:

```
SetViewColor(B_TRANSPARENT_32_BIT);
```

This is very important: if you don't remember to do this, you'll have all kinds of synchronization problems when the Application Server and your drawing code try to draw into the window at the same time.

Note that this sample code doesn't really do anything useful (if all you want to do is have a black window moving around, don't use BDirectWindow—use a regular

BWindow, throw a BView into it, and use `SetViewColor()` to make the view black; it'll be faster and more efficient because it will use hardware graphics acceleration if it's available). However, it serves as a simple example of how to establish a connection to let your own drawing code directly access the screen. Just replace the code inside the drawing loop with something more useful (like a nifty real-time animation).

Hook Functions

`DirectConnected()`

   The `DirectConnected()` hook function is called when the connection to the screen has been made, a change has occurred to the size or format of the frame buffer, a change has occurred to the position, size, or shape of the visible part of the content area of the window, or the connection to the screen is terminated.

Constructor and Destructor

BDirectWindow()

   BDirectWindow(BRect *frame*, const char **title*, window_type *type*, uint32 *flags*,
          uint32 *workspace* = B_CURRENT_WORKSPACE)
   BDirectWindow(BRect *frame*, const char **title*, window_look *look*,
          window_feel *feel*, uint32 *flags*,
          uint32 *workspace* = B_CURRENT_WORKSPACE)

Creates and returns a new BDirectWindow object. This is functionally equivalent to the BWindow constructor, except the resulting BDirectWindow supports direct window operations.

You will probably want to set up a flag to keep track of whether or not the direct window's connection to the screen is viable. In the constructor, you should set this flag (let's call it **fConnectionDisabled**) to `false`, which indicates to both `DirectConnected()` and your drawing thread that the window is not in the process of being deconstructed. The destructor would then set this flag to `true` before terminating the connection to avoid the unlikely possibility of the connection trying to restart while the BDirectWindow is being dismantled.

You'll also need other flags or semaphores (or benaphores) to manage the interaction between the BDirectWindow and your drawing thread.

See the sample code in "Using a Direct Window" for an example.

~BDirectWindow()

   ~BDirectWindow()

Frees all memory the BDirectWindow object allocated for itself. You should never delete a BDirectWindow object; call its `Quit()` or `Close()` function instead.

Your BDirectWindow destructor should begin by setting the **fConnectionDisabled** flag to `true`, to prevent `DirectConnected()` from attempting to reconnect to the direct window while it's being deconstructed.

Then you should call `Hide()` and `Sync()` to force the direct window to disconnect direct access:

```
MyDirectWindow::~BDirectWindow {
    fConnectionDisabled = true;
    Hide();
    Sync();
    /* complete usual destruction here */
}
```

Member Functions

DirectConnected()

> virtual void **DirectConnected** (direct_buffer_info *info*)

This hook function is the core of BDirectWindow. Your application should override this function to learn about the state of the graphics display onto which you're drawing, as well as to be informed of any changes that occur.

This function is also called to suspend and resume your direct access privileges.

Your code in this function should be as short as possible, because what your `DirectConnected()` function does can affect the performance of the entire system. `DirectConnected()` should only handle the immediate task of dealing with changes in the direct drawing context, and shouldn't normally do any actual drawing—that's what your drawing thread is for.

If you have drawing that absolutely has to be done before you can safely return control to the Application Server (see the note below), you may do so, but your code should do the absolute minimum drawing necessary and leave everything else to the drawing thread.

NOTE

> `DirectConnected()` should only return when it can guarantee that the request specified by *info* will be strictly obeyed.

The structure pointed to by *info* goes away after `DirectConnected()` returns, so you should cache the information that interests you.

See "Getting Connected (and Staying That Way)" for more information about the `direct_buffer_info` structure.

GetClippingRegion()

status_t **GetClippingRegion**(BRegion *region*, BPoint *origin* = NULL) const

Sets the specified *region* to match the current clipping region of the direct window. If *origin* is specified, each point in the region is offset by the *origin*, resulting in a BRegion that's localized to your application's vision of where in space the origin is (relative to the origin of the screen's frame buffer).

Although the `direct_buffer_info` structure contains the clipping region of a direct window, it's not in standard BRegion form. This function is provided so you can obtain a standard BRegion if you need one.

WARNING

The `GetClippingRegion()` function can only be called from the `Direct-Connected()` function; calling it from outside `DirectConnected()` will return invalid results.

If you need to cache the clipping region of your window and need a BRegion for clipping purposes, you could use the following code inside your `DirectConnected()` function:

```
BRegion rgn;
GetClippingRegion(&rgn);
```

This serves a double purpose: it obtains the clipping region in BRegion form, and it returns a copy of the region that you can maintain locally. However, it may be more efficient to copy the clipping region by hand, since the clipping rectangle list used by BDirectWindow uses integer numbers, while BRegion uses floating-point.

Return values:
    B_OK. The clipping region was successfully returned.
    B_ERROR. An error occurred while trying to obtain the clipping region.

IsFullScreen(), SetFullScreen()

bool **IsFullScreen**(void) const
status_t **SetFullScreen**(bool *enable*)

`IsFullScreen()` returns `true` if the direct window is in full-screen exclusive mode, or `false` if it's in window mode.

The value returned by `IsFullScreen()` is indeterminate if a call to `SetFullScreen()` is in progress—if this is the case, you shouldn't rely on the resulting value. Instead, it would be safer to maintain a state setting of your own and use that value.

`SetFullScreen()` enables full-screen exclusive mode if the *enable* flag is `true`. To switch to window mode, pass `false`. The `SupportsWindowMode()` function can be used to determine whether or not the video card is capable of supporting window mode. See "Window Mode vs. Full Screen Mode" for a detailed explanation of the differences between these modes.

When your window is in full screen mode, it will always have the focus, and no other window can come in front of it.

`SetFullScreen()` can return any of the following result codes.

Return values:
   B_OK. The mode was successfully changed.
   B_ERROR. An error occurred while trying to switch between full screen and window modes (for example, another window may already be in full-screen exclusive mode in the same workspace).

SetFullScreen() *see* IsFullScreen()

SupportsWindowMode()

   static bool **SupportsWindowMode** (screen_id *id* = B_MAIN_SCREEN_ID)

Returns `true` if the specified screen supports window mode; if you require the ability to directly access the frame buffer of a window (rather than occupying the whole screen), you should call this function to be sure that the graphics hardware in the computer running your application supports it. Because this is a static function, you don't have to construct a BDirectWindow object to call it:

```
if (BDirectWindow::SupportsWindowMode()) {
   /* do stuff here */
}
```

In particular, window mode requires a graphics card with DMA support and a hardware cursor; older video cards may not be capable of supporting window mode.

If window mode isn't supported, but you still select window mode, `DirectConnected()` will never be called (so you'll never be authorized for direct frame buffer access).

Even if window mode isn't supported, you can still use BDirectWindow objects for full-screen direct access to the frame buffer, but it's recommended that you avoid direct video DMA or the use of parallel drawing threads that use both direct frame buffer access and BView calls (because it's likely that such a graphics card won't handle the parallel access and freeze the PCI bus—and that would be bad).

BWindowScreen

Derived from: public BWindow

Declared in: be/game/WindowScreen.h

Library: libgame.so

A BWindowScreen object provides exclusive access to the entire screen, bypassing the Application Server's window system. The object has direct access to the graphics card driver: It can set up the graphics environment on the graphics card, call driver-implemented drawing functions, and directly manipulate the frame buffer.

Screen Access

Like all windows, a BWindowScreen is hidden (off-screen) when it's constructed. By calling Show() to put it on-screen and make it the active window, an application takes over the whole screen. While the BWindowScreen is active, the Application Server's graphics operations are suspended. Nothing except what the application draws will be visible to the user—no other windows and no desktop. When the BWindowScreen gives up active status, the Application Server automatically refreshes the screen with its old contents.

Although the BWindowScreen object provides a connection to the screen, you shouldn't draw from the BWindowScreen's thread. Use the thread only to regulate the access of other threads to the frame buffer.

Keyboard and Mouse

A BWindowScreen object remains a window while it has control of the screen; it stays attached to the Application Server and its message loop continues to function. It gets messages reporting the user's actions on the keyboard and mouse, just like any other active window. Because it covers the whole screen, it's notified of all mouse and keyboard events. You can attach filters to the window to get the messages as they arrive. Or you can call the Interface Kit's get_key_info() function to poll the state of the keyboard and construct a nominal BView so that you can call GetMouse() to poll the mouse.

Workspaces

This class respects workspaces. A BWindowScreen object releases its grip on the screen when the user turns to another workspace and reestablishes its control when the user returns to the workspace in which it's the active window.

Debugging

A BWindowScreen object can be constructed in a debugging mode that lets you switch back and forth between the workspace in which the app is running and a workspace where error messages are printed. See the constructor and the `RegisterThread()` function for details.

Hook Functions

`ScreenConnected()`

Can be implemented to do whatever is necessary when the BWindowScreen object obtains direct access to the frame buffer for the screen, and when it loses that access.

Constructor and Destructor

BWindowScreen()

BWindowScreen(const char *title, uint32 *space*, status_t *error,
            bool *debugging* = false)

Initializes the BWindowScreen object by assigning the window a *title* and specifying a *space* configuration for the screen. The window won't have a visible border or a tab in which to display the title to the user. However, others—such as the Workspaces application—can use the title to identify the window.

The window is constructed to fill the screen; its frame rectangle contains every screen pixel when the screen is configured according to the *space* argument. That argument describes the pixel dimensions and bits-per-pixel depth of the screen that the BWindowScreen object should establish when it obtains direct access to the frame buffer. It should be one of the following constants:

B_8_BIT_640x480	B_16_BIT_640x480	B_32_BIT_640x480
B_8_BIT_800x600	B_16_BIT_800x600	B_32_BIT_800x600
B_8_BIT_1024x768	B_16_BIT_1024x768	B_32_BIT_1024x768
B_8_BIT_1152x900	B_16_BIT_1152x900	B_32_BIT_1152x900
B_8_BIT_1280x1024	B_16_BIT_1280x1024	B_32_BIT_1280x1024
B_8_BIT_1600x1200	B_16_BIT_1600x1200	B_32_BIT_1600x1200

These are the same constants that can be passed to `set_screen_space()`, the Interface Kit function that preference applications call to configure the screen.

The space configuration applies only while the BWindowScreen object is in control of the screen. When it gives up control, the previous configuration is restored.

The constructor assigns the window to the active workspace (B_CURRENT_WORKSPACE). It fails if another BWindowScreen object in any application is already assigned to the same workspace.

To be sure there wasn't an error in constructing the object, check the *error* argument. If all goes well, the constructor sets the *error* variable to B_OK. If not, it sets it to B_ERROR. If there's an error, it's likely to occur in this constructor, not the inherited BWindow constructor. Since the underlying window will probably exist, you'll need to instruct it to quit. For example:

```
status_t error;
MyWindowScreen *screen =
            new MyWindowScreen("Glacier", B_8_BIT_1024x768, &error);
if ( error != B_OK )
    screen->PostMessage(B_QUIT_REQUESTED, screen);
```

If the *debugging* flag is true, the BWindowScreen is constructed in debugging mode. This modifies its behavior and enables three functions, RegisterThread(), Suspend(), and SuspensionHook(). The debugging regime is described under those functions.

See also: RegisterThread(), the BScreen class in the Interface Kit

~BWindowScreen()

virtual ~BWindowScreen()

Closes the clone of the graphics card driver (through which the BWindowScreen object established its connection to the screen), unloads it from the application, and cleans up after it.

Member Functions

CanControlFrameBuffer()

bool CanControlFrameBuffer(void)

Returns true if the graphics card driver permits applications to control the configuration of the frame buffer, and false if not. Control is exercised through these two functions:

```
SetFrameBuffer()
MoveDisplayArea()
```

A return of `true` means that these functions can communicate with the graphics card driver and at least the first will do something useful. A return of `false` means that neither of them will work.

See also: `SetFrameBuffer()`, `MoveDisplayArea()`

CardHookAt()

graphics_card_hook **CardHookAt**(int32 *index*)

Returns a pointer to the graphics card "hook" function that's located at *index* in its list of hook functions. The function returns `NULL` if the graphics card driver doesn't implement a function at that index or the index is out of range.

The hook functions provide accelerated drawing capabilities. The functions (and the `graphics_card_hook` pointer type) are documented under "Graphics Card Hook Functions" in Chapter 11. The first three hook functions (indices 0, 1, and 2) are not available through the Game Kit; if you pass an index of 0, 1, or 2 to `CardHookAt()`, it will return `NULL` even if the function is implemented.

An application can cache the pointers that `CardHookAt()` returns, but it should ask for a new set each time the depth or dimensions of the screen changes and each time the BWindowScreen object releases or regains control of the screen. You'd typically call `CardHookAt()` in your implementation of `ScreenConnection()`.

CardInfo()

graphics_card_info *****CardInfo**(void)

Returns a description of the current configuration of the graphics card, as kept by the driver for the card. The returned `graphics_card_info` structure is defined in *be/add-ons/graphics/GraphicsCard.h* and is documented in "The Entry Point and General Opcodes" in Chapter 11.

See also: `FrameBufferInfo()`

ColorList()   see **SetColorList()**

Disconnect()

void **Disconnect**(void)

Forces the BWindowScreen object to disconnect itself from the screen—to give up its authority over the graphics card driver, allowing the Application Server to reassert control. Normally, you'd disconnect the BWindowScreen only when hiding the app, reducing it to an ordinary window in the background, or quitting. The `Hide()` and `Quit()` functions automatically disconnect the BWindowScreen as part of the process of hiding and quitting. `Disconnect()` allows you to sever the connection before calling those functions.

Before breaking the screen connection, `Disconnect()` causes the BWindowScreen object to receive a `ScreenConnected()` notification with a flag of `false`. It doesn't return until `ScreenConnected()` returns and the connection is broken. `Hide()` and `Quit()` share this behavior.

See also: `Hide()`, `Quit()`

FrameBufferInfo()

frame_buffer_info **FrameBufferInfo**(void)

Returns a pointer to the `frame_buffer_info` structure that holds the driver's current conception of the frame buffer. The structure is defined in *be/add-ons/graphics/GraphicsCard.h* and is documented in "Frame Buffer Opcodes" in Chapter 11.

See also: `SetSpace()`, `SetFrameBuffer()`, `MoveDisplayArea()`, `CardInfo()`

Hide(), Show()

virtual void **Hide**(void)
virtual void **Show**(void)

These functions augment their BWindow counterparts to make sure that the BWindowScreen is disconnected from the screen before it's hidden and that it's ready to establish a connection when it becomes the active window.

`Hide()` calls `ScreenConnected()` (with an argument of `false`) and breaks the connection to the screen when `ScreenConnected()` returns. It then hides the window.

`Show()` shows the window on-screen and makes it the active window, which will cause it to establish a direct connection to the graphics card driver for the screen. Unlike `Hide()`, it may return before `ScreenConnected()` is called (with an argument of `true`).

See also: `BWindow::Hide()`

IOBase()

void **IOBase**(void)

Returns a pointer to the base address for the input/output registers on the graphics card. Registers are addressed by 16-bit offsets from this base address. (This function may not be supported in future releases.)

MoveDisplayArea()

status_t **MoveDisplayArea**(int32 *x*, int32 *y*)

Relocates the display area, the portion of the frame buffer that's mapped to the screen. This function moves the area's left-top corner to (*x, y*); by default, the corner lies at (0, 0). The display area must lie entirely within the frame buffer.

`MoveDisplayArea()` only works if the graphics card driver permits application control over the frame buffer. It must also permit a frame buffer with a total area larger than the display area. If successful in relocating the display area, this function returns B_OK; if not, it returns B_ERROR.

See also: `CanControlFrameBuffer()`

Quit()

virtual void **Quit**(void)

Augments the BWindow version of `Quit()` to force the BWindowScreen object to disconnect itself from the screen, so that it doesn't quit while in control of the frame buffer.

Although `Quit()` disconnects the object before quitting, this may not be soon enough for your application. For example, if you need to destroy some drawing threads before the BWindowScreen object is itself destroyed, you should get rid of them after the screen connection is severed. You can force the object to disconnect itself by calling `Disconnect()`. For example:

```
void MyWindowScreen::Quit()
{
    Disconnect();
    kill_thread(drawing_thread_a);
    kill_thread(drawing_thread_b);
    BWindowScreen::Quit();
}
```

If the screen connection is still in place when `Quit()` is called, it calls `ScreenConnected()` with a flag of `false`. It doesn't return until `ScreenConnected()` returns and the connection is broken.

See also: `ScreenConnected()`

RegisterThread(), Suspend(), SuspensionHook()

void **RegisterThread**(thread_id *thread*)
void **Suspend**(char **label*)
virtual void ****SuspensionHook**(bool *suspended*)

These three functions aid in debugging a Game Kit application. They have relevance only if the BWindowScreen is running in debugging mode. To set up the mode, you must:

- Construct the BWindowScreen with the *debugging* flag set to `true`. The flag is `false` by default.

- Register all drawing threads (all threads that can touch the frame buffer in any way) by passing the `thread_id` to `RegisterThread()` immediately after the thread is spawned—before `resume_thread()` is called to start the thread's execution. The window thread for the BWindowScreen object should not draw and should not be registered.

- Launch the application from the command line in a Terminal window. The window will collect debugging output from the application while the BWindowScreen runs in the "N-1" workspace—for example, if the Terminal is in the fifth workspace, the game will run in the fourth. However, if the Terminal is in the first workspace, the app runs in the second.

The Terminal window is the destination for all messages the app writes to the standard error stream or to the standard output—from `printf()`, for example. You can switch back and forth between the app and Terminal workspaces to check the messages and run your application. When you switch from the app workspace to the Terminal workspace, all registered threads are suspended and the graphics context is saved. When you switch back to the app, the graphics context is restored and the threads are resumed.

Calling `Suspend()` switches to the Terminal workspace programmatically, just as pressing the correct Command–function key combination would. Registered threads are suspended, the Terminal workspace is activated, and the *label* passed as an argument is displayed in a message in the Terminal window. You can resume the app by manually switching back to its workspace.

`SuspensionHook()` is called whenever the app is suspended or resumed—whether by the user switching workspaces or by `Suspend()`. It gives you an opportunity to save and restore any state that would otherwise be lost. `SuspensionHook()` is called with a *suspended* flag of `true` just after the application is suspended and with a flag of `false` just before it's about to be resumed.

`ScreenConnected()` is *not* called when you switch between the Terminal and app workspaces while in debugging mode. However, it is called for all normal app activities—when the BWindowScreen is first activated and when it hides or quits, for example.

Debugging mode can also preserve some information in case of a crash. Hold down all the left modifier keys (Shift, Control, Option, Command, Alt, or whatever the keys may happen to be on your keyboard), and press the F12 key. This restarts the screen with a 640 × 480 resolution and displays a debugger window. You should then be able to switch to the Terminal workspace to check the last set of messages before the crash, modify your code, and start again.

ScreenChanged()

> virtual void **ScreenChanged**(BRect *frame*, color_space *mode*)

Overrides the BWindow version of `ScreenChanged()` so that it does nothing. This function is called automatically when the screen configuration changes. It's not one that you should call in application code or reimplement.

See also: `BWindow::ScreenChanged()`

ScreenConnected()

> virtual void **ScreenConnected**(bool *connected*)

Implemented by derived classes to take action when the application gains direct access to the screen and when it's about to lose that access.

This function is called with the *connected* flag set to `true` immediately after the BWindowScreen object becomes the active window and establishes a direct connection to the graphics card driver for the screen. At that time, the Application Server's connection to the screen is suspended; drawing can only be accomplished through the screen access that the BWindowScreen object provides.

`ScreenConnected()` is called with a flag of `false` just before the BWindowScreen object is scheduled to lose its control over the screen and the Application Server's control is reasserted. The BWindowScreen's connection to the screen will not be broken until this function returns. It should delay returning until the application has finished all current drawing and no longer needs direct screen access.

Note that whenever `ScreenConnected()` is called, the BWindowScreen object is guaranteed to be connected to the screen; if *connected* is `true`, it just became connected, if *connected* is `false`, it's still connected but will be disconnected when the function returns.

Derived classes typically use this function to regulate access to the screen. For example, they may acquire a semaphore when the *connected* flag is `false`, so that application threads won't attempt direct drawing when the connection isn't in place, and release the semaphore for drawing threads to acquire when the flag is `true`. For example:

```
void MyWindowScreen::ScreenConnected(bool connected)
{
    if ( connected == false )
        acquire_sem(directDrawingSemaphore);
    else
        release_sem(directDrawingSemaphore);
}
```

See also: `Disconnect()`

SetColorList(), ColorList()

> void **SetColorList**(rgb_color *colors*, int32 *first* = 0, int32 *last* = 255)
> rgb_color *ColorList(void)

These functions set and return the list of 256 colors that can be displayed when the frame buffer has a depth of 8 bits per pixel (the `B_COLOR_8_BIT` color space). `SetColorList()` is passed an array of one or more *colors* to replace the colors currently in the list. The first color in the array replaces the color in the list at the specified *first* index; all colors up through the *last* specified index are modified. It fails if either index is out of range.

`SetColorList()` alters the list of colors kept on the graphics card. If the BWindowScreen isn't connected to the screen, the new list takes effect when it becomes connected.

`ColorList()` returns a pointer to the entire list of 256 colors. This is not the list kept by the graphics card driver, but a local copy. It belongs to the BWindowScreen object and should be altered only by calling `SetColorList()`.

See also: `BScreen::ColorMap()` in the Interface Kit

SetFrameBuffer()

> status_t **SetFrameBuffer**(int32 *width*, int32 *height*)

Configures the frame buffer on the graphics card so that it's *width* pixel columns wide and *height* pixel rows high. This function works only if the driver for the graphics card allows custom configurations (as reported by `CanControlFrameBuffer()`) and the BWindowScreen object is currently connected to the screen.

The new dimensions of the frame buffer must be large enough to hold all the pixels displayed on-screen—that is, they must be at least as large as the dimensions of the display area. If the driver can't accommodate the proposed *width* and *height*, SetFrameBuffer() returns B_ERROR. If the change is made, it returns B_OK.

This function doesn't alter the depth of the frame buffer or the size or location of the display area.

See also: MoveDisplayArea(), SetSpace()

SetSpace()

status_t **SetSpace**(uint32 *space*)

Configures the screen space to one of the standard combinations of width, height, and depth. The configuration is first set by the class constructor—permitted *space* constants are documented there—and it may be altered after construction only by this function.

Setting the screen space sets the dimensions of the frame buffer and display area. For example, if *space* is B_32_BIT_800x600, the frame buffer will be 32 bits deep and at least 800 pixel columns wide and 600 pixel rows high. The display area (the area of the frame buffer mapped to the screen) will also be 800 pixels × 600 pixels. After setting the screen space, you can enlarge the frame buffer by calling SetFrameBuffer() and relocate the display area in the larger buffer by calling MoveDisplayArea().

If the requested configuration is refused by the graphics card driver, SetSpace() returns B_ERROR. If all goes well, it returns B_OK.

See also: the BWindowScreen constructor, SetFrameBuffer(), MoveDisplayArea()

Suspend() see RegisterThread()

SuspensionHook() see RegisterThread()

WindowActivated()

virtual void **WindowActivated**(bool *active*)

Overrides the BWindow version of WindowActivated() to connect the BWindowScreen object to the screen (give it control over the graphics card driver) when the *active* flag is true.

This function doesn't disconnect the BWindowScreen when the flag is `false`, because there's no way for the window to cease being the active window without the connection already having been lost.

Don't reimplement this function in your application, even if you call the inherited version; rely instead on `ScreenConnected()` for accurate notifications of when the BWindowScreen gains and loses control of the screen.

See also: `BWindow::WindowActivated()`, `ScreenConnected()`

WorkspaceActivated()

virtual void **WorkspaceActivated**(int32 *workspace*, bool *active*)

Overrides the BWindow version of `WorkspaceActivated()` to connect the BWindowScreen object to the screen when the *active* flag is `true` and to disconnect it when the flag is `false`. User's typically activate the app by activating the workspace in which it's running, and deactivate it by moving to another workspace.

Don't override this function in your application; implement `ScreenConnected()` instead.

See also: `BWindow::WorkspaceActivated()`, `ScreenConnected()`

Global Functions

set_mouse_position()

Declared in: be/game/WindowScreen.h

void **set_mouse_position**(int32 *x*, int32 *y*)

Moves the cursor hot spot to (*x*, *y*) in the screen coordinate system, where *x* is a left-to-right index to a pixel column and *y* is a top-to-bottom index to a pixel row. The origin of the coordinate system is the left top pixel of the display area of the main screen.

This function should be called only while the application has a direct connection to the frame buffer through a BWindowScreen object.

CHAPTER EIGHT

The OpenGL Kit

The OpenGL Kit

The OpenGL Kit provides an interface between your BeOS application and the OpenGL graphics library, which is provided with BeOS. The two classes in the OpenGL Kit, BGLView and BGLScreen, let you display graphics rendered using OpenGL on a computer running the BeOS.

The OpenGL Kit Classes

The BGLView class is used to create a view within a window that contains OpenGL-rendered data. Derived from BView, it adds functions for locking and unlocking the OpenGL context associated with the view, as well as for copying pixel data into and out of the graphics buffer, and swapping the front and back buffers.

The BGLScreen class, derived from BWindowScreen, provides most of the same functionality provided by the BGLView class, but is used to take over the full screen instead of presenting OpenGL graphics in a window.

Note that if you want to use OpenGL graphics in a BDirectWindow, you would simply create your BDirectWindow and attach a BGLView to it.

OpenGL On BeOS

BeOS has included an OpenGL implementation since the first Preview Release for PowerPC processors. This implementation of OpenGL is complete, and GLU is supported as well. The optional AUX and GLUT libraries, however, aren't supported at this time.

Also, the current implementation of OpenGL on BeOS supports only 32-bit graphic buffers. Your BGLView or BGLScreen can be in any graphics mode you want, but the graphics buffer offscreen is always 32-bit.

A complete description of the features and use of OpenGL is beyond the scope of this book; however, you can get full documentation of OpenGL as well as sample code at the OpenGL Web site at *http://www.opengl.org*.

There are also some sample OpenGL programs that have already been ported to BeOS available for download on the Be Web site; visit *http://www.be.com/ developers/topics/opengl.html*.

BGLView

Derived from: public BView

Declared in: be/opengl/GLView.h

Library: libGL.so

The BGLView class provides a means for rendering graphics using OpenGL calls in a view.

The Graphics Buffers

A BGLView maintains either one or two BBitmap objects that serve as graphics buffers. If the OpenGL context is single-buffered, there is a single frontbuffer BBitmap. If the context is double-buffered, there's an additional backbuffer BBitmap.

NOTE

The BGLView class currently only supports double-buffered OpenGL contexts.

In a single-buffered context, drawing commands are performed in the frontbuffer. Since the view is attached to the frontbuffer's BBitmap, drawing performed in the frontbuffer appears immediately onscreen.

In double-buffered contexts, drawing is performed in the backbuffer and is not visible onscreen until the `SwapBuffers()` function is called to swap the two buffers and refresh the screen image.

You can get a pointer to a view that encompasses the drawing buffer using the `EmbeddedView()` function.

WARNING

The buffering mechanism is implementation-independent; hardware OpenGL support, when available, will not use BBitmaps, and will not keep the frame buffer in main system memory.

Using OpenGL

It's important to understand how OpenGL fits into the framework of a BeOS application. The example that follows draws a pattern of lines around a central point, as seen in the picture below.

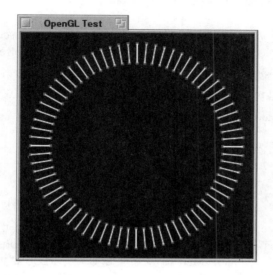

This code has been structured to make it relatively easy to port sample programs from the OpenGL Web site; however, most of those samples use GLUT features, which aren't available yet in the BeOS implementation of OpenGL. In particular, most of the samples on the OpenGL Web site use GLUT functions to handle user interface of some form. You'll have to add code for this yourself.

The first thing that's needed, as always, is an application object, which we establish as follows:

```
class SampleGLApp : public BApplication {
   public:
                SampleGLApp();
      private:
         SampleGLWindow theWindow;
};
```

The SampleGLApp class has a constructor and a private pointer to the application's window. The constructor looks like this:

```
SampleGLApp::SampleGLApp()
         : BApplication("application/x-vnd.Be-GLSample") {
   BRect windowRect;
   uint32 type;
```

```
        // Set type to the appropriate value for the
        // sample program you're working with.

        type = BGL_RGB|BGL_DOUBLE;

        windowRect.Set(50,50,350,350);
        theWindow = new SampleGLWindow(windowRect, type);
}
```

The first thing the constructor does is set the variable type to describe the context we need. In this example, we want an RGB context with double-buffering, so we specify BGL_RGB and BGL_DOUBLE.

The SampleGLWindow class is almost as simple:

```
class SampleGLWindow : public BWindow {
   public:
                    SampleGLWindow(BRect frame, uint32 type);
        virtual bool QuitRequested();

   private:
        SampleGLView *theView;
};
```

The constructor accepts a frame rectangle for the window and the OpenGL context type parameter that will be passed to SampleGLView's constructor. As usual, QuitRequested() is overridden to post a B_QUIT_REQUESTED message to the application and return true. A pointer to the SampleGLView object is maintained as well.

The constructor is fairly trivial:

```
SampleGLWindow::SampleGLWindow(BRect frame, uint32 type)
        : BWindow(frame, "OpenGL Test", B_TITLED_WINDOW, 0) {
   AddChild(theView=new SampleGLView(Bounds(), type));
   Show();
   theView->Render();
}
```

This code establishes the window, then creates the SampleGLView and adds it as a child of the window. Once that's done, the window is made visible by calling Show(). Finally, the SampleGLView's contents are drawn by calling the SampleGLView's Render() function.

The meat of this program is in the SampleGLView class, which follows:

```
class SampleGLView : public BGLView {
   public:
                    SampleGLView(BRect frame, uint32 type);
        virtual void AttachedToWindow(void);
        virtual void FrameResized(float newWidth, float newHeight);
        virtual void ErrorCallback(GLenum which);

        void      Render(void);
```

```
private:
    void       gInit(void);
    void       gDraw(void);
    void       gReshape(int width, int height);

    float      width;
    float      height;
};
```

The SampleGLView class implements the constructor and reimplements three of the functions of the BGLView class: `AttachedToWindow()`, `FrameResized()`, and `ErrorCallback()`. An additional public method, `Render()`, will contain the actual code for drawing the contents of the view.

In addition, there are three private methods that will contain the actual OpenGL calls for initializing, drawing, and resizing the BGLView's contents and a pair of values to represent the width and height of the BGLView.

The constructor is very simple:

```
SampleGLView::SampleGLView(BRect frame, uint32 type)
        : BGLView(frame, "SampleGLView", B_FOLLOW_ALL_SIDES, 0,
            type) {
    width = frame.right-frame.left;
    height = frame.bottom-frame.top;
}
```

For the most part, the constructor defers to the BGLView constructor, setting the resizing mode to **B_FOLLOW_ALL_SIDES** and the OpenGL context type to the value specified.

The only addition is that the width and height of the view are cached, based upon the frame rectangle specified. This is done because we'll need that information when the view is attached to the window, and the BGLView class doesn't include `Width()` and `Height()` functions.

The `AttachedToWindow()` function, which is called when the SampleGLView is attached to its parent window, looks like this:

```
void SampleGLView::AttachedToWindow(void) {
    LockGL();
    BGLView::AttachedToWindow();
    gInit();
    gReshape(width, height);
    UnlockGL();
}
```

This performs the initialization of the OpenGL context. First, `LockGL()` is called to lock the context and let the OpenGL Kit know which view should be targeted by future OpenGL calls. Then the inherited version of `AttachedToWindow()` is called to let BGLView set up the view normally.

Once that's done, the `gInit()` and `gReshape()` functions are called. `gInit()`, as we'll see shortly, is responsible for initializing the context. `gReshape()` is called to configure the OpenGL coordinate system for the BGLView given the current width and height of the view.

Finally, `UnlockGL()` is called to release the OpenGL context for the SampleGLView and to indicate that we're done using the context for the time being.

The `FrameResized()` function is called automatically whenever the SampleGLView is resized:

```
void SampleGLView::FrameResized(float newWidth, float newHeight) {
    LockGL();
    BGLView::FrameResized(width, height);
    width = newWidth;
    height = newHeight;

    gReshape(width,height);

    UnlockGL();
    Render();
}
```

As always, this function begins by locking the OpenGL context. It then calls the inherited version of `FrameResized()` to let BGLView perform whatever tasks it may need to do.

The new width and height of the view are saved in the `width` and `height` variables, then the `gReshape()` function is called to adjust the OpenGL context given the new size of the view.

Finally, the context is unlocked, and `Render()` is called to redraw the view's contents at the new size.

Although the default `ErrorCallback()` function provided by BGLView would be acceptable, we include one of our own anyway:

```
void SampleGLView::ErrorCallback(GLenum whichError) {
    fprintf(stderr, "Unexpected error occured (%d):\n", whichError);
    fprintf(stderr, "    %s\n", gluErrorString(whichError));
}
```

Note the use of the `gluErrorString()` OpenGL function to obtain an appropriate error message for the error code. You can use this function to avoid displaying error messages for errors that are acceptable or expected.

The `gInit()` function sets up the OpenGL context and initializes variables that will be used later:

```
void SampleGLView::gInit(void) {
    glClearColor(0.0, 0.0, 0.0, 0.0);
    glLineStipple(1, 0xF0E0);
```

```
      glBlendFunc(GL_SRC_ALPHA, GL_ONE);
      use_stipple_mode = GL_FALSE;
      use_smooth_mode = GL_TRUE;
      linesize = 2;
      pointsize = 4;
}
```

Briefly, this sets the clear color (the background color) of the view to black, configures the pattern for stippled lines and the blending function to be used when blending is enabled. It also selects not to use stippled lines (you can change this by setting use_stipple_mode to GL_TRUE) and to use anti-aliasing when drawing the lines (you can change this by setting use_smooth_mode to GL_FALSE). It also chooses to use 2 pixel wide lines, and 4 pixel wide points.

This function doesn't call LockGL() and UnlockGL(), so they must be called by the calling function (and if you look at the AttachedToWindow() code above, you'll see that this is the case).

There are some global variables used by this program (some of them accessed in the code above), so let's take a quick look at those:

```
GLenum use_stipple_mode;// GL_TRUE to use dashed lines
GLenum use_smooth_mode;// GL_TRUE to use anti-aliased lines
GLint linesize; // Line width
GLint pointsize;// Point diameter

float pntA[3] = {
    -160.0, 0.0, 0.0
};
float pntB[3] = {
    -130.0, 0.0, 0.0
};
```

The variables use_stipple_mode, use_smooth_mode, linesize, and pointsize are discussed in the gInit() function, above. The two float arrays define points in three-dimensional space. These points will be used as the endpoints of the lines drawn by the gDraw() function.

The gDraw() function does the actual drawing into the OpenGL context:

```
void SampleGLView::gDraw(void) {
    GLint i;

    glClear(GL_COLOR_BUFFER_BIT);
    glLineWidth(linesize);

    if (use_stipple_mode) {
      glEnable(GL_LINE_STIPPLE);
    } else {
      glDisable(GL_LINE_STIPPLE);
    }
```

```
  if (use_smooth_mode) {
    glEnable(GL_LINE_SMOOTH);
    glEnable(GL_BLEND);
  } else {
    glDisable(GL_LINE_SMOOTH);
    glDisable(GL_BLEND);
  }

  glPushMatrix();

  for (i = 0; i < 360; i += 5) {
    glRotatef(5.0, 0,0,1);// Rotate right 5 degrees
    glColor3f(1.0, 1.0, 0.0);// Set color for line
    glBegin(GL_LINE_STRIP);// And create the line
        glVertex3fv(pntA);
        glVertex3fv(pntB);
    glEnd();

    glPointSize(pointsize);// Set size for point
    glColor3f(0.0, 1.0, 0.0);// Set color for point
    glBegin(GL_POINTS);
        glVertex3fv(pntA);// Draw point at one end
        glVertex3fv(pntB);// Draw point at other end
    glEnd();
  }

  glPopMatrix();// Done with matrix
}
```

Without getting too deeply involved in OpenGL specifics, this code begins by clearing the context's buffer and setting the line width. It then enables the features selected by the **use_stipple_mode** and **use_line_mode** variables.

Once that's done, it establishes a matrix to be used for rotating the lines and draws the lines with points at each end, drawing one every five degrees in a 360-degree circle around the center of the window. After drawing all the lines, the matrix is destroyed and the function returns.

The **gReshape()** function handles adjusting the OpenGL context's coordinate system and viewport when the SampleGLView is first created, and whenever the view is resized:

```
void SampleGLView::gReshape(int width, int height) {
    glViewport(0, 0, width, height);
    glMatrixMode(GL_PROJECTION);
    glLoadIdentity();
    gluOrtho2D(-175, 175, -175, 175);
    glMatrixMode(GL_MODELVIEW);
}
```

This code simply sets the viewport's coordinate system to reflect the new width and height of the view, and establishes a projection matrix such that no matter what the size and shape of the window, the center of the window is considered to be (0,0) and the window is 300 units wide and 300 units tall. This lets the rendering code draw without having to worry about scaling; OpenGL handles it for us.

The details of how this works are, again, beyond the scope of this chapter.

Finally, the `Render()` function is the high-level function used to actually update the contents of the SampleGLView whenever we wish to redraw it:

```
void SampleGLView::Render(void) {
   LockGL();
   gDraw();
   SwapBuffers();
   UnlockGL();
}
```

`LockGL()` is called to lock the context before calling `gDraw()` to do the actual OpenGL calls to draw the view. Then the `SwapBuffers()` function is called to swap the backbuffer that was just drawn to the screen, and the context is unlocked.

Adapting OpenGL Sample Code

The program described above can easily be adapted to be used with other sample code from the OpenGL Web site. First, replace the code in the `gInit()`, `gDraw()`, and `gReshape()` functions with the code from the `Init()`, `Draw()`, and `Reshape()` functions in the sample code (some of the sample programs give these functions slightly different names).

Keep in mind that the current implementation of OpenGL under BeOS doesn't support single-buffered graphics, so you'll need to make whatever adjustments are necessary to use double-buffering.

Once these functions have been implemented, copy any global variables from the sample program into your project. Finally, in the SampleGLApp constructor, fix the OpenGL context type and window size information to match that used by the sample program.

Hook Functions

`ErrorCallback()`
   Can be implemented to handle OpenGL errors.

Constructor and Destructor

BGLView()

> BGLView(BRect *frame*, const char **name*,
>   int32 *resizingMode*,
>   int32 *flags*, int32 *type*)

Initializes the view, then creates a new OpenGL drawing context and attaches it to the view. The *type* argument specifies the OpenGL type specification for the view:

BGL_RGB (the default) *or* BGL_INDEX	Use RGB graphics or indexed color. Currently, indexed color (BGL_INDEX) isn't supported.
BGL_SINGLE (the default) *or* BGL_DOUBLE	Use single-buffering (direct rendering) or double-buffering. In the latter, all rendering is done to an offscreen buffer and only becomes visible when the SwapBuffers() function is called. Currently, direct rendering (BGL_SINGLE) isn't supported.
BGL_ACCUM	Requests that the view have an accumulation buffer.
BGL_ALPHA	Requests that the view's color buffer include an alpha component.
BGL_DEPTH	Requests that the view have a depth buffer.
BGL_STENCIL	Requests that the view have a stencil buffer.

~BGLView()

> virtual ~BGLView()

Disposes of the OpenGL context for the view.

Member Functions

AttachedToWindow()

> virtual void AttachedToWindow(void)

Calls the inherited version of AttachedToWindow() and sets the view color to B_TRANSPARENT_32_BIT (this improves performance by preventing the Application Server from erasing the view, since OpenGL takes over responsibility for drawing into the view).

CopyPixelsIn(), CopyPixelsOut()

> status_t CopyPixelsIn(BBitmap **source*, BPoint *dest*)
> status_t CopyPixelsOut(BPoint *source*, BBitmap **dest*)

These functions copy pixel data into and out of the OpenGL draw buffer for the context.

`CopyPixelsIn()` copies the entire contents of the *source* BBitmap into the OpenGL context, offset such that the top-left corner of the BBitmap is drawn at the point *dest* in the OpenGL buffer.

`CopyPixelsOut()` copies from the OpenGL draw buffer into the specified BBitmap. The area copied is the size of the *dest* bitmap and contains all data from the specified *source* point to the bottom-right corner of the buffer.

If the source is larger than the destination, it's clipped at the bottom and right edges to fit; no scaling is performed Also, the OpenGL context and the BBitmap must be in the same color space.

Return values:
B_OK. The data was copied without error.
B_BAD_VALUE. The current draw buffer is not valid, or the destination buffer's width or height is less than or equal to zero.
B_BAD_TYPE. The source and destination are in different color spaces.

CopyPixelsOut() *see* CopyPixelsIn()

Draw()

virtual void **Draw**(BRect *updateRect*)

Refreshes the contents of the BGLView by copying the frontbuffer to the screen.

If the view's color space is eight bits deep and the `GL_DITHER` OpenGL option is enabled, the display is dithered.

EmbeddedView()

BView ****EmbeddedView**(void)

Returns a pointer to an embedded view that encompasses the current OpenGL drawing buffer, as defined by OpenGL, for the BGLView. If the view is single-buffered, this will be the frontbuffer, and if the view is double-buffered, the embedded view will encompass the backbuffer.

NOTE

`EmbeddedView()` returns `NULL` if, for any reason, BView functions can't be used in the GL buffer.

ErrorCallback()

> virtual void **ErrorCallback**(GLenum *errorCode*)

Called when an OpenGL error occurs. By default, this function invokes the debugger with an error message reading "GL: Error code $xxxx." You can (and probably should) reimplement this function to cope with errors more gracefully.

FrameResized()

> virtual void **FrameResized**(float *width*, float *height*)

Calls the inherited version of `FrameResized()`, releases tables that need to be recalculated, and resizes the OpenGL buffers.

You can augment this function to perform other necessary tasks, such as adjusting your BGLView's coordinate system.

LockGL(), UnlockGL()

> void **LockGL**(void)
> void **UnlockGL**(void)

These functions lock and unlock the OpenGL context. You must lock the context before issuing any OpenGL commands, and unlock it when you're done—this is how OpenGL knows which context the drawing commands are intended for, since OpenGL itself isn't encapsulated within the BGLView class. For example:

```
LockGL();     /* lock the OpenGL context */
glEnable(GL_DITHER);/* turn on dithering support */
UnlockGL();
```

Failing to lock and unlock the context appropriately will result in unpredictable behavior and may cause your application to crash.

SwapBuffers()

> void **SwapBuffers**(void)

Swaps the front buffer and back buffer, then redraws the contents of the BGLView.

This function has no effect if the view is single-buffered.

UnlockGL() see LockGL()

BGLScreen

Derived from:	public BWindowScreen
Declared in:	be/opengl/GLView.h
Library:	libGL.so

The BGLScreen class provides an interface to the OpenGL graphics system just like the BGLView class. The only difference is that BGLScreen displays its images in a BWindowScreen for full-screen graphics, while BGLView displays in a view.

Hook Functions

ErrorCallback()
   Can be implemented to handle OpenGL errors.

Constructor and Destructor

BGLScreen()

   BGLScreen(char *name, int32 screenMode, int32 type,
                   status_t *error, bool debug = **false**)

Initializes the object's BWindowScreen and creates the OpenGL drawing context for it.

The *name*, *screenMode*, *error*, and *debug* parameters are the same as those for the BWindowScreen class.

The *type* parameter is a set of flags that specifies the desired OpenGL options for the new context:

BGL_RGB (the default) *or* **BGL_INDEX**	Use RGB graphics or indexed color. Currently, indexed color (BGL_INDEX) isn't supported.
BGL_SINGLE (the default) *or* **BGL_DOUBLE**	Use single-buffering (direct rendering) or double-buffering. In the latter, all rendering is done to an offscreen buffer and only becomes visible when the **SwapBuffers**() function is called. Currently, direct rendering (BGL_SINGLE) isn't supported.
BGL_ACCUM	Requests an accumulation buffer.
BGL_ALPHA	Requests that the color buffer include an alpha component.
BGL_DEPTH	Requests a depth buffer.
BGL_STENCIL	Requests a stencil buffer.

~BGLScreen()

virtual ~BGLScreen()

Disposes of the OpenGL context that's attached to the BWindowScreen.

Member Functions

ErrorCallback()

virtual void **ErrorCallback**(GLenum *errorCode*)

Called when an OpenGL error occurs. By default, this function invokes the debugger with an error message reading "GL: Error code $xxxx." You can (and probably should) reimplement this function to cope with errors more gracefully.

FrameResized()

virtual void **FrameResized**(float *width*, float *height*)

Calls the inherited version of `FrameResized()` and resizes the OpenGL buffers.

LockGL(), UnlockGL()

void **LockGL**(void)
void **UnlockGL**(void)

These functions lock and unlock the OpenGL context. You must lock the context before issuing any OpenGL commands, and unlock it when you're done—this is how OpenGL knows which context the drawing commands are intended for, since OpenGL itself isn't encapsulated within the BGLScreen class. For example:

```
LockGL();      /* lock the OpenGL context
glEnable(GL_DITHER);/* turn on dithering support */
UnlockGL();
```

Failing to lock and unlock the context appropriately will result in unpredictable behavior and may cause your application to crash.

ScreenConnected()

void **ScreenConnected**(bool *connected*)

Calls the inherited version of `ScreenConnected()`, then, if the connection is being established (*connected* is `true`), sets the OpenGL buffers to be the correct size for the screen.

SwapBuffers()

void **SwapBuffers**(void)

Swaps the front buffer and back buffer, thereby making the back buffer visible.

This function has no effect if the display is single-buffered.

UnlockGL() see LockGL()

The Device Kit

The Device Kit

The Device Kit contains software for controlling hardware that's connected to the computer.

- A BSerialPort object represents a RS-232 serial port.

The other classes pertain to BeBox hardware only:

- A BJoystick object represents a joystick connection to the BeBox.
- The BA2D class is the programming interface to the GeekPort's analog-to-digital converter (ADC) and BD2A is the interface to its digital-to-analog converter (DAC).
- The BDigitalPort class provides access to the two digital ports that are part of the GeekPort.

If you're interested in the interface to a serial port or joystick, you can turn directly to the BSerialPort or BJoystick class. If you're interested in a GeekPort interface, there's a small section that introduces the port and its three classes; look at it before turning to the particular class that interests you.

The GeekPort and Its Classes

WARNING

This documentation applies to the BeBox hardware only.

The GeekPort is a piece of hardware on the back of the BeBox that communicates with external devices. Depending on how you use the GeekPort's ports, you can get up to 24 independent data paths:

- Four 12-bit analog input channels
- Four 8-bit analog output channels

- Two 8-bit wide digital ports (16 paths, total) that can act as inputs or outputs

To provide high-level access to these data paths, the Device Kit defines three classes:

- The BA2D class ("analog to digital") lets you get at the analog input channels.
- The BD2A class ("digital to analog") does the same for the analog output channels.
- The BDigitalPort class lets you configure, read, and write the digital ports.

The signals and data that these classes read and write appear at the GeekPort connector, a 37-pin female connector that you'll find at the back of every BeBox. In addition to the pins that correspond to the analog and data paths, the GeekPort provides power and ground pins. Everything you need to feed your external gizmo is right there.

The GeekPort connector's pins are assigned thus:

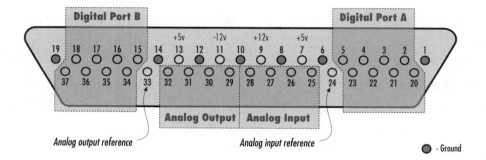

The ADC and DAC

The GeekPort provides four channels of simultaneous analog-to-digital (a/d) and four channels of simultaneous digital-to-analog (d/a) conversion. The signals that feed the ADC arrive on pins 25-28 of the GeekPort connector; the signals that are produced by the DAC depart through pins 29-32 (as depicted below). Pins 24 and 33 are DC reference levels (ground) for the a/d and d/a signals, respectively (*don't* use pins 24 or 33 as power grounds):

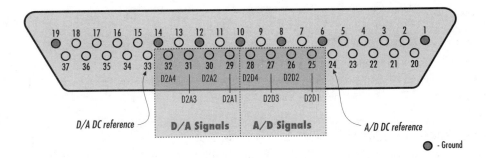

In the illustration, the a/d and d/a pins are labelled ("A2D1", "A2D2", etc.) as they are known to the BA2D and BD2A classes.

If you've read the GeekPort hardware specification, you'll have discovered that the ADC can be placed in a few different modes (the DAC is less flexible). The BA2D and BD2A classes (more accurately, the ADC and DAC drivers) refine the GeekPort specification, as described in the following sections.

NOTE

Keep in mind that the a/d and d/a converters that the GeekPort uses are *not* part of the Crystal codec that's used by the audio software (and brought into your application through the Media Kit). The two sets of converters are completely separate and can be used independently and simultaneously. If you're doing on-board high-fidelity sound processing (or generation) in real time, you should stick with the Crystal convertors.

The ADC

The ADC accepts signals in the range [0, +4.096] Volts, performs a linear conversion, and spits out unsigned 12-bit data. The 4.096V to 12-bit conversion produces a convenient one-digital-step per milliVolt of input.

A/d conversion is performed on-demand: When you read a value from the ADC, the voltage that lies on the specified pin is immediately sampled (this is the "Single Shot" mode described in the GeekPort hardware specification). In other words, the ADC doesn't perform a sample and hold—it doesn't constantly and regularly measure the voltages at its inputs. Nonetheless, you *can't* retrieve samples at an arbitrarily high frequency simply by reading in a tight loop. This is because of the "sampling latency": When you ask for a sample, it takes the driver about ten microseconds to process the request, not counting the (slight) overhead imposed by the C++ call (from your BA2D object). Therefore, the fastest rate at which you can get samples from the ADC is a bit less than 100 kHz.

Furthermore, the ADC driver "fakes" the four channels of a/d conversion. In reality, there's only one ADC data path; the driver multiplexes the path to create four independent signals. This means that the optimum 100 kHz sampling frequency is divided by the number of channels that you want to read. If all four channels are being read at the same time, you'll find that successive samples on a *particular* channel arrive slightly less often than once every 40 microseconds (a rate of < 25 kHz).

Finally, the ADC hardware is shared by the GeekPort and the two joysticks. This cooperative use shouldn't affect your application—you can treat the ADC as if it were all your own—but this increases the multiplexing. In general, joysticks shouldn't need to sample very often, so while the theoretical "worst hit" on the ADC is a sample every 60 microseconds, the reality should be much better. If we can assume that a joystick-reading application isn't oversampling, then the BA2D "sampling latency" should stay near the 10 microseconds per channel measurement.

The DAC

The DAC accepts 8-bit unsigned data and converts it, in 16 mV steps, to an analog signal in the range [0, +4.080] Volts. Again, the quantization is linear. The DAC output isn't filtered; if you need to smooth the stair-step output, you have to build a filter into the gizmo that you're connecting to the GeekPort.

Each of the d/a pins is protected by an in-series 4.7 kOhm resistor; however, pin 33, the d/a DC reference (ground) pin, is not similarly impeded. If you want to attach an op-amp circuit to the DAC output, you should hang a 4.7 kOhm resistor on the ground pin that you're using.

When you write a digital sample to the DAC, the specified pin is immediately set to the converted voltage. The pin continues to produce that voltage until you write another sample.

Unlike the ADC, the DAC is truly a four-channel device, so there's no multiplexing imposition to slow things down. Furthermore, writing to the DAC is naturally faster than writing to the ADC. You should be able to write to the DAC as frequently as you want, without worrying about a hardware-imposed "sampling latency."

The Digital Ports

The following illustration shows the disposition of the GeekPort connector pins as they are assigned to the digital ports:

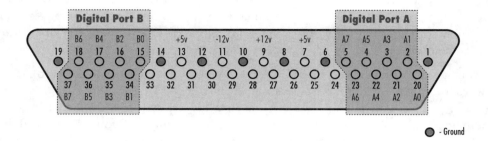

Each pin in a digital port transmits the value of a single bit; the pins are labelled by bit position. Thus, A0 is the least significant bit of digital port A, and A7 is its most significant bit. You can use any of the seven ground pins (1, 6, 8, 10, 12, 14, and 19) in your digital port circuit.

Devices that you connect to the digital ports should send and (expect to) receive voltages that are below 0.8 Volts or above 2.0 Volts. These thresholds correspond, respectively, to the greatest value for digital 0 and the least for digital 1 (as depicted below). The correspondence to bit value for voltages between these limits is undefined.

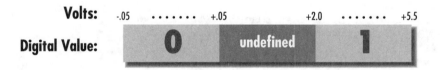

Although there's no lower voltage limit for digital 0, nor upper limit for digital 1, the BeBox outputs voltages that are no less than 0 Volts, nor no more than +5 Volts. Your input device can exceed this range without damaging the BeBox circuitry: Excessive input emf is clipped to fall within [-0.5V, +5.5V].

Be aware that behind each digital port pin lies a 1 kOhm resistor.

BA2D

Derived from: *none*

Declared in: be/device/A2D.h

Library: libdevice.so

The BA2D class lets you create objects that can read the GeekPort's a/d channels. Each BA2D object can read a single channel at a time; if you want to read all four channels simultaneously, you have to create four separate objects.

To retrieve a value from one of the a/d channels, you create a new BA2D object, open it on the channel you want, and then (repeatedly) invoke the object's `Read()` function. When you're through reading, you call `Close()` so some other object can open the channel.

Reading is a one-shot deal: For each `Read()` invocation, you get a single `uint16` that stores the 12-bit ADC value in its least significant 12 bits. To get a series of successive values, you have to put the `Read()` call in a loop. Keep in mind that there's no sampling rate or other automatic time tethering. For example, if you want to read the ADC every thousandth of a second, you have to impose the waiting period yourself (by snoozing between reads, for example).

The outline of a typical a/d-reading setup is shown below:

```
#include <A2D.h>

void ReadA2D1()
{
    uint16 val;
    BA2D a2d;

    if (a2d.Open("A2D1") <= 0)
        return;

    while ( /* whatever */ ) {

        /* Read() returns the number of bytes that were
         * read; a successful read returns 2.
         */
        if (a2d.Read(&val) != 2)
            break;
        ...
        snooze(1000);
    }
    a2d.Close();
}
```

Constructor and Destructor

BA2D()

BA2D(void)

Creates a new object that can open an ADC channel. The particular channel is specified in a subsequent `Open()` call. Constructing a new BA2D object doesn't affect the state of the ADC.

~BA2D()

virtual ~**BA2D**()

Closes the channel that the object holds open (if any) and then destroys the object.

Member Functions

Open(), IsOpen(), Close()

status_t **Open**(const char *name)
bool **IsOpen**(void)
void **Close**(void)

Open() opens the named ADC channel. The channel names are:

BA2D Channels

"A2D1"

"A2D2"

"A2D3"

"A2D4"

See "The ADC and DAC" for an illustration that shows the correspondences between the channel names and the GeekPort connector pins.

Each channel can only be held open by one object at a time; you should close the channel as soon as you're finished with it. Furthermore, each BA2D object can only hold one channel open at a time. When you invoke Open(), the channel that the object currently has open is automatically closed—even if the channel that you're attempting to open is the channel that the object already has open. Opening an ADC channel doesn't affect the data in the channel itself.

IsOpen() returns true if the object holds an ADC channel open. Otherwise, it returns false.

Close() closes the object's connection to the channel without affecting the state of the hardware.

Return values:

Open() returns a positive integer if the channel is successfully opened; otherwise, it returns B_ERROR.

Read()

ssize_t **Read**(uint16 *adc_12_bit)

Causes the ADC to sample and convert (within a 12-bit range) the voltage level on the GeekPort pin that corresponds to the object's ADC channel. The 12-bit unsigned value is returned by reference in the *adc_12_bit* argument.

The object must `Open()` an ADC channel before calling `Read()`.

Return values:

`Read()` return B_ERROR if a channel isn't open, or if, for any other reason, the read failed. Otherwise it returns 2 (the number of bytes that were read).

BD2A

Derived from:	*none*
Declared in:	be/device/D2A.h
Library:	libdevice.so

The BD2A class lets you write to (and, less importantly, read from) the GeekPort's digital-to-analog converter (DAC). Each BD2A object can write a single channel at a time; if you want to read all four channels simultaneously, you have to create four separate objects.

To write a value to one of the d/a channels, you create a new BD2A object, open it on the channel you want, and then (repeatedly) invoke the object's `Write()` function. When you're through reading, you call `Close()` so some other object can open the channel. The `Write()` function writes a single byte at each call and returns 1 if it was successful:

```
#include <D2A.h>

void WriteD2A1()
{
   uint8 val;
   BD2A d2a;

   if (d2a.Open("D2A1") <= 0)
      return;

   while ( /* whatever */ ) {
      /* Get a byte from somewhere. */
      val = ...;

      if (d2a.Write(val) != 1)
         break;
      snooze(1000);
```

```
    }
    d2a.Close();
}
```

The DAC performs a "sample and hold": The voltage that the DAC produces is maintained until another `Write()` call (on that channel) changes the setting. Furthermore, the "hold" persists across BD2A objects: Neither closing nor deleting a BD2A object affects the voltage that's held by the corresponding GeekPort pin.

The BD2A class also implements a `Read()` function. This function returns the value that was most recently written to the particular DAC channel.

Constructor and Destructor

BD2A()

BD2A(void)

Creates a new object that can open a DAC channel. The particular channel is specified in a subsequent `Open()` call. Constructing a new BD2A object doesn't affect the state of the DAC.

~BD2A()

virtual **~BD2A**()

Closes the channel that the object holds open (if any) and then destroys the object.

Deleting a BD2A object *doesn't* affect the DAC channel's output voltage. If you want the voltage cleared (for example), you have to set it to 0 explicitly before deleting (or otherwise closing) the BD2A object.

Member Functions

Open(), IsOpen(), Close()

status_t **Open**(const char *name)
bool **IsOpen**(void)
void **Close**(void)

`Open()` opens the named DAC (BD2A) channel. The channel names are:

BD2A Channels

"D2A1"

"D2A2"

"D2A3"

"D2A4"

See "The ADC and DAC" for an illustration that shows the correspondences between the channel names and the GeekPort connector pins.

Each channel can only be held open by one object at a time; you should close the channel as soon as you're finished with it. Furthermore, each BD2A object can only hold one channel open at a time. When you invoke `Open()`, the channel that the object currently has open is automatically closed—even if the channel that you're attempting to open is the channel that the object already has open.

Opening a DAC channel doesn't affect the data in the channel itself. In particular, when you open a DAC channel, the channel's output voltage isn't changed.

`IsOpen()` returns `true` if the object holds a DAC channel open. Otherwise, it returns `false`.

`Close()` does the obvious without affecting the state of the ADC or DAC channel. If you want to set a DAC channel's output voltage to 0 (for example), you must explicitly write the value before invoking `Close()`.

Return values:
> `Open()` returns a positive integer if the channel is successfully opened; otherwise, it returns `B_ERROR`.

Read()

> ssize_t **Read**(uint8 **dac_8_bit*)

Returns, by reference in *dac_8_bit*, the value that was most recently written to the object's DAC channel. The value needn't have been written by this object—it could have been written by the channel's previous opener.

WARNING

The BD2A `Read()` function returns a value that's cached by the DAC driver—it doesn't actually tap the GeekPort pin to see what value it's currently carrying. This should only matter to the clever few who will attempt (unsuccessfully) to use the d/a pins as input paths.

The object must open a DAC channel before calling `Read()`.

Return values:
> `Read()` return `B_ERROR` if a channel isn't open, or if, for any other reason, the read failed. Otherwise it returns 1 (the number of bytes that were read).

Write()

> ssize_t **Write**(uchar *dac_8_bit*)

Sends the *dac_8_bit* value to the object's DAC channel. The DAC converts the value to an analog voltage in the range [0, +4.080] Volts and sets the corresponding GeekPort pin. The pin continues to produce the voltage until another `Write()` call—possibly by a different BD2A object—changes the setting.

The DAC's conversion is linear: Each digital step corresponds to 16 mV at the output. The analog voltage midpoint, +2.040V, can be approximated by a digital input of 0x7F (which produces +2.032V) or 0x80 (+2.048V).

Return values:

If the object isn't open, this function returns B_ERROR, otherwise it returns 1 (the number of bytes that were written).

BDigitalPort

Derived from: *none*

Declared in: be/device/DigitalPort.h

Library: libdevice.so

The BDigitalPort class is an interface to the GeekPort's two *digital ports*. Each digital port is an 8-bit wide device that can be set for input or output. See "The Digital Ports" for an illustration of the GeekPort's digital port pins.

To access a digital port, you construct a BDigitalPort object, open it on the port you want, assign the object to work as either an input or an output, and then read or write a series of bytes from or to the object.

In the following example, we open and read from digital port A:

```
#include <DigitalPort.h>

void ReadDigitalPortA()
{
   char val;
   BDigitalPort dPortA;

   if (dPortA.Open("DigitalA") <= 0 ||
       dPortA.SetAsInput() != B_NO_ERROR)
       return;

   while ( /* whatever */ ) {
       /* Read() returns the number of bytes that were
        * read; a successful read returns 1.
        */
       if (dPortA.Read(&val) != 1)
          break;
       ...
       snooze(1000);
```

```
   }
   dPortA.Close();
}
```

As shown here, the BDigitalPort is constructed without reference to a specific port. It's not until you actually open the object (through Open()) that you have to identify the port that you want. Identification is by name, "DigitalA" or "DigitalB". The Read() function returns only one value per invocation, and is untimed—if you don't provide some sort of tethering (as we do with snooze(), above) the read loop will spin as fast as possible.

To safeguard against an inadvertent burst of equipment-destroying output, the digital port is set to be an input when it's opened, and automatically reset to be an input when you close it.

Using Both Digital Ports at the Same Time

To access both digital ports at the same time, you have to construct two BDigitalPort objects. One of the objects can be used as an output and the other an input, both as outputs, or both as inputs.

In the following example, digital port A is used to write data to an external device, while digital port B is used for acknowledgment signalling: Before each write we set port B to 0, and after the write we wait for port B to be set to 1. We're assuming that the external device will write a 1 to port B when it's ready to receive the next 8-bits of data.

```
void WriteAndAck()
{
   char val;
   BDigitalPort dPortA;
   BDigitalPort dPortB;

   if (dPortA.Open("DigitalA") <= 0 ||
       dPortA.SetAsOutput() != B_OK ||
       dPortB.Open("DigitalB") <= 0 ||
       dPortB.SetAsOutput() != B_OK)
       goto exit_tag;

   while ( /* whatever */ ) {

       /* Clear the acknowledgment signal. */
       val = 0;
       if (dPortB.Write(&val) != 1)
          break;

       /* Reset val to the data we want to send. */
       val = ...;
```

```
      if (dPortA.Write(val) != 1)
         break;

      /* Reset digital port B to be an input. */
      if (dPortB.SetAsInput() != B_OK)
         break;

      /* Wait for the acknowledgment. */
      while (1) {
         if (dPortB.Read(&val) != 1)
            goto exit_tag;
         if (val == 1)
            break;
         snooze(1000);
      }

      /* Reset digital port B to be an output. */
      if (dPortB.SetAsOutput() != B_OK)
         break;
   }
exit_tag:
   dPortA.Close();
   dPortB.Close();
}
```

Notice that the acknowledgment signal only takes one bit of digital port B. This leaves seven bits that the external device can use to send additional data (triggers or gates, for example). The restriction in this scheme, given the structure shown above, is that this additional data would have to be synchronized with the acknowledgment signal.

By extension, if the data that you want to write to the external device is, at most, only seven-bits wide, then you could rewrite this example to use a single port: You would mask one of the bits as the acknowledgment carrier, and let the other seven bits carry the data, toggling the port between input and output as needed.

Overdriving an Output Pin

One of the features of the digital ports is that you can "overdrive" a pin from the outside. This means that you can set a port to be an output, and then force a voltage back onto the pin from an external device and read that voltage with the Read() function *without having to reset the port to be an input.* Keep in mind that there's a 1 kOhm resistor behind the pin (on the BeBox side), so your "overdrive" circuit has to be hot enough to balance the resistance.

When you overdrive an output pin, the voltage on the pin is altered for as long as the external force keeps it there. If you write an "opposing" value to an overdriven pin (through Write()), the written value won't pull the pin—the overdriven value will still be enforced. As soon as the overdrive voltage is removed, the pin will produce the voltage that was more recently written to it by the `Write()` function.

Constructor and Destructor

BDigitalPort()

BDigitalPort(void)

Creates a new object that can open one of the digital ports. The particular port is specified in a subsequent `Open()` call.

~BDigitalPort

virtual ~BDigitalPort()

Closes the port the object has open and destroys the object.

Deleting a BDigitalPort object sets the port (at the driver level) to be an input. The values at the port's pins are, at that point, undefined.

Member Functions

Open(), IsOpen(), Close()

status_t **Open**(const char *name*)

bool **IsOpen**(void)

void **Close**(void)

`Open()` opens the named digital port; the *name* argument should be either "DigitalA" or "DigitalB". "The Digital Ports" shows you where the two ports appear among the GeekPort's pins.

A digital port can only be held open by one BDigitalPort object at a time; you should close the port as soon as you're finished with it. Furthermore, each BDigitalPort object can only hold one port open at a time. When you invoke `Open()`, the port that the object currently has open is automatically closed—even if the port that you're attempting to open is the port that the object already has open.

When you open a digital port, the device is automatically set to be an input. If you want the port to be an output, you must follow this call with a call to `SetAsOutput()`. Just to be safe, it couldn't hurt to explicitly set the port to be an input (through `SetAsInput()`) if that's what you want.

`IsOpen()` returns `true` if the object currently has a port open, and `false` if not.

`Close()` closes the object's connection to its port. The digital port is set to be an input at the driver level.

Return values:

    `Open()` returns a positive integer if the port is successfully opened; otherwise, it returns `B_ERROR`.

Read()

    ssize_t **Read**(uint8 **buf*)

Reads the data that currently lies on the digital ports pins, and returns the data in *buf.* Although you usually read a digital port that's been set to be an input, it's also possible to read an output port. In any case, the port must be open.

Return values:

    If the port was successfully read, the function returns 1 (the number of bytes read). Otherwise, it returns `B_ERROR`.

SetAsInput(), SetAsOutput(), IsInput(), IsOutput()

    status_t **SetAsInput**(void)
    status_t **SetAsOutput**(void)

    bool **IsInput**(void)
    bool **IsOutput**(void)

`SetAsInput()` and `SetAsOutput()` set the object's port to act as an input or output. They return `B_ERROR` if the object isn't open, and `B_OK` otherwise.

`IsInput()` and `IsOutput()` tell you the input/output state of the object. They both return `false` if the object isn't open.

Write()

    ssize_t **Write**(uint8 *value*)

Sends *value* to the object's port. The port continues to produce the value until another `Write()` call changes the setting. The object must be open as an output for this function to succeed.

Return values:

    `Write()` return `B_ERROR` if a port isn't open, or if, for any other reason, the write failed. Otherwise it returns 1 (the number of bytes that were read).

BJoystick

Derived from: *none*

Declared in: be/device/Joystick.h

Library: libdevice.so

A BJoystick object provides an interface to a joystick (or other game controller) connected to the BeBox. There are two game ports on the back of the machine, one above the other. With a Y adaptor, each port can support two joysticks.

The interface to a joystick is demand-driven. An application must repeatedly poll the state of the joystick by calling the BJoystick object's `Update()` function. `Update()` queries the port and updates the object's data members to reflect the current state of the joystick.

Data Members

bigtime_t **timestamp**
> The time of the most recent update, as measured in microseconds from the beginning of 1970.

int16 **horizontal**
> The horizontal position of the joystick at the time of the last update. Values increase as the joystick moves from right to left.

int16 **vertical**
> The vertical position of the joystick at the time of the last update. Values increase as the joystick moves forward and decrease as it's pulled back.

bool **button1**
> `true` if the first button was pressed at the time of the last update.

bool **button2**
> `true` if the second button was pressed at the time of the last update.

The `horizontal` and `vertical` data members record values read directly from the ports, values that simply digitize the analog output of the joysticks. This class makes no effort to translate the values to a standard scale or range. Values can range from 0 through 4,095, but joysticks typically don't use the full range and some don't register all values within the range that is used. The scale is not linear—identical increments in different parts of the range can reflect differing amounts of horizontal and vertical movement. The exact variance from linearity and the extent of the usable range are partly characteristics of the individual joystick and partly functions of the BeBox hardware.

Constructor and Destructor

BJoystick()

> **BJoystick**(void)

Initializes the BJoystick object so that all values are set to 0. Before using the object, you must call `Open()` to open a particular joystick port. For the object to register any meaningful values, you must call `Update()` to query the open port.

~BJoystick()

> virtual **~BJoystick**()

Closes the port and destroys the object.

Member Functions

CountDevices(), GetDeviceName()

> int32 **CountDevices**(void)
> status_t **GetDeviceName**(int32 *n*, char **name*,
> size_t *bufSize* = B_OS_NAME_LENGTH)

These two function work together to let you retrieve the names of all joystick ports. `CountDevices()` returns the number of joystick ports (devices) that are supported by the machine. `GetDeviceName()` returns, in *name*, the name of the *n*'th joystick port. *bufSize* is the length of the *name* buffer, in bytes. It needn't be longer than `B_OS_NAME_LENGTH` (defined in OS.h).

Return values:
> `GetDeviceName()` returns...
> `B_OK`. Success.
> `B_BAD_VALUE`. *n* is out of range.
> `B_NAME_TOO_LONG`. The device name length is greater than *bufSize*.

Open(), Close()

> status_t **Open**(const char **name*)
> void **Close**(void)

`Open()` opens the *name* joystick port. There are two ports on the back panel of the BeBox; by attaching a Y cables to these ports, your BeBox can support two more joysticks. If the port is already open, `Open()` tries to close it first.

`Close()` closes the joystick port that the object holds open.

Return values:

> Open() returns B_ERROR if it couldn't open the named port. Otherwise it returns a positive integer.

Update()

status_t **Update**(void)

Updates the data members of the object so that they reflect the current state of the joystick.

Return values:

> Update() returns B_ERROR if the BJoystick object doesn't have a port open, and B_OK if it does.

BSerialPort

Derived from: *none*

Declared in: be/device/SerialPort.h

Library: libdevice.so

A BSerialPort object represents an RS-232 serial connection to the computer. Through BSerialPort functions, you can read data received at a serial ports and write data over the connection. You can also configure the connection—for example, set the number of data and stop bits, determine the rate at which data is sent and received, and select the type of flow control (hardware or software) that should be used.

To read and write data, a BSerialPort object must first open one of the serial ports by name. To find the names of all the serial ports on the computer, use the CountDevices() and GetDeviceName() functions:

```
BSerialPort serial;
char devName[B_OS_NAME_LENGTH];
int32 n = 0;

for (int32 n = serial.CountDevices()-1; n >= 0; n--) {
   serial.GetDeviceName(n, devName);

   if ( serial.Open(devName) > 0 )
     ....
}
```

The BSerialPort object communicates with the driver for the port it has open. The driver maintains an input buffer to collect incoming data and a smaller output buffer to hold outgoing data. When the object reads and writes data, it reads from and writes to these buffers.

The serial port drivers, and therefore BSerialPort objects, send and receive data asynchronously only.

Constructor and Destructor

BSerialPort()

> BSerialPort(void)

Initializes the BSerialPort object to the following default values:

- Hardware flow control (see `SetFlowControl()`)
- A data rate of 19,200 bits per second (see `SetDataRate()`)
- A serial unit with 8 bits of data, 1 stop bit, and no parity (see `SetDataBits()`)
- Blocking with no time limit—an infinite timeout—for reading data (see `Read()`)

The new object doesn't represent any particular serial port. After construction, it's necessary to open one of the ports by name.

The type of flow control must be decided before a port is opened. But the other default settings listed above can be changed before or after opening a port.

See also: `Open()`

~BSerialPort()

> virtual ~BSerialPort()

Makes sure the port is closed before the object is destroyed.

Member Functions

ClearInput(), ClearOutput()

> void **ClearInput**(void)
> void **ClearOutput**(void)

These functions empty the serial port driver's input and output buffers, so that the contents of the input buffer won't be read (by the `Read()` function) and the contents of the output buffer (after having been written by `Write()`) won't be transmitted over the connection.

The buffers are cleared automatically when a port is opened.

See also: `Read()`, `Write()`, `Open()`

Close() see Open()

DataBits() see SetDataBits()

DataRate() see SetDataRate()

FlowControl() see SetFlowControl()

IsCTS()

bool IsCTS(void)

Returns `true` if the Clear to Send (CTS) pin is asserted, and `false` if not.

IsDCD()

bool IsDCD(void)

Returns `true` if the Data Carrier Detect (DCD) pin is asserted, and `false` if not.

IsDSR()

bool IsDSR(void)

Returns `true` if the Data Set Ready (DSR) pin is asserted, and `false` if not.

IsRI()

bool IsRI(void)

Returns `true` if the Ring Indicator (RI) pin is asserted, and `false` if not.

Open(), Close()

status_t Open(const char *name)

void Close(void)

These functions open the *name* serial port and close it again. To get a serial port name, use the GetDeviceName() function; an example is shown in the introduction.

To be able to read and write data, the BSerialPort object must have a port open. It can open first one port and then another, but it can have no more than one open at a time. If it already has a port open when Open() is called, that port is closed before an attempt is made to open the *name* port. (Thus, both Open() and Close() close the currently open port.)

Open() can't open the *name* port if some other entity already has it open. (If the BSerialPort itself has *name* open, Open() first closes it, then opens it again.)

When a serial port is opened, its input and output buffers are emptied and the Data Terminal Ready (DTR) pin is asserted.

Return values:
> *positive integers* (not 0). Success.
> B_PERMISSION_DENIED. The port is already open.
> B_ERROR. The port couldn't be opened for some other reason.

ParityMode()   see SetDataBits()

Read(), SetBlocking(), SetTimeout()

> ssize_t **Read**(void *buffer*, size_t *maxBytes*)

> void **SetBlocking**(bool *shouldBlock*)

> status_t **SetTimeout**(bigtime_t *timeout*)

Read() takes incoming data from the serial port driver and places it in the data *buffer* provided. In no case will it read more than *maxBytes*—a value that should reflect the capacity of the *buffer*. The input buffer of the driver, from which Read() takes the data, holds a maximum of 2,024 bytes (2048 on Mac hardware). This function fails if the BSerialPort object doesn't have a port open.

The number of bytes that Read() will read before returning depends not only on *maxBytes*, but also on the *shouldBlock* flag and the *timeout* set by the other two functions.

- SetBlocking() determines whether Read() should block and wait for *maxBytes* of data to arrive at the serial port if that number isn't already available to be read. If the *shouldBlock* flag is true, Read() will block. However, if *shouldBlock* is false, Read() will take however many bytes are waiting to be read, up to the maximum asked for, then return immediately. If no data is waiting at the serial port, it returns without reading anything.

  The default *shouldBlock* setting is true.

- SetTimeout() sets a time limit on how long Read() will block while waiting for data to arrive at the port's input buffer. The *timeout* is relevant to Read() only if the *shouldBlock* flag is true. However, the time limit also applies to the WaitForInput() function, which always blocks, regardless of the *shouldBlock* setting.

  There is no time limit if the *timeout* is set to B_INFINITE_TIMEOUT—Read() (and WaitForInput()) will block forever. Otherwise, the *timeout* is expressed in microseconds and can range from a minimum of 100,000 (0.1 second) through a maximum of 25,500,000 (25.5 seconds); differences less than 100,000 microseconds are not recognized; they're rounded to the nearest tenth of a second.

The default *timeout* is B_INFINITE_TIMEOUT.

Return values:
Read() returns...
non-negative integer. Success; the value is the number of bytes that were read.
B_INTERRUPTED. The operation was interrupted by a signal.
B_FILE_ERROR. The BSerialPort doesn't have a port open.

Return values:
SetTimeout() returns...
B_OK. Success.
B_BAD_VALUE. Out-f-range value passed to SetTimeout().
(Note that it's not considered an error if a timeout expires.)

SetBlocking()   see Read()

SetDataBits(), SetStopBits(), SetParityMode(), DataBits(), StopBits(), ParityMode(), data_bits, stop_bits, parity_mode

void **SetDataBits**(data_bits *count*)
void **SetStopBits**(stop_bits *count*)
void **SetParityMode**(parity_mode *mode*)

data_bits **DataBits**(void)
stop_bits **StopBits**(void)
parity_mode **ParityMode**(void)

typedef enum { **B_DATA_BITS_7**, **B_DATA_BITS_8** } data_bits
typedef enum { **B_STOP_BITS_1**, **B_STOP_BITS_2** } stop_bits
typedef enum { **B_EVEN_PARITY**, **B_ODD_PARITY**, **B_NO_PARITY** } parity_mode

These functions set and return characteristics of the serial unit used to send and receive data.

• SetDataBits() sets the number of bits of data in each unit; the default is B_DATA_BITS_8.

• SetStopBits() sets the number of stop bits in each unit; the default is B_STOP_BITS_2.

• SetParityMode() sets whether the serial unit contains a parity bit and, if so, the type of parity used; the default is B_NO_PARITY.

SetDataRate(), DataRate(), data_rate

status_t **SetDataRate**(data_rate *bitsPerSecond*)

data_rate **DataRate**(void)

typedef enum { **B_0_BPS, B_50_BPS, B_75_BPS, B_110_BPS, B_134_BPS, B_150_BPS, B_200_BPS, B_300_BPS, B_600_BPS, B_1200_BPS, B_1800_BPS, B_2400_BPS, B_4800_BPS, B_9600_BPS, B_19200_BPS, B_31250_BPS, B_38400_BPS, B_57600_BPS, B_115200_BPS, B_230400_BPS** } data_rate

These functions set and return the rate (in bits per second) at which data is both transmitted and received.

The default data rate is `B_19200_BPS`. If the rate is set to 0 (`B_0_BPS`), data will be sent and received at an indeterminate number of bits per second.

`SetDataRate()` returns...

`B_OK`. The rate was successfully set.

`B_NO_INIT`. The BSerialPort object doesn't have a port open.

`B_ERROR`. The data rate couldn't be set for any other reason.

SetDTR()

status_t **SetDTR**(bool *pinAsserted*)

Asserts the Data Terminal Ready (DTR) pin if the *pinAsserted* flag is `true`, and de-asserts it if the flag is `false`. The function should always returns `B_OK`.

SetFlowControl(), FlowControl()

void **SetFlowControl**(uint32 *mask*)

uint32 **FlowControl**(void)

These functions set and return the type of flow control the driver should use. There are four possibilities:

Control Code	Meaning
B_SOFTWARE_CONTROL	Control is maintained through XON and XOFF characters inserted into the data stream.
B_HARDWARE_CONTROL	Control is maintained through the Clear to Send (CTS) and Request to Send (RTS) pins.
B_SOFTWARE_CONTROL + B_HARDWARE_CONTROL	Both of the above.
0 (zero)	No control.

`SetFlowControl()` should be called before a specific serial port is opened. You can't change the type of flow control the driver uses in midstream.

SetParityMode()   see SetDataBits()

SetRTS()

> status_t **SetRTS**(bool *pinAsserted*)

Asserts the Request to Send (RTS) pin if the *pinAsserted* flag is `true`, and de-asserts it if the flag is `false`. The function always returns `B_OK`.

SetStopBits()   see SetDataBits()

SetTimeout()   see Read()

StopBits()   see SetDataBits()

WaitForInput()

> ssize_t **WaitForInput**(void)

Waits for input data to arrive at the serial port and returns the number of bytes available to be read. If data is already waiting, the function returns immediately.

This function doesn't respect the flag set by `SetBlocking()`; it blocks even if blocking is turned off for the `Read()` function. However, it does respect the timeout set by `SetTimeout()`. If the timeout expires before input data arrives at the serial port, it returns 0.

Write()

> ssize_t **Write**(const void **data*, size_t *numBytes*)

Writes up to *numBytes* of *data* to the serial port's output buffer. This function will be successful in writing the data only if the BSerialPort object has a port open. The output buffer holds a maximum of 512 bytes (1024 on Mac hardware).

Return values:

> *non-negative integer.* Success; the value is the number of bytes that were written.
> `B_INTERRUPTED`. The operation was interrupted by a signal.
> `B_FILE_ERROR`. The BSerialPort doesn't have a port open.

Playing with Tracker

Playing with Tracker

This chapter describes how you can control the Tracker application through the use of scripts, and how to apply your own add-on modules to the files that Tracker displays in its windows.

Tracker Scripting

Each Tracker window defines a "Poses" property representing the contents of the window. Each poses, in turn, defines the two properties "Entry" and "Selection". An "Entry" is an item in the window, e.g. either a file or a directory, while a "Selection" represents a selected "Entry".

When a Tracker window receives a scripting message with a "Poses" property, it pops the current specifier off the specifier stack and then forwards the scripting message to the view handling the "Poses" property. From there, the "Entry" and "Selection" properties are processed. For example, the following function returns the number of entries present in a given Tracker window:

```
int32 CountEntries(const char *name)
{
   int32 count;
   BMessage message, reply;

   // form scripting request
   message.what = B_COUNT_PROPERTIES;
   message.AddSpecifier("Entry");
   message.AddSpecifier("Poses");
   message.AddSpecifier("Window", name);

   // deliver request and fetch response
   BMessenger("application/x-vnd.Be-TRAK").SendMessage(&message, &reply);
```

```
    // return result
    if (reply.FindInt32("result", &count) == B_OK)
        return count;

    return -1;
}
```

The Tracker scripting API defines a number of ways of specifying entries in a Poses. These methods are summarized below:

Specifier	Description
B_DIRECT_SPECIFIER	Used for specifying the entire Poses or selection as appropriate.
B_INDEX_SPECIFIER	"index" contains int32 index of file in the Poses. Ranges are specified with a pair of indices.
'sref'	"refs" contains entry_refs of specified files.
'sprv'	Refers to item immediately following file whose entry_ref is found in "data."
'snxt'	Refers to item immediately preceding file whose entry_ref is found in "data."

Always remember that other programs (or the user) may also be adding or removing entries to the view and selection, so do not rely upon indices as a safe method of referring to a specific file. Instead, use entry_refs.

The Entry Property

Message	Specifiers	Meaning
B_COUNT_PROPERTIES	B_DIRECT_SPECIFIER	Counts entries in a Poses.
B_DELETE_PROPERTY	'sref', B_INDEX_SPECIFIER	Moves the specified entry to the Trash.
B_EXECUTE_PROPERTY	'sref', B_INDEX_SPECIFIER	Perform the equivalent action of opening the specified items in the Tracker.
B_GET_PROPERTY	B_DIRECT_SPECIFIER	Returns entry_refs of all entries in current Poses.
B_GET_PROPERTY	B_INDEX_SPECIFIER	Returns specified entry_ref.
B_GET_PROPERTY	'sprv', 'snxt'	Returns entry_ref of entry prior to or following specified entry_ref. Also returns index of file in "index."

The Selection Property

Message	Specifiers	Meaning
B_COUNT_PROPERTIES	B_DIRECT_SPECIFIER	Counts the number of selected items in the Poses.
B_CREATE_PROPERTY	B_DIRECT_SPECIFIER	Adds items to the current selection. These can be specified as either entry_refs or int32s in the "data" array.
B_DELETE_PROPERTY	'sref', B_INDEX_SPECIFIER	Removes items from the current selection.
B_GET_PROPERTY	B_DIRECT_SPECIFIER	Returns entry_refs of items in selection.
B_GET_PROPERTY	'sprv', 'snxt'	Returns entry_ref of file prior to or following given item. Returns the index of the file in "index."
B_SET_PROPERTY	B_DIRECT_SPECIFIER	Clears the current selection and set it to the range given in "data." Also accepts entry_refs in "data" to determined the new selection.
B_SET_PROPERTY	'sprv', 'snxt'	Clears the current selection and sets it to the entry_refs prior to or following those specified in "data."

Tracker Add-on Protocol

The Tracker provides a convenient shortcut mechanism through the use of add-ons. A user can access a special add-ons menu by right-clicking in the Tracker. The Tracker interacts with an add-on through the process_refs() function described below.

Tracker add-ons should be placed in */boot/home/config/add-ons/Tracker*. A shortcut key can be associated with the add-on by appending a dash followed by the shortcut key to the filename of the add-on.

process_refs()

Declared in: be/add-ons/tracker/TrackerAddOn.h

> void **process_refs**(entry_ref *dir_ref*, BMessage **msg*, void **reserved*)

The Tracker calls this function when the user invokes the add-on. The current directory is found in *dir_ref*. *msg* is a standard B_REFS_RECEIVED BMessage with the "*refs*" array containing the entry_refs of the files selected by the user. The third argument is currently unused.

`process_refs()` runs in a separate thread within the Tracker's team, so if your add-on crashes, the Tracker goes too.

A simple Tracker add-on follows. It simply takes the contents of the arguments to `process_refs()` and outputs them in a window.

```
#include <Application.h>
#include <InterfaceKit.h>
#include <StorageKit.h>

#include <stdio.h>
#include <string.h>

#include <be/add-ons/tracker/TrackerAddon.h>

void process_refs(entry_ref dir_ref, BMessage *msg, void *)
{
    BWindow *window = new BWindow(BRect(100,100,300,300),
        "Sample Tracker Add-on", B_TITLED_WINDOW, 0);
    BTextView *view = new BTextView(BRect(0,0,200,200), "view",
        BRect(0,0,200,200), B_FOLLOW_ALL_SIDES, B_WILL_DRAW |
        B_FULL_UPDATE_ON_RESIZE);

    BPath path;
    BEntry entry(&dir_ref);
    entry.GetPath(&path);
    view->Insert("Current Directory: ");
    view->Insert(path.Path());
    view->Insert("\n");

    int refs;
    entry_ref file_ref;
    for (refs=0;msg->FindRef("refs", refs, &file_ref) == B_NO_ERROR;refs++) {
        if (refs == 0)
            view->Insert("Selected files:\n");
        entry.SetTo(&file_ref);
        entry.GetPath(&path);
        view->Insert(path.Path());
        view->Insert("\n");
    }

    if (refs == 0)
        view->Insert("No files selected.\n");

    view->MakeEditable(false);
    window->AddChild(view);
    window->Show();
}

main()
{
    new BApplication("application/x-sample-tracker-add-on");
    (new BAlert("", "Sample Tracker Add-on", "swell"))->Go();
    delete be_app;
}
```

Graphics Card Drivers

Graphics Card Drivers

A graphics card driver is the interface between the system and a specific graphics card. The driver is implemented as an add-on that's loaded by the Application Server when the Server starts up. Once the driver is loaded, it remains loaded until the machine is shut down.

Basic communication with a graphics card driver is performed through a single function called `control_graphics_card()`. The Application Server tells the driver which operation to perform by passing an opcode through this function. The driver can also implement a set of "hook" functions that the Server can invoke directly. (The locations of the hook functions are retrieved through a particular opcode passed to `control_graphics_card()`.)

The Application Server is the primary "consumer" of a graphics card driver's functionality. However, the Game Kit, through its BWindowScreen class, can also access and modify the graphics card's frame buffer, and can call the card's accelerated graphics functions.

This chapter explains how to use `control_graphics_card()`, lists and describes the opcodes and hook functions, and explains how to build a graphics card driver:

- "The Entry Point and General Opcodes" describes the `control_graphics_card()` function and the fundamental opcodes.

- "Graphics Card Hook Functions" describes the hook functions.

- The Game Kit gains access to a driver's hook functions through a driver "clone." The section "Driver Cloning Opcodes" describes the opcodes that are sent when the Game Kit clones a driver.

- "Frame Buffer Opcodes" are also used by the Game Kit, when it accesses the frame buffer.

- "Building and Installing a Driver" explains how to build a driver add-on, and where to put it.

NOTE

This documentation is valid for PCI-based cards only.

The Entry Point and General Opcodes

Declared in: be/add-ons/graphics/GraphicsCard.h

The primary means by which the Application Server and Game Kit communicate with a graphics card driver—the driver's "entry point"—is the `control_graphics_card()` function; every graphics card driver must implement this function:

>   int32 **control_graphics_card**(uint32 *opcode*, void **data*)

The first argument, *opcode*, specifies the operation the driver is to perform. The second argument, *data*, is used to pass data to the driver, or to return information from it; the type of data depends on the nature of the operation.

The return value is an error code. In general, the control function should return `B_OK` or `B_ERROR` to indicate success or failure. It should also return `B_ERROR` for *op* codes that it doesn't understand.

Only the Application Server and Game Kit objects can (effectively) call `control_graphics_card()`; random applications can't load the driver and invoke the function themselves.

General Opcodes and Structures

Listed below are descriptions of the general opcodes and structures that examine and configure a graphics card driver. Briefly, the opcodes are:

Opcode	Description
B_OPEN_GRAPHICS_CARD B_CLOSE_GRAPHICS_CARD	Initiates and terminates communication with the driver.
B_GET_GRAPHICS_CARD_INFO, B_GET_GRAPHICS_CARD_HOOKS, B_GET_SCREEN_SPACES B_GET_REFRESH_RATES	Queries the driver for information such as the location of the hook functions, the supported screen configurations, and so on.
B_SET_INDEXED_COLOR, B_SET_SCREEN_GAMMA	Tells the driver to poke entries into its color map, and to set its color correction table.
B_CONFIG_GRAPHICS_CARD	Tells the driver to configure the frame buffer and turn on the display.

B_OPEN_GRAPHICS_CARD, graphics_card_spec

Tells the driver to open and initialize the graphics card specified by the *data* argument. *data* points to a **graphics_card_spec** structure, which has the following fields:

void *screen_base	The beginning of the card's memory.
void *io_base	The base address for the I/O registers that control the graphics card. Registers are at 16-bit offsets from the base address.
uint32 vendor_id	A number that identifies the manufacturer of the card's graphics chip, (as given by a register on the card).
uint32 device_id	A number that identifies the particular graphics chip of that manufacturer (as given by a register on the card).

The driver can initialize structures and perform other startup routines, but should wait for the B_CONFIG_GRAPHICS_CARD opcode before initializing the frame buffer or turning on the video display.

Return values:
> The function should return B_OK if the driver can open the card, and B_ERROR if not. If the driver returns B_ERROR, it will immediately get a B_CLOSE_GRAPHICS_CARD opcode.

B_CLOSE_GRAPHICS_CARD

Notifies the graphics card driver that it's about to be unloaded. The *data* argument and return value are ignored. .

B_GET_GRAPHICS_CARD_HOOKS

Asks the driver to supply a set of hook functions that the Application Server can call to carry out specific graphics tasks. See "Graphics Card Hook Functions" for more information.

A driver can expect this opcode soon after it's opened, and again any time the screen configuration changes.

Return values:
> The function should return B_OK if the driver can supply any hooks; a return of B_ERROR sets all the hook pointers to NULL.

B_GET_GRAPHICS_CARD_INFO, graphics_card_info

Asks the driver to supply information about itself and the current configuration of the screen. The driver provides this information by filling in the fields of the graphics_card_info structure that's passed through the *data* argument. *All* fields must be filled in, and they must *all* be valid:

int16 **version**	The version of the Be architecture for graphics cards that the driver was designed to work with.
int16 **id**	A driver-defined identifier for the driver.
void *frame_buffer	A pointer to the first byte of the frame buffer.
char **rgba_order**[4]	This field, which is intended to encode color component order, is currently ignored. The order of components is "bgra" for Intel processors and the BeBox, and "argb" for Power Mac-compatible machines.
int16 **flags**	A mask containing flags that describe the ability of the graphics card driver to perform particular tasks. (See below.)
int16 **bits_per_pixel**	The depth of the screen in bits per pixel—one of 8,15,16, or 32. Note that 15 bpp designates 5-5-5-1 encoding, as opposed to "true" 16-bit which designates 5-6-5 encoding. The nominal 15-bit format actually *uses* 16 bits; other "bits per pixel" API returns 16 bits for both formats, and differentiates the encodings through some other field (typically named "color space", or the like).
int32 **bytes_per_row**	The number of bytes required to represent a single row of pixel data in the frame buffer.
int16 **width**	The width of the display area in pixels.
int16 **height**	The height of the display area in pixels.

There are four `flags`:

B_CRT_CONTROL	Indicates that the driver is able to control in software, to any extent, the position or the size of the CRT display on the monitor.
B_GAMMA_CONTROL	Indicates that the driver is able to make gamma corrections that compensate for the particular characteristics of the display device.
B_FRAME_BUFFER_CONTROL	Indicates that the driver accepts the frame buffer opcodes (described in "Frame Buffer Opcodes").
B_PARALLEL_BUFFER_ACCESS	Enables parallel access to the frame buffer. If the card doesn't allow parallel access, the Game Kit's BDirectWindow class won't work in "window mode" (the class will still work in "full screen mode").

The driver will receive frequent `B_GET_GRAPHICS_CARD_INFO` requests. The `graphics_card_info` structure it supplies should always reflect the values currently in effect.

Return values:
> The function should return B_OK if the driver has filled in all fields with valid info. A return of B_ERROR causes the info structure to be ignored.

B_GET_REFRESH_RATES, refresh_rate_info

Asks the driver to place the current refresh rate, as well as the maximum and minimum rates, in the **refresh_rate_info** structure referred to by the *data* pointer. The structure contains these fields:

float **current**	The current refresh rate in Hertz.
float **min**	The minimum refresh rate (Hz) that the graphics card is capable of, given the current configuration.
float **max**	The maximum refresh rate (Hz) that the graphics card is capable of, given the current configuration.

Return values:
> The return value is ignored.

B_GET_SCREEN_SPACES

Asks the driver to provide a mask containing all possible configurations of pixel depth and screen dimensions (in pixels) that it supports. The mask is formed from the following constants (defined in *interface/GraphicsDefs.h*) and is returned through the *data* pointer:

B_8_BIT_640x480	B_15_BIT_640x480	B_16_BIT_640x480	B_32_BIT_640x480
B_8_BIT_800x600	B_15_BIT_800x600	B_16_BIT_800x600	B_32_BIT_800x600
B_8_BIT_1024x768	B_15_BIT_1024x768	B_16_BIT_1024x768	B_32_BIT_1024x768
B_8_BIT_1152x900	B_15_BIT_1152x900	B_16_BIT_1152x900	B_32_BIT_1152x900
B_8_BIT_1280x1024	B_15_BIT_1280x1024	B_16_BIT_1280x1024	B_32_BIT_1280x1024
B_8_BIT_1600x1200	B_15_BIT_1600x1200	B_16_BIT_1600x1200	B_32_BIT_1600x1200

WARNING

> Don't use the two reserved screen space constants (B_8_BIT_640x400 and B_FAKE_DEVICE) that are also defined in *interface/GraphicsDefs.h*.

Return values:
> The return value is ignored.

B_SET_INDEXED_COLOR, indexed_color

Tells the driver to poke a 32-bit RGB color value into a slot in its 8-bit color map. The index into the map and the color value are encoded in the fields of the **indexed_color** structure that's pointed to by *data*:

int32 **index**	The index (0-based) into the map.
rgb_color **color**	The full 32-bit color that should be associated with the index.

A driver can expect a series of these calls (one for each index in the color map) at startup time. Thereafter, it might get indexed color requests when an application modifies the color map, or when a Game Kit window returns control to the Application Server.

Return values:

The return value is ignored.

B_SET_SCREEN_GAMMA, screen_gamma

WARNING

This opcode is currently unused.

Tells the driver to set up a table for adjusting color values to correct for the peculiarities of the display device. This opcode is only meaningful to drivers that can make gamma corrections (i.e. those that set the `B_GAMMA_CONTROL` flag in response to a `B_GET_GRAPHICS_CARD_INFO` request).

The *data* argument points to a `screen_gamma` structure that contains "replacement arrays" for the three color components:

uint8 **red**[256]	Mappings for the red component.
uint8 **green**[256]	Mappings for the green component.
uint8 **blue**[256]	Mappings for the blue component.

The value at a given index replaces the index taken as a value. For example, if the value at `blue[152]` is 154, all blue component values of 152 are displayed as 154.

Return values:

The return value is ignored.

B_CONFIG_GRAPHICS_CARD, graphics_card_config

Tells the driver to configure the frame buffer and enable the display according to the values set in the **graphics_card_config** structure that the *data* argument points to. The structure contains the following fields:

uint32 **space**	A "screen space" constant that describes the size and depth of the frame buffer. The constants are listed under B_GET_SCREEN_SPACES, above.
float **refresh_rate**	The refresh rate of the screen in Hertz.
uint8 **h_position**	The horizontal position of the CRT display on the monitor.
uint8 **v_position**	The vertical position of the CRT display on the monitor.
uint8 **h_size**	The horizontal size of the CRT display on the monitor.
uint8 **v_size**	The vertical size of the CRT display on the monitor.

The `space` setting must be precisely adhered to. The driver should come as close as it can to the requested `refresh_rate`, but precise adherence isn't mandatory.

The last four fields are only meaningful to drivers that can control CRT positioning (i.e. those that set the B_CRT_CONTROL flag in response to a B_GET_GRAPHICS_CARD_INFO request). The values in these fields range from 0 through 100, with 50 as the default. Values less than 50 for `h_position` and `v_position` should move the display toward the left and top; greater than 50 should move it to the right and bottom. Values of less than 50 for `h_size` and `v_size` should make the display narrower and shorter, squeezing it into a smaller area; values greater than 50 should make it wider and taller.

The driver receives this opcode during the startup routine, and, thereafter, whenever the screen configuration needs to change (when the user plays with the Screen preferences, for example).

Return values:

> If the driver can configure the frame buffer as described by the `space` value, the function should return B_OK; otherwise, it should return B_ERROR.

Graphics Card Hook Functions

Declared in: be/add-ons/graphics/GraphicsCard.h

A graphics card driver can implement a set of hook functions that perform specific tasks on behalf of the Application Server and the Game Kit's BWindowScreen object. Drivers should implement as many of these functions as they can.

The Application Server asks the driver for the locations of its hook functions by passing the B_GET_GRAPHICS_CARD_HOOKS opcode. In response to this request, the driver writes an array of function pointers to *data*, cast as a `graphics_card_hook` pointer (described below). The `B_GET_GRAPHICS_CARD_HOOKS` request is made whenever the configuration of the frame buffer changes. The driver can thus provide hook functions that are tailored to specific frame buffer configurations.

The system can accommodate B_GRAPHICS_HOOK_COUNT (48) hook functions. Currently, only the first 14 functions are used. These functions fall into four groups:

- **Indices 0-2: Cursor management**. Drivers must implement all three of these functions, or none of them.

- **Indices 3-9, 12, and 13: Drawing functions**. These are specific drawing tasks, such as drawing a line or filling a rectangle. A driver can implement as many of these as it wishes.

- **Index 10: Driver/Application Server synchronization**. Drivers should implement this function only if the other hook functions are performed asynchronously.

- **Index 11: Color inversion**. This function inverts the colors in a rectangle.

The graphics_card_hook Type

All pointers in the hook function array are declared to be of type `graphics_card_hook`:

>   typedef void (***graphics_card_hook**)(void)

The code that fills *data* will look something like this:

```
int32 control_graphics_card(uint32 opcode, void *data)
{
    switch (opcode) {
    ...
    case B_GET_GRAPHICS_CARD_HOOKS:
        ((graphics_card_hook *)data)[0] = (graphics_card_hook)define_cursor;
        ((graphics_card_hook *)data)[1] = (graphics_card_hook)move_cursor;
    ...
    }
}
```

Despite the `graphics_card_hook` declaration, each function has its own set of arguments and returns an integer error code. All functions should return `B_OK` if they're successful, and `B_ERROR` if not.

Unimplemented Functions

All hook functions that the driver doesn't implement (including indices 14–47) should be set to `NULL`. For example:

```
((graphics_card_hook *)data)[14] = (graphics_card_hook)NULL;
```

A driver can chose to nullify functions it *does* implement if it wants to defer to the Application Server version.

WARNING

Don't implement a function to simply (always) return B_ERROR. If you want to declare a hook as a no-op, you must pass NULL as the pointer.

Coordinate Spaces

Most hook function coordinates are in depth-independent "frame buffer space" (the exceptions are well noted below). In other words, a coordinate pair gives the location of a pixel in the frame buffer independent of the buffer's depth; pixel (0, 0) is at the left top corner of the frame buffer.

Naming

You can name the functions whatever you wish—the Application Server finds the functions by index in the hook function array. For convenience and clarity, the following descriptions suggest default names.

Hook Functions

Index 0: define_cursor()

```
int32 define_cursor(uchar *xorMask, uchar *andMask,
                    int32 width, int32 height,
                    int32 hotX, int32 hotY)
```

Tells the driver to create a cursor image as defined by the arguments. The first two arguments, *xorMask* and *andMask*, are bit vectors that represent the cursor image laid out in concatenated, byte-aligned rows (top to bottom). Parallel bits from the two vectors define the color of a single cursor pixel:

xorMask	andMask	Meaning
0	0	Transparent; let the color of the underlying screen pixel show through.
1	0	Inversion; invert the color of the screen pixel.
0	1	White; replace the screen pixel with a white cursor pixel.
1	1	Black; replace the screen pixel with a black cursor pixel.

The second two arguments, *width* and *height*, are the size of the cursor image in pixels. (Currently, the Application Server supports only 16x16 cursors.)

The (*hotX*, *hotY*) arguments define the "hot spot"—the pixel that precisely locates the cursor. Hot spot coordinates are relative to the cursor rectangle itself, where the pixel at the left top corner of the cursor image is (0, 0) and the one at the right bottom corner is (*width*-1, *height*-1).

If the cursor is currently showing (i.e. not hidden), this function should display the cursor image.

Index 1: move_cursor()

> int32 **move_cursor**(int32 *screenX*, int32 *screenY*)

Tells the driver to move the cursor so the hot spot corresponds to (*screenX*, *screenY*). The arguments are display area coordinates (*not* frame buffer coordinates).

Index 2: show_cursor()

> int32 **show_cursor**(bool *flag*)

If the *flag* argument is `true`, the driver should show the cursor image on-screen; if it's `false`, it should remove the cursor from the screen.

If the driver is asked to show the cursor before `define_cursor()` is called, it should show it at (0, 0).

Index 3: draw_line_with_8_bit_depth()

> int32 **draw_line_with_8_bit_depth**(int32 *startX*, int32 *endX*,
>   int32 *startY*, int32 *endY*,
>   uint8 *colorIndex*,
>   bool *clipToRect*,
>   int16 *clipLeft*, int16 *clipTop*, int16 *clipRight*, int16 *clipBottom*)

Tells the driver to draw a straight, 8-bit color, minimally thin line.

* The line begins at (*startX*, *startY*) and ends at (*endX*, *endY*), inclusive. The arguments are frame buffer coordinates.
* *colorIndex* gives the color of the line as an index into the 8-bit color table.
* If *clipToRect* is `true`, the function should draw only the portion of the line that lies within the clipping rectangle defined by the last four arguments. The sides of the rectangle are included in the drawing area. If *clipToRect* is `false`, the final four arguments should be ignored.

To produce minimal thinness, the line should color only one pixel per row or column, as the absolute slope of the line is more or less than 45 degrees; in other words, the line should move between rows or columns on the diagonal, not by overlapping. Here's how you should (and shouldn't) produce a mostly vertical line; for the mostly horizontal version, turn your head sideways:

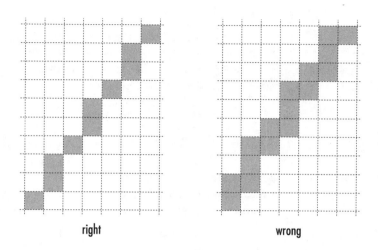

right   **wrong**

Index 4: draw_line_with_32_bit_depth()

> int32 **draw_line_with_32_bit_depth**(int32 *startX*, int32 *endX*,
>   int32 *startY*, int32 *endY*,
>   uint32 *color*,
>   bool *clipToRect*,
>   int16 *clipLeft*, int16 *clipTop*, int16 *clipRight*, int16 *clipBottom*)

This is the same as `draw_line_with_8_bit_depth()` except for the *color* argument. Here, *color* is a 32-bit value with 8-bit red, green, blue, and alpha components. The components are arranged in the order that the driver specified when it received the B_GET_GRAPHICS_CARD_INFO request.

See also: "B_GET_GRAPHICS_CARD_INFO, graphics_card_info"

Index 5: draw_rect_with_8_bit_depth()

> int32 **draw_rect_with_8_bit_depth**(int32 *left*, int32 *top*, int32 *right*, int32 *bottom*,
>   uint8 *colorIndex*)

Tells the driver to fill a rectangle, specified by the first four arguments, with the color at *colorIndex* in the 8-bit color table. The arguments are frame buffer coordinates. The sides of the rectangle should be included in the area being filled.

Index 6: draw_rect_with_32_bit_depth()

> int32 **draw_rect_with_32_bit_depth**(int32 *left*, int32 *top*, int32 *right*, int32 *bottom*,
> uint32 *color*)

This is the same as `draw_rect_with_8_bit_depth()` except for the *color* argument. Here, *color* is a 32-bit value with 8-bit red, green, blue, and alpha components. The components are arranged in the order that the driver specified when it received the `B_GET_GRAPHICS_CARD_INFO` request.

See also: "B_GET_GRAPHICS_CARD_INFO, graphics_card_info"

Index 7: blit()

> int32 **blit**(int32 *sourceX*, int32 *sourceY*,
> int32 *destinationX*, int32 *destinationY*,
> int32 *width*, int32 *height*)

Tells the driver to copy pixel data from a source rectangle to a destination rectangle. All coordinates and sizes are in frame buffer space. The left top pixel of the source rectangle is at (*sourceX, sourceY*) in the frame buffer. The left top pixel of the destination rectangle is at (*destinationX, destinationY*) in the frame buffer. Both rectangles are *width* pixels wide and *height* pixels high. The *width* and *height* arguments will always contain positive values, and the rectangles are guaranteed to lie wholly within the frame buffer.

Index 8: draw_array_with_8_bit_depth(), indexed_color_line

> int32 **draw_array_with_8_bit_depth**(indexed_color_line **array*, int32 *numItems*,
> bool *clipToRect*,
> int16 *clipLeft*, int16 *clipTop*, int16 *clipRight*, int16 *clipBottom*)

Tells the driver to draw an array of lines in 8-bit depth. The line *array* holds a total of *numItems*. Each item is specified as an `indexed_color_line` structure, which contains the following fields (all coordinates are in frame buffer space):

int16 **x1**	The *x* coordinate of one end of the line.
int16 **y1**	The *y* coordinate of one end of the line.
int16 **x2**	The *x* coordinate of the other end of the line.
int16 **y2**	The *y* coordinate of the other end of the line.
uint8 **color**	The color of the line, expressed as an index into the color map.

If *clipToRect* is `true`, the function should draw only the portions of the lines that lie within the clipping rectangle defined by the last four arguments. The sides of the rectangle are included in the drawing area. If *clipToRect* is `false`, the final four arguments should be ignored.

The lines should be minimally thin, as described under "Index 3: draw_line_with_8_bit_depth()".

Index 9: draw_array_with_32_bit_depth(), rgb_color_line

> int32 **draw_array_with_32_bit_depth**(rgb_color_line **array*, int32 *numItems*,
>   bool *clipToRect*,
>   int16 *clipLeft*, int16 *clipTop*, int16 *clipRight*, int16 *clipBottom*)

Except for the color specification, which is encoded in the `rgb_color_line` structure, this is the same as `draw_array_with_8_bit_depth()`. The `rgb_color_line` structure contains these fields:

int16 **x1**	The *x* coordinate of one end of the line.
int16 **y1**	The *y* coordinate of one end of the line.
int16 **x2**	The *x* coordinate of the other end of the line.
int16 **y2**	The *y* coordinate of the other end of the line.
rgb_color **color**	The color of the line, expressed as a full 32-bit value.

Index 10: sync()

> int32 **sync**(void)

The driver should implement this function to block until all other currently-executing hook functions have finished. (More accurately, you only have to wait for those hook functions that actually touch the frame buffer.) The return value is ignored.

You should only implement this function if the card can perform any of the hook functions asynchronously. If all hook functions are synchronous, you should set the index 10 function to NULL.

After receiving a `sync()` call, your driver won't receive anymore hook functions until `sync()` returns. Thus, you don't have to guard against in-coming hook functions while sitting in `sync()`.

Index 11: invert_rect()

> int32 **invert_rect**(int32 *left*, int32 *top*, int32 *right*, int32 *bottom*)

Tells the driver to invert the colors in the rectangle specified by the arguments. The sides of the rectangle are included in the inversion.

Index 12: draw_line_with_16_bit_depth()

int32 **draw_line_with_16_bit_depth**(int32 *startX*, int32 *endX*,
                int32 *startY*, int32 *endY*,
                uint16 *color*,
                bool *clipToRect*,
                int16 *clipLeft*, int16 *clipTop*, int16 *clipRight*, int16 *clipBottom*)

This is the same as `draw_rect_with_8_bit_depth()` except for the *color* argument. Here, *color* is a 16-bit value with red, green, blue, and (possibly) alpha components. The components are arranged in the order that the driver specified when it received the `B_GET_GRAPHICS_CARD_INFO` request.

See also: "B_GET_GRAPHICS_CARD_INFO, graphics_card_info"

Index 13: draw_rect_with_16_bit_depth()

int32 **draw_rect_with_16_bit_depth**(int32 *left*, int32 *top*, int32 *right*, int32 *bottom*,
                uint16 *color*)

This is the same as `draw_rect_with_8_bit_depth()` except for the *color* argument. Here, *color* is a 16-bit value with red, green, blue, and (possibly) alpha components. The components are arranged in the order that the driver specified when it received the `B_GET_GRAPHICS_CARD_INFO` request.

See also: "B_GET_GRAPHICS_CARD_INFO, graphics_card_info"

Driver Cloning Opcodes

Declared in: be/add-ons/graphics/GraphicsCard.h

The Game Kit's BWindowScreen class gives an application access to the graphics card's accelerated graphics functions ("hook" functions) by "cloning" the graphics driver that was initially loaded by the Application Server. The clone is created and managed through the four opcodes:

- `B_GET_INFO_FOR_CLONE` and `B_GET_INFO_FOR_CLONE_SIZE` are sent to the "source" driver to retrieve information that's used to create the clone.

- `B_SET_CLONED_GRAPHICS_CARD` and `B_CLOSE_CLONED_GRAPHICS_CARD` are sent to the clone to tell it to initialize itself, and to tell it that it's about to be closed.

While the clone is active, the Server suspends its graphic operations. When the clone is finished, the Server resumes control—and assumes that the card is in the same state as it was before the clone took over. In other words, the clone must leave the card in the same state that it found it.

Opcodes

B_GET_INFO_FOR_CLONE

Tells the driver to write information about its current state into the location referred to by the *data* pointer. This information is passed to the clone (in a B_SET_CLONED_GRAPHICS_CARD request) so the clone can duplicate the state of the driver.

The structure of the information is defined by the driver. The structure should contain the driver's software settings, such as the screen configuration and frame buffer location. Hardware settings, such as the color map, don't need to be cloned.

For example, if the structure is called info_for_clone, driver code might look something like this:

```
case B_GET_INFO_FOR_CLONE:
    ((info_for_clone *)data)->depth = info.bits_per_pixel;
    ((info_for_clone *)data)->height = info.height;
    ((info_for_clone *)data)->width = info.width;
    ((info_for_clone *)data)->row_byte = info.bytes_per_row;
    ((info_for_clone *)data)->frame_base = info.frame_buffer;
    ((info_for_clone *)data)->io_base = spec.io_base;
    ((info_for_clone *)data)->available_mem = unused_memory;
    ((info_for_clone *)data)->refresh_rate = rate.current;
    . . .
    break;
```

The driver can receive numerous B_GET_INFO_FOR_CLONE requests while the clone is active.

Return values:

If the driver can provide the clone info, the function should return B_OK. If it returns B_ERROR, the clone won't be created.

B_GET_INFO_FOR_CLONE_SIZE

Asks the driver for the size (in bytes) of its "clone info" structure (the structure it will provide in response to a B_GET_INFO_FOR_CLONE opcode). The size should be written to the *data* pointer as an int32. For example:

```
*((int32 *)data) = sizeof(info_for_clone);
```

Return values:

If the driver can provide the size of the clone info, the function should return B_OK. If it returns B_ERROR, the clone won't be created.

B_SET_CLONED_GRAPHICS_CARD

Sent to the clone to tell it to initialize itself. The *data* pointer contains (a copy of) the structure that the driver provided in response to a `B_GET_INFO_FOR_CLONE` request. The clone should read the structure and set all the parameters that are provided.

Note that this is the first opcode that the clone will receive; it *doesn't* receive a `B_OPEN_GRAPHICS_CARD` opcode. It subsequently will receive this opcode many more times—whenever it must be synchronized with the driver loaded by the Application Server.

B_CLOSE_CLONED_GRAPHICS_CARD

Tells the clone that it's about to be unloaded. The *data* pointer and return value are ignored. The clone should implement this function to restore the previous (i.e. "pre-clone") state of the driver.

Frame Buffer Opcodes

Declared in: be/add-ons/graphics/GraphicsCard.h

If the graphics card driver allows it, the BWindowScreen class in the Game Kit will provide direct control of the frame buffer. A driver announces that it allows this control by including the `B_FRAME_BUFFER_CONTROL` constant when responding to a `B_GET_GRAPHICS_CARD_INFO` request. (See also "B_GET_GRAPHICS_CARD_INFO, graphics_card_info".)

The Game Kit's frame buffer control is performed through the four opcodes described below. All four opcodes use the **frame_buffer_info** structure to pass data to the driver. The structure contains eight fields:

int16 **bits_per_pixel**	The frame buffer depth.
int16 **bytes_per_row**	The size (in bytes) of a frame buffer row.
int16 **width**	The width of the frame buffer, in pixels.
int16 **height**	The height of the frame buffer, in pixels.
int16 **display_width**	The width of the display area, in pixels.
int16 **display_height**	The height of the display area, in pixels.
int16 **display_x**	The frame buffer column that's mapped to the leftmost column on the screen, where columns are indicated by a left-to-right index beginning with 0.
int16 **display_y**	The frame buffer row that's mapped to the topmost row on the screen, where rows are indicated by a top-to-bottom index beginning with 0.

The first four fields describe the frame buffer itself (these are the "frame buffer fields"); the final four describe the the part of the frame buffer that's displayed on-screen (these are the "display area fields"). This distinction permits the display area to be moved within a (possibly) much larger frame buffer, and also facilitates buffered drawing (since you can set up display area partitions).

In all cases, the driver should return B_OK if it can comply with the request, and B_ERROR if not.

Opcodes

B_PROPOSE_FRAME_BUFFER

Asks the driver if it can handle a particular frame buffer width and depth, as encoded in the width and bits_per_pixel fields of the frame_buffer_info argument. If the driver accepts, it should set the other two frame buffer fields and return B_OK:

- In the bytes_per_row field, it should write the minimum number of bytes required to store each row of pixel data given the proposed depth and width.
- In the height field, it should report the maximum number of pixel rows it can provide given the other dimensions

The driver shouldn't actually configure the frame buffer yet; it should wait for a B_SET_FRAME_BUFFER opcode. (But note that B_PROPOSE_FRAME_BUFFER *isn't* guaranteed to be sent before a B_SET_FRAME_BUFFER request.)

If the driver can't accommodate the proposed dimensions, it should place –1 in the bytes_per_row and height fields and return B_ERROR.

The display area fields needn't be set in either case.

B_SET_FRAME_BUFFER

Tells the driver to configure the frame buffer according to the description in the frame_buffer_info argument. All eight fields in the structure contain meaningful values.

B_MOVE_DISPLAY_AREA

Tells the driver to move the display area so its left top pixel is at the location specified by the display_x and display_y fields of the frame_buffer_info argument. The other fields should be ignored.

Building and Installing a Driver

The section tells you how to prepare, compile, and install your graphics driver.

- In your source code, export the `control_graphics_card()` declaration:

```
__declspec(dllexport)
int32 control_graphics_card(uint32 op, void *data);
```

- Tell the linker to produce a shared library. If you're using the BeIDE, go to the **Settings** window, pop open the **Project** list, click on **PPC Project** or **x86 Project**, and select "Shared Library" in the **Project Type** popup menu. If you're using `make`, include the `-G` option.

- Since it's loaded by the Application Server (which is, itself, a user-level app), your graphics card drivers can link against any of the BeOS libraries.

- You can name driver whatever you wish except for "stub", which is reserved for the generic driver provided by Be.

The Application Server looks for an appropriate graphics card driver in the following directories (in this order):

1. */fd/beos/system/add-ons/app_server* (on a floppy)

2. */boot/home/config/add-ons/app_server*

3. */boot/beos/system/add-ons/app_server*

Finished, publishable drivers should be installed in #2, */boot/home/config/add-ons/app_server*. Do *not* install in the *beos/system* directory. While you're working on your driver, you'll probably want to load it from one of the floppy directories (so you don't overwrite a working driver with your experimental one).

For each driver it tries to load, the Application Server prints a message to the serial port:

```
Try to hire add-on name as graphic driver...
```

Where *name* is the path of the candidate driver. If the driver is rejected, the Server prints:

```
name refuse the job
```

When it finds an acceptable driver, it prints:

```
name is the new graphic driver...
```

If it can't find a driver, the Server looks for the generic driver called "stub".

Device Drivers

Device Drivers

WARNING

The device driver architecture will change in BeOS Release 4. The API described here will continue to be supported, but the new API will be easier to use and more efficient.

A device driver ties an input/output hardware device to the computer's operating system. All drivers are created as add-ons that are loaded by a running application. This chapter discusses drivers that are loaded by the kernel.

The drivers that the kernel loads must play by these rules:

- The driver must implement a set of pre-defined entry points functions. The kernel invokes these functions as it loads and runs the driver. The entry point functions are described within the context of an example driver implementation in the section "A Sample Device Driver".

- In addition to the functions that it defines and implements itself, a driver can only call system functions that the kernel specifically exports for driver use. Exported system functions are described in "Functions for Kernel Drivers".

- To find the hardware that it's driving, a driver has to ask the system for the devices that are attached to the system. The functions and macros that search for PCI and Plug and Play devices are described in "PCI Functions" and "Plug and Play".

- The driver must be compiled as an add-on module and it must be installed in a directory where the kernel can find it. See "Building and Installing a Kernel Driver" for details.

A Sample Device Driver

The best way to learn something is to do it, so let's explore the design of a simple device driver. This section will lead you through the process of creating a device driver for a fictional PCI card called a BeGadget. Although this sample examines the creation of a PCI device driver, the basic concepts are similar for all types of devices.

The BeGadget card supports four logical devices, each of which can be individually opened and accessed. The card has a single base register, which serves as a pointer to the memory-mapped control registers for the four logical devices. Each of these four logical devices is capable of both reading from and writing to system memory via DMA.

The card has two special-purpose registers, both of which are 32 bits wide. The first is a special self-test register, which can be examined to determine whether or not the card is functioning properly. It is located at offset 0x80 in PCI configuration space on the card. The value in the register is zero if the card is functioning properly and non-zero otherwise. The other special-purpose register is a reset register, located at 0x84. Writing to this register resets the BeGadget card to its default status. These registers will be referred to as `GADGET_CONFIG_STATUS` and `GADGET_CONFIG_RESET`, respectively, and are defined with these names in the source code for the driver.

Reads from and writes to these devices are initiated using a 32-bit command register. There is one command register for each of the four logical devices on the card. To perform I/O, the BeGadget card requires that we write to this register three times. The first write specifies the command to issue (read or write). The second write to the register specifies the address of the buffer in memory. The third write specifies the number of bytes to read or write.

In addition, each of the virtual devices has a speed register, which controls the rate at which data transfers between the BeGadget card and the computer.

This sample driver will allow us to investigate the use of interrupts for managing device I/O operations, coping with memory-mapped I/O in virtual memory space, and using semaphores to synchronize access to the hardware.

NOTE

Because the BeGadget device is fictional, there is no actual hardware on which the BeGadget driver can be tested. The `DEBUG_NO_HW` #define is provided to allow us to build and run the driver without a BeGadget card; if `DEBUG_NO_HW` is 1, extra code is compiled which allows the driver to simulate functioning without a card available.

Entry Points

These entry points are called by the kernel to manage your driver as a whole. Functions by these names must exist in your driver, since the kernel calls them explicitly. These entry points are:

Entry Point	Description
init_hardware()	Called once by the kernel during system startup to allow the driver to reset the hardware to a known default state. If your device doesn't need initialization, you don't have to provide this function.
init_driver()	Called whenever the driver is loaded into memory. This allows the driver to set up any memory space needed, as well as to initialize any global variables it uses. If your driver doesn't need to be initialized, you don't have to provide this function.
uninit_driver()	Called whenever the driver is unloaded from memory. This can be used to release any system resources allocated by init_driver(). If your driver doesn't need to be uninitialized, you don't have to provide this function.
publish_devices()	Called by the kernel to obtain a list of device names supported by the driver.
find_device()	Called by the kernel when it needs to obtain a list of the hook functions for a particular device.

init_hardware()

The init_hardware() function is called by the kernel when the BeOS first starts up, and is only called once. This allows the driver to put the device into a known initial state. The init_hardware() function should verify that the device is attached to the computer, then initialize it to a stable state.

This function should return B_OK if the hardware was successfully initialized or B_ERROR if an error occurred or the device is not present; if B_OK is not returned, the kernel will not use the driver.

In the case of the BeGadget card, there are three steps to initializing the device:

- Verify that a BeGadget card is installed in the computer.
- Check the self-test register on the card to ensure that it is functioning properly.
- Reset the card by writing to the reset register on the BeGadget card.

Before we look at the init_hardware() function, let's look at the lookup_pci_device() function, which is used by the BeGadget driver to search the PCI bus for specific devices.

```
static bool lookup_pci_device (short vendor, short device, pci_info
*returned_info)
{
```

```
    int i;

    for (i = 0; ; i++) {
        if (get_nth_pci_info (i, returned_info) != B_OK)
            return false;/* Error or end of device list */

        /* Compare the vendor ID and device ID of the scanned
           device with the desired information. If it is a
           match, break out of the loop so we can return it. */

        if (returned_info->vendor_id == vendor &&
            returned_info->device_id == device)
            break;
    }
    return true; /* Device was found */
}
```

This code iterates through all available PCI devices by calling the `get_nth_pci_info()` function provided by the kernel, each time passing in the index number into the device list and a pointer to the `pci_info` structure called *returned_info*. If an error is reported by `get_nth_pci_info()`, `lookup_pci_device()` returns `false`, thereby indicating that no matching device was found. Each device's vendor and device ID numbers are compared with those specified by the input parameters *vendor_id* and *device_id*. When a match is found, `true` is returned, with the `pci_info` structure filled out with the information about the BeGadget card.

Now let's have a look at the `init_hardware()` handler.

```
status_t init_hardware (void)
{
    pci_infoinfo;
    int32  val;

    /* Get the device information */

    if (!lookup_pci_device (GADGET_DEV_VENDOR_ID,
                            GADGET_DEV_DEVICE_ID, &info))
        return ENODEV;

#if DEBUG_NO_HW
    return true;/* for debugging purposes */
#endif

    /* Check the self-test register */

    val = read_pci_config (info.bus, info.device, info.function,
        GADGET_CONFIG_STATUS,/* offset in config space */
        4         /* size of register */
    );

    if (val)      /* Check the self-test result */
        return ENODEV;/* Return no device found if failed */
```

```
    /* Reset the BeGadget card */

    write_pci_config (info.bus, info.device, info.function,
        GADGET_CONFIG_RESET,/* offset in config space */
        4,          /* size of register */
        0           /* initialization value */
    );

    return B_OK;/* We've successfully initialized the device */
}
```

This function starts by calling the `lookup_pci_device()` function to obtain the PCI device information record about the BeGadget card. As a helpful side effect, we know that if it reports an error, the device was not found on the PCI bus, so we can immediately return the `ENODEV` return code, which tells the kernel there is no BeGadget installed in the computer.

Once it has been determined that the BeGadget device is installed, `read_pci_config()` is used to read the value of the BeGadget's self-test register. If the self-test register reports a non-zero result, which indicates that the card is malfunctioning, we again report an `ENODEV` result code.

Finally, the device is reset by using the `write_pci_config()` function to write to the 32-bit reset register on the BeGadget card. Then the result code `B_OK` is returned to tell the kernel that the device has been initialized.

init_driver()

The `init_driver()` function is called by the kernel whenever the driver is loaded from disk into memory. This function is used to initialize global variables used by the driver and to allocate any system resources required by the driver as a whole, such as semaphores or memory. This function should return `B_OK` if the driver is safely initialized, or `B_ERROR` if the driver should not be used for whatever reason.

If individual logical devices have system resource needs of their own, it is usually better to allocate those resources when the device is opened, to preserve system resources when they aren't needed.

For devices that utilize memory-mapped I/O, the driver must map the physical memory locations into the virtual memory system. This should be done when initializing the driver, and the memory should be unmapped when `uninit_driver()` is called.

The BeGadget `init_driver()` function will perform the following three tasks:

* Verify that the BeGadget card is still installed, just to be safe.
* Obtain the address of the memory-mapped I/O space assigned to the device.

- Map the memory-mapped I/O locations for the device into the virtual memory system.

Let's have a look at the code.

```
status_t
init_driver (void)
{
    pci_info  info;
    int32     base;
    int32     size;

    /* Get the info record for the device */

    if (!lookup_pci_device (GADGET_DEV_VENDOR_ID,
                            GADGET_DEV_DEVICE_ID, &info))
        return ENODEV;

    /* Get the base address and size of the registers */

    base = info.u.h0.base_registers[0];/* get address of the reg */
    size = info.u.h0.base_register_sizes[0];/* get reg size */

    /* Round the base address of the register down to
       the nearest page boundary. */
    base = base & ~(B_PAGE_SIZE - 1);

    /* Adjust the size of our register space based on
       the rounding we just did. */
    size += info.u.h0.base_registers[0] - base;

    /* And round up to the nearest page size boundary,
       so that we occupy only complete pages, and not
       any partial pages. */
    size = (size + (B_PAGE_SIZE - 1)) & ~(B_PAGE_SIZE - 1);

    /* Now we ask the kernel to create a memory area
       which locks this I/O space in memory. */

    reg_area = map_physical_memory (
        "gadget_pci_device_regs",
        (void *) base,
        size,
        B_ANY_KERNEL_ADDRESS,
        B_READ_AREA + B_WRITE_AREA,
        &reg_base
    );

    /* Negative results from map_physical_memory() are
       errors. If we got an error, return that. */

    if (reg_area < 0)
        return reg_area;
```

```
   /* Note that there are no open devices on the card and
      return B_OK */

   is_open = 0;/* no devices open yet */
   return B_OK;
}
```

The `lookup_pci_device()` function is used to obtain the `pci_info` record for the BeGadget device. Again, it has the beneficial side effect of verifying the presence of the BeGadget card. We then look into the `pci_info` record for the device to obtain the physical address assigned to the card's base registers in memory as well as the size of the physical memory range into which the registers are mapped.

Then we round the physical address down to the beginning of the page on which the registers lie, and round the size up to the nearest full page, so that we know exactly which pages of memory need to be mapped.

Once we know which pages need to be mapped, we use the `map_physical_memory()` call to map the I/O registers into the virtual address space. This function creates a new area named "gadget_pci_device_regs". The physical address is specified by *base*, and the address as mapped into virtual memory is returned in *reg_base*. We specify through flags that the memory is readable and writable (`B_READ_AREA` + `B_WRITE_AREA`) and that it can be located anywhere within the kernel's address space (`B_ANY_KERNEL_ADDRESS`).

If `map_physical_memory()` returns a negative number, it is an error code, and we return that error code. Otherwise we zero the `is_open` variable, which is a bitfield representing which logical devices we control are open; at this point, none of them are open. Finally, we return the `B_OK` result code, since we have successfully initialized the driver.

uninit_driver()

When your driver is about to be unloaded from memory by the kernel, your `uninit_driver()` function is called. This function should dispose of any system resources allocated by your `init_driver()` function, including memory areas used to manage your I/O memory.

The BeGadget `uninit_driver()` function doesn't need to do much; the I/O memory which was mapped by `init_driver()` must be released.

```
void
uninit_driver (void)
{
   delete_area (reg_area);/* Dispose of I/O space memory area */
}
```

The BeGadget driver simply deletes the memory area created in `init_driver()` for the purpose of mapping the I/O memory into virtual memory. This is the only system resource allocated by our `init_driver()` function, so that's all we have to release here.

publish_devices()

The `publish_devices()` function is called by the kernel when the kernel needs to know the names of the devices your driver supports. This function's responsibilities are very simple:

- Determine the names of the devices supported by the driver. This can be done either by having a preset static list of device names, or by constructing a list of names on the fly.

- Return a pointer to the device name list.

The `publish_devices()` function in the BeGadget driver simply returns a pointer to a static list of four device names. The code looks like this:

```
const char**
publish_devices(void)
{
    return name_list;/* Return a pointer to the device name list */
}
```

The `name_list`, which contains the names of the devices, is:

```
static char*name_list[] = {
    "begadget/gadget1",
    "begadget/gadget2",
    "begadget/gadget3",
    "begadget/gadget4",
    0
};
```

These names represent a portion of a pathname located in the */dev* directory. Each of these names is appended to */dev*, so the devices are accessed by client applications via their full names:

- */dev/begadget/gadget1*
- */dev/begadget/gadget2*
- */dev/begadget/gadget3*
- */dev/begadget/gadget4*

When a client application wants to open the second virtual device on the BeGadget card for writing, it would call the POSIX `open()` function like this:

```
int fd = open("/dev/begadget/gadget2", O_WRONLY);
```

find_device()

When a request is made for access to a particular device, the kernel calls the driver's `find_device()` function to obtain pointers to the hook functions which handle specific I/O operations. The kernel passes into this function the name of the device it is trying to locate. The `find_device()` function returns a pointer to a structure that lists the driver's hook functions.

These hook functions are called by the kernel to handle specific operations, such as opening, closing, reading, and writing the device. If the device is not handled by the driver, the `find_device()` function should return NULL.

Before we look at the BeGadget driver's `find_device()` function, let's take a quick look at an internal utility function implemented by BeGadget for determining the virtual device number of a device based on its name.

```
static int
lookup_device_name (const char *name)
{
    int i;

    for (i = 0; name_list[i]; i++)
        if (!strcmp (name_list[i], name))
            return i;
    return -1;    /* Invalid device name */
}
```

The `lookup_device_name()` function accepts as input a virtual device name (such as *begadget/gadget3*) and returns the virtual device number of that device, or -1 if the device isn't handled by the BeGadget driver.

All this code does is scan the static list of device names supported by the BeGadget driver and return the index number into the array of the matching device name. The result is therefore an integer between zero and three. If no matching name is found, -1 is returned.

This function is used in several places throughout the BeGadget driver, including the `find_device()` hook function, to which we now turn our attention.

```
device_hooks *
find_device (const char *name)
{
    if (lookup_device_name (name) >= 0)
        return &my_device_hooks;/* Return hooks list */

    return NULL; /* Device not found */
}
```

Because of the useful `lookup_device_name()` function we've already implemented, all `find_device()` needs to do is call `lookup_device_name()` to determine whether or not the device exists. If it returns a non-negative number, we return a pointer to `my_device_hooks`, which is a structure that lists the hook functions required by the kernel. Otherwise we return `NULL`, indicating to the kernel that the BeGadget driver does not support the device requested.

Since all four devices handled by the BeGadget driver can be handled by the same hook functions, we always return a pointer to the same list of hooks.

The device hooks are specified as follows.

```
static device_hooks my_device_hooks = {
    &pci_open,
    &pci_close,
    &pci_free,
    &pci_control,
    &pci_read,
    &pci_write
};
```

These functions provide support for the C `open()`, `close()`, `read()`, and `write()` functions, all of which are POSIX-compliant, plus the `ioctl()` function. The free hook function (called `pci_free()` in the BeGadget driver) is a special hook which operates in conjunction with the close hook. This will be discussed in greater detail when we look into the `pci_close()` and `pci_free()` functions later in this section.

Hook Functions

When the BeOS kernel needs to perform a specific operation on a device, it does so by calling a hook function provided by the driver for that device. The hook functions your driver must provide are:

Hook	Description
open	Handles the POSIX `open()` function. This function should prepare a device for reading or writing.
close	Handles the POSIX `close()` function. This function is called by a client program when it has finished using the device.
free	The free hook releases a device after all I/O transactions have been completed. It does not directly correspond to any POSIX or other C function.
read	Handles the POSIX `read()` function. This function reads data from the device into system memory.
write	Handles the POSIX `write()` function. This function writes data from system memory to the device.
control	Handles the `ioctl()` function. This function provides the mechanism by which the system, and client programs, can control how the device functions.

The difference between the close and free hooks is a critical one. In a multithreaded environment such as the BeOS, it is entirely possible for a client program to close a driver before all I/O transactions have completed. Because of this, it is important that the close hook not perform any actions that might interrupt the flow of data.

This is why there is also a free hook function. The free hook is called by the kernel after all I/O operations on a closed device have been concluded. The free handler should perform any necessary deallocation of resources or other activities related to closing the device after a transaction.

To better understand how these hook functions operate, let's take a look at the BeGadget driver's implementations of each them.

pci_open()

This function handles the open hook for the BeGadget driver, and is called by the kernel to handle the POSIX `open()` call. The kernel passes the `pci_open()` function the name of the virtual device to open, such as *begadget/gadget2*, as well as the open flags. Also provided is a pointer to a 32-bit space in which we can store a pointer to a "cookie."

A cookie is a device-specific piece of information which can be used to track device status information. The open hook function creates the cookie for the device when it is opened; from then on, all other hook functions receive a pointer to this cookie for identification and data storage purposes.

The cookies used by the BeGadget driver have the PCI information record stored in them, as well as a copy of the device's ID number and a pointer to the registers for the device.

Let's have a look at the open hook function for the BeGadget driver, then examine how it works.

```
static status_t
pci_open(const char *name, uint32 flags, void **cookie)
{
    dev_info*d;
    int        id;
    int32  mask;
    status_terr;
    char    sem_name [B_OS_NAME_LENGTH];

    /* Get the device ID by looking at the name. */
    id = lookup_device_name (name);
    if (id < 0)
        return EINVAL;/* Invalid device name */

    /* Check to be sure if the device is in use; if not,
        set the flag that says it is */

    mask = 1 << id;/* Construct a mask for the bit */
```

```
        if (atomic_or (&is_open, mask) & mask)
            return B_BUSY;/* The device is already in use */

        /* Allocate a cookie for the device */

        err = B_NO_MEMORY;
        d = (dev_info *) malloc (sizeof (dev_info));
        if (!d)
            goto err0;/* Unable to allocate the cookie */

        /* Locate the device and fill out the rest of the cookie */

        err = ENODEV;/* If we fail, we'll report this error */
        if (!lookup_pci_device (GADGET_DEV_VENDOR_ID,
                                GADGET_DEV_DEVICE_ID, &d->pci))
            goto err1;/* We couldn't find the device */

        /* Set up other fields in the cookie */
        d->id = id;
        d->regs = (dev_regs *) reg_base + id;

        /* Allocate the hardware locking semaphore and make the
           system team its owner */

        sprintf (sem_name, "gadget dev %d hw_lock", id);/* create the sem name */
        d->hw_lock = err = create_sem (1, sem_name);/* create the semaphore */
        if (err < 0) /* If an error occurred, bail out */
            goto err1;
        set_sem_owner(err, B_SYSTEM_TEAM);

        /* Allocate the semaphore for waiting until I/O is done
           and transfer it to the system team */

        sprintf (sem_name, "gadget dev %d io_done", id);
        d->io_done = err = create_sem (0, sem_name);
        if (err < 0) /* Bail out if an error occurred */
            goto err2;
        set_sem_owner(err, B_SYSTEM_TEAM);

        *cookie = d;  /* Let the kernel know where the
                         cookie is */

        /* Install and enable the interrupt handler */

        set_io_interrupt_handler (
            d->pci.u.h0.interrupt_line,/* interrupt number */
            gadget_dev_inth,/* Pointer to interrupt handler */
            d           /* pass this to handler */
        );
        enable_io_interrupt (d->pci.u.h0.interrupt_line);

        return B_OK; /* We're open for business */

err2:               /* Error handler when HW lock
                       semaphore is installed */
    delete_sem (d->hw_lock);
```

```
err1:
   free (d);     /* Error handler when no
                     semaphores are installed yet */
err0:
   atomic_and(&is_open, ~mask);
   return err;
}
```

The very first thing the `pci_open()` function does is determine the ID number of the virtual device which is to be opened. As described earlier, the BeGadget card has four virtual devices. These four devices have ID numbers of zero through three. We make this determination by calling the `lookup_device_name()` function we defined earlier. If it returns -1, indicating that the device does not exist, we return the `EINVAL` return code to let the kernel know that an error occurred.

BeGadget devices can only be accessed by one client at a time, so we maintain flags to keep track of which of the four devices are already open. These flags are stored in a variable called `is_open`. This variable's lowest four bits are used for this purpose; for example, if the value of bit 0 is set to 1, the first BeGadget device (*/dev/begadget/gadget1*) is currently open. The bits of the `is_open` variable are diagrammed below.

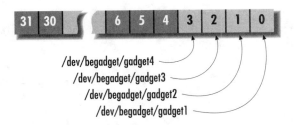

Before we can proceed to open the requested virtual device, we need to ensure that the device is not already open by examining the state of the `is_open` variable. If the device is not already open, we need to set the appropriate flag to indicate that it is now open, so that future `open()` calls on this virtual device will fail.

To do this safely, without risking a dangerous race condition, we make use of the `atomic_or()` function exported by the kernel. This allows us to examine and alter the value of the `is_open` variable in a single atomic operation. We construct a mask in which all bits are zero except the one that represents the device to be checked, then use `atomic_or()` to set that bit to 1. The `atomic_or()` function returns the previous value of the variable. If the previous value of the variable already specified that the device is open, we return the `B_BUSY` result code. Otherwise, we have safely set the flag indicating that the device is open.

Now we need to create the "cookie" to represent this virtual device. We simply call `malloc()` to do this. If the `malloc()` call fails, we report the `B_NO_MEMORY` result code and return immediately. The cookie's memory is allocated in the kernel's heap, which is always locked, so we know it will never be paged out by the virtual memory system.

Once we have allocated the memory to contain the cookie, we need to fill out the various fields therein. We begin by locating the BeGadget device, using the `lookup_pci_device()` function we have already written. If `lookup_pci_device()` returns `false`, we immediately return the `ENODEV` result code, since the device was not found on the PCI bus.

The PCI info record returned by `lookup_pci_device()` is stored in the cookie. The device ID and a pointer to the command register for this device are also stored in the cookie. Recall that each of the four virtual devices controlled by the BeGadget card has a single 32-bit command register. This pointer, stored within the cookie, provides easy access to this register when we need it.

This device requires two semaphores. The first is used to enforce exclusive access to the device. We call `create_sem()` to establish this semaphore, called `hw_lock`, which is a component of the device's cookie. We then call `set_sem_owner()` to transfer ownership of the semaphore to the system team. This is critical, since otherwise the semaphore is created in the team of the application that called `open()`. This team goes away when the application is shut down. If the device is still open at that time—possibly while still in use by another team—its semaphores would go away as well. By transferring the semaphores to the system team, we avoid this problem.

WARNING

> Failure to transfer ownership of the locking semaphores to the system team can cause unpredictable behavior and system crashes.

We set the initial value of the `hw_lock` semaphore to 1 so that it will not block the first time an attempt is made to acquire it.

A semaphore will also be used to block I/O calls until transactions with the device are completed, so we call `create_sem()` to create the `io_done` semaphore, which is also stored in the cookie for this device. We set the initial value of the semaphore to 0 so it will block the first time an `aquire_sem()` call is issued. The interrupt handler which monitors I/O with the BeGadget card will release the semaphore when the I/O transaction is finished. Again, we call `set_sem_owner()` to transfer ownership of the semaphore to the system team.

Now that the cookie has been created and filled out, a pointer to it is stored in the location passed to us by the kernel, so that the kernel can pass a reference to this cookie when requesting that operations be performed on this open device.

Finally, the interrupt handler for the BeGadget device is installed by calling `set_io_interrupt_handler()`. The interrupt number is obtained from the PCI info structure for the device. Also passed into the `set_io_interrupt_handler()` function are a pointer to the interrupt handler function, called `gadget_dev_inth()`, which is implemented by the BeGadget driver, as well as a pointer to the cookie for this device, which allows the interrupt handler to get access to this information.

Once the interrupt handler has been installed, the `enable_io_interrupt()` function is called to activate the interrupt for the device.

At this point, the device has been opened successfully, so the `B_OK` return code is returned to the kernel.

After this are three error-handling exit points, which are branched to using goto commands upon errors earlier in the code; these points handle removing the `hw_lock` semaphore, freeing up the cookie memory, and turning off the device open flag for the device, depending on where in the code the error occurred.

pci_close()

The `pci_close()` hook function handles the POSIX `close()` function for BeGadget devices, which is called when the client program has finished issuing read, write, and control calls to the device.

NOTE

In a multithreaded world such as the BeOS, it is entirely possible for the close hook to be called even though there are pending I/O requests for the device. The close hook should therefore not deallocate anything; instead, use the free hook to do this, which is called after all I/O transactions for a closed device have been completed.

```
static status_t
pci_close(void *cookie)
{
    return B_OK;
}
```

The BeGadget driver doesn't need to do anything when the POSIX `close()` function is called. Instead, we wait until the free hook is called after all I/O on the device is complete.

pci_free()

The free hook does not correspond to any POSIX call. This hook is called when all I/O transactions on a closed device are completed. Since the BeOS is a multithreaded operating system, it is possible for a situation to arise in which read or write operations are queued up for a device even after `close()` is called.

The free hook allows us to finish closing down the device after those transactions are finished. This includes releasing system resources used by the device, including interrupts, semaphores, and memory; among other things, the device's cookie should be released by this function.

NOTE

The driver is not necessarily being unloaded after this hook is called. The free hook's sole responsibility is to clean up when a particular device handled by the driver is closed. The uninit_driver() entry point is responsible for cleanup prior to the entire driver being unloaded from memory.

The BeGadget driver's free hook must perform the following actions, in order to undo those actions performed by the open hook:

- Disable and remove the interrupt handler.
- Mark the device as not open in the is_open flag variable.
- Delete the hw_lock and io_done semaphores.
- Release the memory occupied by the cookie for the device.

```
static status_t
pci_free(void *cookie)
{
    dev_info *d = (dev_info *) cookie;

    /* Disable and remove the interrupt handler for the device */

    disable_io_interrupt (d->pci.u.h0.interrupt_line);
    set_io_interrupt_handler (
        d->pci.u.h0.interrupt_line,
        NULL,
        NULL
    );

    /* Mark the device as not open */

    atomic_and (&is_open, ~(1 << d->id));

    /* Dispose of the hw_lock and io_done semaphores */

    delete_sem (d->hw_lock);
    delete_sem (d->io_done);
    free (d);

    return B_OK;
}
```

In the BeGadget driver, the pci_free() function is nearly the exact opposite of the pci_open() function. It begins by disabling the interrupt for the device by passing the interrupt number stored in the cookie to the disable_io_interrupt() kernel function. Once the interrupt is disabled, set_io_interrupt_handler() is called to remove the interrupt handler entirely by setting the interrupt handler for that interrupt number to NULL.

Having removed the interrupt handler for the device, `atomic_and()` is used to clear the appropriate bit in the `is_open` variable to zero. This lets us keep track of the fact that this device is no longer open.

Finally, the `hw_lock` and `io_done` semaphores are deleted and the cookie is disposed of. The `B_OK` return code is returned to the kernel.

pci_control()

When the C `ioctl()` function is called for an open BeGadget device, the kernel passes the call along to the BeGadget driver's control hook, which is handled by the `pci_control()` function.

The BeGadget device supports three control calls:

GADGET_DEV_RESET	Resets the BeGadget device to its default state.
GADGET_DEV_SET_SPEED	Sets the speed of the BeGadget device.
GADGET_DEV_GET_SPEED	Returns the current speed of the BeGadget device.

Recall that the BeGadget card provides a reset register which, when written to, resets the entire card to its default state.

The `GADGET_DEV_SET_SPEED` and `GADGET_DEV_GET_SPEED` commands are handled by accessing the speed register for the device whose cookie is passed in to the `pci_control()` function.

```
static status_t
pci_control(void *cookie, uint32 op, void *data, size_t len)
{
    dev_info *d = (dev_info *) cookie;

    switch (op) {

    case GADGET_DEV_RESET:/* reset the device */
        write_pci_config (d->pci.bus, d->pci.device,
            d->pci.function,
            GADGET_CONFIG_RESET,/* offset in config space */
            4,    /* size of register */
            0     /* initialization value */
        );
        break;

    case GADGET_DEV_SET_SPEED:/* set device speed */
        d->regs->speed = *(int32 *)data;
        break;
```

```
case GADGET_DEV_GET_SPEED:/* return current speed */
    *(int32 *)data = d->regs->speed;
    break;

default:
    return EINVAL;
}

return B_OK;
}
```

If the GADGET_DEV_RESET operation is requested, we use the write_pci_config() kernel function to store a zero into the reset register on the BeGadget card. Since any write to the reset register will perform the desired reset, this is all it takes to do the job.

If the GADGET_DEV_SET_SPEED operation is requested, we store the 32-bit integer pointed to by the *data* parameter in the speed register.

If the GADGET_DEV_GET_SPEED operation is requested, the value of the speed register is retrieved and stored in the 32-bit memory location pointed to by the *data* parameter.

pci_read()

The POSIX read() function is handled by the BeGadget driver's pci_read() hook function, which looks like this:

```
static status_t
pci_read(void *cookie, off_t pos, void *data, size_t *len)
{
    return do_device_io ((dev_info *)cookie, GADGET_DEV_READ,
        data, len);
}
```

For convenience, the BeGadget driver uses a single function for both reading and writing. This function, called do_device_io(), is described below, after we look briefly at the pci_write() function.

To perform a read, we simply call do_device_io() and forward the pointer to the cookie for the device to read from, the opcode GADGET_DEV_READ, which specifies to the do_device_io() function that it should perform a read, and a pointer to the buffer into which to read as well as a count for the number of bytes to read.

We ignore the *pos* parameter, which specifies the position within the input data to begin reading, since the BeGadget device doesn't support random-access operations.

pci_write()

The POSIX `write()` function is handled by the BeGadget driver's `pci_write()` hook, the code for which follows.

```
static status_t
pci_write(void *cookie, off_t pos, const void *data, size_t *len)
{
    return do_device_io ((dev_info *)cookie, GADGET_DEV_WRITE,
        (void *)data, len);
}
```

As discussed in the section on `pci_read()` above, the `pci_write()` function calls `do_device_io()` to perform the actual work of writing to the BeGadget device. We pass the opcode `GADGET_DEV_WRITE` to request the write activity.

The *pos* parameter is ignored, since random-access writes are not permitted by the BeGadget hardware.

Let's have a look at the `do_device_io()` function. This is where both read and write operations get their start. It accepts, as input, a pointer to the cookie for the device being accessed, an operation opcode (either `GADGET_DEV_READ` or `GADGET_DEV_WRITE`), a pointer to a data buffer into which the data will be read, or from which the data will be written, and the number of bytes to transfer.

```
static status_t
do_device_io (dev_info *d, dev_op op, void *data, size_t *len)
{
    status_t  err;
    size_t    xfer_count = 0;
    int32     flags;

    ddprintf ("do_device_io: data=%.8x *len = %.8x\n", data, *len);

    /* If the requested transfer is zero bytes long,
       just exit immediately */

    if (!*len)
        return B_OK;

    /* Lock down the client buffer in memory */

    flags = B_DMA_IO;/* It's a DMA operation */
    if (op == GADGET_DEV_READ)
        flags |= B_READ_DEVICE;/* And we're reading, too */

    /* Tell the kernel to lock the memory down and why */

    err = lock_memory (data, *len, flags);
    if (err != B_OK)
        goto err0;/* Unable to lock the memory */
```

```
    /* Block until the BeGadget hardware is available */

    err = acquire_sem_etc (d->hw_lock, 1, B_CAN_INTERRUPT, 0);
    if (err != B_OK)
        goto err1;/* Couldn't get the lock */

    d->xfer_count = 0;/* No data has been transferred */

    /* Get a list of pages comprising the client buffer */

    err = get_memory_map (data, *len, d->scatter, MAX_SCATTER);
    if (err != B_OK)
        goto err2;/* Couldn't get the map */
#if DEBUG_NO_HW
    {
        int j;
        for (j = 0; j < MAX_SCATTER; j++)
            ddprintf ("do_device_io: scatter[j] = %.8x %.8x\n",
            d->scatter[j].address, d->scatter[j].size);
    }
#endif

    /* Start up the I/O on the first scatter/gather entry */

    d->scat_index = 0;
    d->op = op;
    start_io (d);

#if DEBUG_NO_HW
    /* start up the gadget interrupt provoker thread */
    d->DEBUG_INT_SEM = create_sem (0, "gadget int sem");
    resume_thread (spawn_kernel_thread (gadget_interrupter,
        "gadget_interrupter", B_NORMAL_PRIORITY, d));
#endif

    /* Block until the entire transfer is complete */

    err = acquire_sem_etc (d->io_done, 1, B_CAN_INTERRUPT, 0);
    if (err != B_OK)
        goto err2;

#if DEBUG_NO_HW
    /* stop the gadget interrupter thread */
    release_sem (d->DEBUG_INT_SEM);
#endif
    xfer_count = d->xfer_count;/* Update the transfer count */
    err = B_OK;   /* And note that no error occurred */

    /* Handle errors which occurred at various points */

err2:
    release_sem (d->hw_lock);
err1:
    unlock_memory (data, *len, flags);
err0:
```

```
    *len = xfer_count;

    return err;
}
```

The first thing `do_device_io()` does is check to see if the size of the requested transfer is larger than zero bytes long. If it's zero bytes long, the `B_OK` result code is immediately returned, since we don't have to do anything to successfully fulfill a zero-byte request.

Since the BeGadget driver uses DMA to transfer information between the client buffer and the BeGadget card on the PCI bus, we need to tell the kernel this is the case because some computers don't maintain cache coherency during DMA operations. On these computers, the kernel marks the client buffer's memory as non-cachable for the duration of the operation.

Also, if this is a read operation, we need to tell the kernel that the DMA activity may alter the contents of the memory so it can mark the altered memory as dirty for virtual memory purposes.

This is accomplished by calling `lock_memory()` on the data buffer, passing in the `B_DMA_IO` flag to tell the kernel why we're locking the buffer down. The `B_READ_DEVICE` flag is added if the request is going to be reading into the memory, so that the memory will be marked as dirty by the kernel. If an error occurs, we branch to an exit point which handles cleaning up and returning the appropriate error code.

Next, exclusive access to the BeGadget virtual device is obtained by acquiring the `hw_lock` semaphore for this virtual device. All but the first request will block here. This ensures that only one thread at a time is manipulating the device. This `acquire_sem_etc()` call blocks until the hardware is not in use (i.e., when the `hw_lock` semaphore has been released). If an error occurs, the code immediately routes to code that cleans up and returns an error code.

The transfer count—the number of bytes of data that have been transferred between the BeGadget device and memory—is cleared to zero.

Once the hardware has been acquired, a list of memory pages which the client buffer spans is requested. Our cookie contains an array called a scatter/gather table (named `scatter`) into which this list will be stored.

In order to keep the scatter/gather table small, I/O transactions are limited to 32k by the BeGadget driver; larger requests will be broken down into numerous requests no larger than 32k. This maximum, as well as the number of pages in the scatter/gather list, is defined as follows in the source code for the BeGadget driver:

```
#define MAX_IO0x8000/* biggest single i/o we do */
#define MAX_SCATTER((MAX_IO/B_PAGE_SIZE) + 1)
```

MAX_IO is the number of bytes to which we limit a single transaction. MAX_SCATTER is the number of entries in our scatter/gather table.

As data is actually transferred to or from system memory, the addresses of the pages into which the data will be stored are obtained from this list.

If the get_memory_map() call fails, an error is immediately returned.

Once this has been done, we note that the scatter table entry currently being addressed is the first one, by setting the cookie's scat_index field to 0. The operation to perform (GADGET_DEV_READ or GADGET_DEV_WRITE) is stored in the op field of the cookie, so that the actual I/O routines know which operation to perform. Finally, the start_io() function (which is internal to the BeGadget driver) is called with a pointer to the cookie. This function actually issues the I/O request to the BeGadget hardware, and we'll have a look at it in a moment.

Once the start_io() call is issued, we block by attempting to acquire the io_done semaphore for this driver. The interrupt handler will handle completing the request by starting the I/O for the remainder of the pages in the scatter/gather table, and will unblock the io_done semaphore when the entire table has been processed.

After the io_done semaphore unblocks, the hw_lock semaphore is released, the data buffer's memory is unlocked, and the transfer count, which is in the variable xfer_count, is stored at the address pointed to by the *len* parameter to the do_device_io() function. Finally, the return code is returned to the caller.

The actual interfacing with the hardware is done by the start_io() function. This function performs the task of writing the needed commands into the 32-bit command register for a given virtual device on the BeGadget card in order to transfer a single contiguous chunk of data either from the client buffer to the BeGadget device or vice versa.

The start_io() function is called by do_device_io() initially, as we have already seen, to transfer the first page. After that, it is called repeatedly by the driver's interrupt handler to transfer the remaining pages.

Exclusive access to the hardware has already been obtained via the hw_lock semaphore, so we don't have to lock down the hardware in here.

start_io() returns true if a page transfer has been performed or false if there are no more pages to transfer. A pointer to the cookie for the device being accessed is passed into this function.

```
static bool
start_io (dev_info *d)
{
    int i;

    /* Check to see if the access has been completed */
    ddprintf ("start_io: index = %.8x\n", d->scat_index);
```

```
    i = d->scat_index;
    if (i == MAX_SCATTER || d->scatter[i].size == 0)
       return false;

    d->scat_index++;/* Increment the entry # to access */

    /* Issue the command by writing the opcode, address,
       and data size to the command register. */


#if DEBUG_NO_HW
    return true;
#endif
    d->regs->cmd = d->op;/* Send the opcode */
    __eieio();    /* Wait until it's sent */
    d->regs->cmd = (int32) ram_address (d->scatter[i].address);
                  /* Send the address */
    __eieio();    /* Wait until it's sent */
    d->regs->cmd = d->scatter[i].size;
                  /* Send the size */
    __eieio();    /* Wait until it's sent */
    return true;
}
```

First, this code checks to make sure that there is actually data left to transfer, by comparing the scat_index value in the cookie to the number of entries in the scatter/gather table for the device, as well as the maximum number of entries possible in the scatter/gather table. If the page to be transferred is outside the range of existing pages, false is returned, which indicates that the entire transfer has been completed. Otherwise, the scat_index field is incremented so that the next time start_io() is called, the next block will be transferred.

Recall that I/O transactions are performed by writing three times to the virtual device's command register. The first write is the opcode (GADGET_DEV_READ or GADGET_DEV_WRITE), the second is the address of the data buffer in main system memory, and the third is the number of bytes of data to transfer. These three values are 32-bit integers, and are written one after the other into the command register.

The __eieio() intrinsic function must be used after each of these three writes because the PowerPC processor, which is capable of reordering operations to improve efficiency, needs to be told not to reorder these operations, since they have to be performed in order. The __eieio() function issues the eieio (Enforce Inorder Execution of I/O) PowerPC instruction, which forces all pending memory accesses to complete before the processor proceeds to handle the next instruction.

WARNING

When creating a driver that requires I/O to be performed in a particular order, be sure to use the eieio operation to ensure that the order of the I/O is maintained, or your driver may not function reliably.

The `ram_address()` function, which is exported by the kernel, translates an address in main system memory into the equivalent address as viewed from the PCI bus. When we pass the address of the buffer to the BeGadget card, we need to first convert it into the PCI equivalent address.

Finally, `start_io()` returns `true` to indicate that the request has been issued to the BeGadget card.

gadget_dev_inth()

The final component of the BeGadget device driver is the `gadget_dev_inth()` function, which is the interrupt handler used by the driver to issue repeated calls to `start_io()` each time a chunk of a data transfer is completed.

`gadget_dev_inth()` is called each time a chunk transfer from or to the BeGadget card is completed. Let's have a look.

```
static bool
gadget_dev_inth(void *data)
{
    dev_info*d = (dev_info *)data;

    /* start_io() returns false if the transaction is complete */

    if (!start_io (d))
        release_sem_etc(d->io_done, 1, B_DO_NOT_RESCHEDULE);

    return true;
}
```

When `gadget_dev_inth()` is called, a pointer to the cookie for the virtual device is passed in the *data* parameter—this was established when the interrupt handler was installed by the `pci_open()` hook function. A local pointer, properly typecast to the type `dev_info *`, is created for convenience.

`start_io()` is called with a pointer to the cookie. As discussed previously, `start_io()` attempts to transfer another chunk of data to or from the BeGadget device; all the necessary parameters are located within the cookie.

If `start_io()` returns `true`, the entire transaction has been completed; there are no further entries in the scatter table for the transaction. The `io_done` semaphore is released, which indicates that the transaction has been completed. Recall that the `do_device_io()` call, once a transaction is initiated, blocks until this semaphore is released. Once the interrupt handler releases the semaphore, `do_device_io()` is unblocked and knows that the transaction is finished, so it can clean up and return to the caller.

Note that when we release the semaphore, we use the `B_DO_NOT_RESCHEDULE` flag. This is a must if anything of significance is done after the call to release the semaphore. If this flag is not set, the release call could reschedule the current thread that is processing the interrupt. When it wakes up, possibly much later, other driver operations may have been done by other threads, which could lead to unexpected behavior.

Although careful thought and planning could be used to avoid using B_DO_NOT_RESCHEDULE, it's much easier to do it this way. The release call will always return right away.

The interrupt handler returns `true` since the interrupt was handled.

Functions for Kernel Drivers

The kernel exports a number of functions that device drivers can call. The device driver accesses these functions directly in the kernel, not through a library.

Remember when writing a driver that calls one of these functions to link against either _KERNEL_.LIB_ (for x86) or a copy of the kernel named _KERNEL_ (for PPC). This will instruct the loader to dynamically locate the symbols in the current kernel when the driver is loaded.

Functions

acquire_spinlock(), release_spinlock(), spinlock

Declared in: be/drivers/KernelExport.h

    typedef vlong **spinlock**

    void **acquire_spinlock**(spinlock *_lock_)
    void **release_spinlock**(spinlock *_lock_)

Spinlocks are mutually exclusive locks that are used to protect sections of code that must execute atomically. To create a spinlock, simply declare a `spinlock` variable and initialize it 0:

```
spinlock lock = 0;
```

The functions acquire and release the _lock_ spinlock. When you acquire and release a spinlock, you _must_ have interrupts disabled; the structure of your code will look like this:

```
cpu_status former = disable_interrupts();
acquire_spinlock(&lock);
/* critical section goes here */
release_spinlock(&lock);
restore_interrupts(former);
```

The spinlock should be held as briefly as possible, and acquisition must not be nested within the critical section.

Spinlocks are designed for use in a multi-processor system (on a single processor system simply turning off interrupts is enough to guarantee that the critical section will be atomic). Nonetheless, you *can* use spinlocks on a single processor—you don't have to predicate your code based on the number of CPUs in the system.

add_debugger_command() *see* kernel_debugger()

disable_interrupts(), restore_interrupts(), cpu_status

Declared in: be/drivers/KernelExport.h

    typedef ulong **cpu_status**

    cpu_status **disable_interrupts**(void)
    void **restore_interrupts**(cpu_status *status*)

These functions disable and restore interrupts on the CPU that the caller is currently running on. `disable_interrupts()` returns its previous state (i.e. whether or not interrupts were already disabled). `restore_interrupts()` restores the previous *status* of the CPU, which should be the value that `disable_interrupts()` returned:

```
cpu_status former = disable_interrupts();
...
restore_interrupts(former);
```

As long as the cpu state is properly restored (as shown here), the disable/restore functions can be nested.

See also: `install_io_interrupt_handler()`

dprintf(), set_dprintf_enabled(), panic()

Declared in: be/drivers/KernelExport.h

    void **dprintf**(const char **format*, ...)
    bool **set_dprintf_enabled**(bool *enabled*)

    void **panic**(const char **format*, ...)

`dprintf()` is a debugging function that has the same syntax and behavior as standard C `printf()`, except that it writes its output to the fourth serial port ("/dev/serial4") at a data rate of 19,200 bits per second. By default, `dprintf()` is disabled.

set_dprintf_enabled() enables dprintf() if the *enabled* flag is true, and disables it if the flag is false. It returns the previous enabled state, thus permitting intelligent nesting:

```
/* Turn on dprintf */
bool former = set_dprintf_enabled(true);
...
/* Now restore it to its previous state. */
set_dprintf_enabled(former);
```

panic() is similar to dprintf(), except it hangs the computer after printing the message.

get_memory_map(), physical_entry

Declared in: be/drivers/KernelExport.h

> long **get_memory_map**(const void *address*, ulong *numBytes*,
>   physical_entry **table*, long *numEntries*)

> typedef struct {   void **address*;
>   ulong **size*;
>   } **physical_entry**

Returns the physical memory chunks that map to the virtual memory that starts at *address* and extends for *numBytes*. Each chunk of physical memory is returned as a physical_entry structure; the series of structures is returned in the *table* array. (which you have to allocate yourself). *numEntries* is the number of elements in the array that you're passing in. As shown in the example, you should lock the memory that you're about to inspect:

```
physical_entry table[count];
lock_memory(addr, extent, 0);
get_memory_map(addr, extent, table, count);
. . .
unlock_memory(someAddress, someNumberOfBytes, 0);
```

The end of the *table* array is indicated by (size == 0):

```
long k;
while (table[k].size > 0) {
   /* A legitimate entry */
   if (++k == count) {
      /* Not enough entries */
      break; }
}
```

If all of the entries have non-zero sizes, then table wasn't big enough; call get_memory_map() again with more table entries.

Return values:
     The function always returns B_NO_ERROR.

See also: `lock_memory()`, `start_isa_dma()`

has_signals_pending()

Declared in: be/drivers/KernelExport.h

int **has_signals_pending**(struct thread_rec *thr*)

Returns a bitmask of the currently pending signals for the current thread. *thr* should always be **NULL**; passing other values will yield meaningless results. `has_signals_pending()` returns 0 if no signals are pending.

install_io_interrupt_handler(), remove_io_interrupt_handler()

Declared in: be/drivers/KernelExport.h

long **install_io_interrupt_handler**(long *interrupt_number,* interrupt_handler *handler,*
                void **data,* ulong *flags*)

long **remove_io_interrupt_handler**(long *interrupt_number,*
                interrupt_handler *handler*)

`install_io_interrupt_handler()` adds the handler *function* to the chain of functions that will be called each time the specified *interrupt* occurs. This function should have the following syntax:

bool `handler`(void **data*)

The *data* passed to `install_io_interrupt_handler()` will be passed to the handler function each time it's called. It can be anything that might be of use to the handler, or **NULL**. If the interrupt handler returns **true**, the system bypasses the remaining handlers in the interrupt chain; if it returns **false**, the next handler in the chain is dispatched.

The *flags* parameter is a bitmask of options. The only option currently defined is **B_NO_ENABLE_COUNTER**. By default, the OS keeps track of the number of functions handling a given interrupt. If this counter changes from 0 to 1, then the system enables the IRQ for that interrupt. Conversely, if the counter changes from 1 to 0, the system disables the IRQ. Setting the **B_NO_ENABLE_COUNTER** flag instructs the OS to ignore the handler for the purpose of enabling and disabling the IRQ.

`install_io_interrupt_handler()` returns **B_NO_ERROR** if successful in installing the handler, and **B_ERROR** if not. An error occurs when either the *interrupt_number* is out of range or there is not enough room left in the interrupt chain to add the handler.

`remove_io_interrupt()` removes the named *interrupt* from the interrupt chain. It returns **B_NO_ERROR** if successful in removing the handler, and **B_ERROR** if not.

io_card_version()   see motherboard_version()

kernel_debugger()   see dprintf()

kernel_debugger(), add_debugger_command(), load_driver_symbols(), kprintf(), parse_expression()

Declared in: be/drivers/KernelExport.h

> void **kernel_debugger**(const char **string*)
> int **add_debugger_command**(char **name*, int (**func*)(int, char **), char **help*)
> int **load_driver_symbols**(const char **driverName*)
> void **kprintf**(const char **format*, ...)
> ulong **parse_expression**(const char **string*)

`kernel_debugger()` drops the calling thread into a debugger that writes its output to the fourth serial port at 19,200 bits per second, just as `dprintf()` does. This debugger produces *string* as its first message; it's not affected by `set_dprintf_enabled()`.

`kernel_debugger()` is identical to the `debugger()` function documented in the Kernel Kit, except that it works in the kernel and engages a different debugger. Drivers should use it instead of `debugger()`.

`add_debugger_command()` registers a new command with the kernel debugger. When the user types in the command *name*, the kernel debugger calls *func* with the remainder of the command line as *argc*/*argv*-style arguments. The help string for the command is set to *help*.

`load_driver_symbols()` loads symbols from the specified kernel driver into the kernel debugger. *driver_name* is the path-less name of the driver which must be located in one of the standard kernel driver directories. The function returns B_NO_ERROR on success and B_ERROR on failure.

`kprintf()` outputs messages to the serial port. It should be used instead of `dprintf()` from new debugger commands because `dprintf()` depends too much upon the state of the kernel to be reliable from within the debugger.

`parse_expression()` takes a C expression and returns the result. It only handles integer arithmetic. The logical and relational operations are accepted. It can also supports variables and assignments. This is useful for strings with multiple expressions, which should be separated with semicolons. Finally, the special variable "." refers to the value from the previous expression. This function is designed to help implement new debugger commands.

See also: `debugger()` in the Kernel Kit

kprintf()   see kernel_debugger()

load_driver_symbols()   see kernel_debugger()

lock_isa_dma_channel(), unlock_isa_dma_channel()

Declared in: be/drivers/KernelExport.h

>   long **lock_isa_dma_channel**(long *channel*)
>   long **unlock_isa_dma_channel**(long *channel*)

These functions reserve an ISA DMA *channel* and release a channel previously reserved. They return `B_NO_ERROR` if successful, and `B_ERROR` if not. Like semaphores, these functions work only if all participating parties adhere to the protocol.

There are 8 ISA DMA channels. In general, they're used as follows:

Channel	Use
0	Unreserved, available
1	Unreserved, available
2	Reserved for the floppy disk controller
3	Reserved for the parallel port driver
4	Reserved by system, cannot be used
5	Reserved for IDE
6	Reserved for sound
7	Reserved for sound

lock_memory(), unlock_memory()

Declared in: be/drivers/KernelExport.h

>   long **lock_memory**(void *address, ulong *numBytes*, ulong *flags*)
>   long **unlock_memory**(const void *address, ulong *numBytes*, ulong *flags*)

`lock_memory()` makes sure that all the memory beginning at the specified virtual *address* and extending for *numBytes* is resident in RAM, and locks it so that it won't be paged out until `unlock_memory()` is called. It pages in any of the memory that isn't resident at the time it's called. It is typically used in preparation for a DMA transaction.

The *flags* field contains a bitmask of options. Currently, two options, `B_DMA_IO` and `B_READ_DEVICE`, are defined. `B_DMA_IO` should be set if any part of the memory range will be modified by something other than the CPU while it's locked, since that change won't otherwise be noticed by the system and the modified pages may not be written to disk by the virtual memory system. Typically, this sort of change is performed through DMA. B_READ_DEVICE, if set, indicates that the caller intends to fill the memory (read *from* the device). If cleared, it indicates the memory will be written to the device and will not be altered.

unlock_memory() releases locked memory and should be called with the same flags as passed into the corresponding lock_memory() call.

Each of these functions returns B_NO_ERROR if successful and B_ERROR if not. The main reason that lock_memory() would fail is that you're attempting to lock more memory than can be paged in.

make_isa_dma_table() see start_isa_dma()

map_physical_memory()

Declared in: be/drivers/KernelExport.h

area_id **map_physical_memory**(const char *areaName*, void **physicalAddress*,
                size_t *numBytes*, uint32 *spec*, uint32 *protection*,
                void ***virtualAddress*)

This function allows you to map the memory in physical memory starting at *physicalAddress* and extending for *numBytes* bytes into your team's address space. The kernel creates an area named *areaName* mapped into the memory address *virtualAddress* and returns its area_id to the caller. *numBytes* must be a multiple of B_PAGE_SIZE (4096).

spec must be either B_ANY_KERNEL_ADDRESS or B_ANY_KERNEL_BLOCK_ADDRESS. If *spec* is B_ANY_KERNEL_ADDRESS, the memory will begin at an arbitrary location in the kernel address space. If *spec* is B_ANY_KERNEL_BLOCK_ADDRESS, then the memory will be mapped into a memory location aligned on a multiple of B_PAGE_SIZE.

protection is a bitmask consisting of the fields B_READ_AREA and B_WRITE_AREA, as discussed in create_area().

The error codes are the same as those for create_area().

See also: create_area()

motherboard_version(), io_card_version()

Declared in: be/drivers/KernelExport.h

long **motherboard_version**(void)
long **io_card_version**(void)

These functions return the current versions of the motherboard and of the I/O card.

panic()   see dprintf()

parse_expression()   see kernel_debugger()

platform()

Declared in: be/drivers/KernelExport.h

   platform_type **platform**(void)

Returns the current platform, as defined in *be/kernel/OS.h*.

ram_address()

Declared in: be/drivers/KernelExport.h

   void ***ram_address**(const void **physicalAddress*)

Returns the address of a physical block of system memory (RAM) as viewed from the PCI bus. If passed NULL as the *physicalAddress*, this function returns a pointer to the first byte of RAM; otherwise it returns a pointer to the *physicalAddress*.

This information is needed by bus masters—components, such as the ethernet and some SCSI controllers, that can perform DMA reads and writes (directly read from and write to system memory without CPU intervention).

Memory must be locked when calling this function. For example:

```
physical_entry table[count];
void *where;

lock_memory(someAddress, someNumberOfBytes, FALSE);
get_memory_map(someAddress, someNumberOfBytes, table, count);
where = ram_address(table[i].address)
. . .
unlock_memory(someAddress, someNumberOfBytes);
```

See also: get_memory_map(), lock_memory()

read_io_8(), write_io_8(), read_io_16(), write_io_16(), read_io_32(), write_io_32()

Declared in: be/drivers/KernelExport.h

   uint8 **read_io_8**(int *port*)
   void **write_io_8**(int *port*, uint8 *value*)

uint16 **read_io_16**(int *port*)
void **write_io_16**(int *port*, uint16 *value*)

uint32 **read_io_32**(int *port*)
void **write_io_32**(int *port*, uint32 *value*)

These functions provide an interface for reading and writing from i/o ports.

register_kernel_daemon(), unregister_kernel_daemon()

Declared in: be/drivers/KernelExport.h

int **register_kernel_daemon**(void (**func)(void *, int), void *arg, int *freq*)
int **unregister_kernel_daemon**(void (**func)(void *, int), void *arg)

Adds or removes daemons from the kernel. A kernel daemon function is executed approximately once every *freq*/10 seconds. The kernel calls *func* with the arguments *arg* and an iteration value that increases by *freq* on successive calls to the daemon function.

release_spinlock()   see acquire_spinlock()

remove_io_interrupt_handler()   see install_io_interrupt_handler()

restore_interrupts()   see disable_interrupts()

set_dprintf_enabled()   see dprintf()

spawn_kernel_thread()

Declared in: be/drivers/KernelExport.h

thread_id **spawn_kernel_thread**(thread_entry *func*, const char *name,
                    long *priority*, void *data)

This function is a counterpart to `spawn_thread()` in the Kernel Kit, which is not exported for drivers. It has the same syntax as the Kernel Kit function, but is able to spawn threads in the kernel itself.

See also: `spawn_thread()` in the Kernel Kit

spin()

Declared in: be/drivers/KernelExport.h

void **spin**(bigtime_t *microseconds*)

Executes a delay loop lasting at least the specified number of *microseconds*. It could last longer, due to rounding errors, interrupts, and context switches.

start_isa_dma(), start_scattered_isa_dma(), make_isa_dma_table(), isa_dma_entry

Declared in: be/drivers/KernelExport.h

> long **start_isa_dma**(long *channel*, void *address, long *transferCount*, uchar *mode*,
>   uchar *eMode*)

> long **start_scattered_isa_dma**(long *channel*, const isa_dma_entry *table, uchar *mode*,
>   uchar *eMode*)

> long **make_isa_dma_table**(const void *address, long *numBytes*,
>   ulong *numTransferBits*, isa_dma_entry *table, long *numEntries*)

> struct {...} **isa_dma_entry**;

These functions initiate ISA DMA memory transfers for the specified *channel*. They engage the ISA 8237 DMA controller.

`start_isa_dma()` starts the transfer of a contiguous block of physical memory beginning at the specified *address*. It requests *transferCount* number of transfers, which cannot be greater than `B_MAX_ISA_DMA_COUNT`. Each transfer will move 8 or 16 bits of memory, depending on the *mode* and *eMode* flags. These arguments correspond to the mode and extended mode flags recognized by the DMA controller.

The physical memory *address* that's passed to `start_isa_dma()` can be obtained by calling `get_memory_map()`.

`start_scattered_isa_dma()` starts the transfer of a memory buffer that's physically scattered in various pieces. The separate pieces of memory are described by the *table* passed as a second argument and provided by `make_isa_dma_table()`.

`make_isa_dma_table()` provides a description of the separate chunks of physical memory that make up the contiguous virtual buffer that begins at *address* and extends for *numBytes*. This function anticipates a subsequent call to `start_scattered_isa_dma()`, which initiates a DMA transfer. It ensures that the information it provides is in the format expected by the 8237 DMA controller. This depends in part on how many bits will be transferred at a time. The third argument, *numTransferBits*, provides this information. It can be `B_8_BIT_TRANSFER` or `B_16_BIT_TRANSFER`.

Each chunk of physical memory is described by a `isa_dma_entry` structure, which contains the following fields (not that its arcane details matter, since you don't have to do anything with the information except pass it to `start_scattered_isa_dma()`:

Field	Meaning
ulong address	A physical memory address (in little-endian format).
ushort transfer_count	The number of transfers it will take to move all the physical memory at that address, minus 1 (in little-endian format). This value won't be greater than `B_MAX_ISA_DMA_COUNT`.
int flags.end_of_list:1	A flag that's set to mark the last chunk of physical memory corresponding to the virtual buffer.

`make_isa_dma_table()` is passed a pointer to a *table* of `isa_dma_entry` structures. It fills in the table, stopping when the entire buffer of virtual memory has been described or when *numEntry* entries in the table have been written, whichever comes first. It returns the number of bytes from the virtual *address* buffer that it was able to account for in the *table*.

`start_isa_dma()` and `start_scattered_isa_dma()` both return B_NO_ERROR if successful in initiating the transfer, and B_ERROR if the channel isn't free.

unlock_isa_dma_channel() see lock_isa_dma_channel()

unlock_memory() see lock_memory()

unregister_kernel_daemon() see register_kernel_daemon()

write_io_8() see read_io_8()

write_io_16() see read_io_8()

write_io_32() see read_io_8()

write_pci_config() see read_pci_config()

xpt_ccb_alloc(), xpt_ccb_free(), xpt_action(), xpt_bus_register(), xpt_bus_deregister()

Declared in: be/drivers/CAM.h

```
CCB_HEADER *xpt_ccb_alloc(void)
void xpt_ccb_free(void *ccb)
long xpt_action(CCB_HEADER *ccbHeader)
long xpt_bus_register(CAM_SIM_ENTRY *entryPoints)
long xpt_bus_deregister(long pathID)
```

These functions conform to the SCSI common access method (CAM) specification. See the draft ANSI standard *SCSI-2 Common Access Method Transport and SCSI Interface Modules* for information.

Although `xpt_init()` is exported by the kernel, your code never needs to call it; the BeOS does this for you at bootup.

WARNING

The current implementation doesn't support asynchronous callback functions. All CAM requests are executed synchronously in their entirety.

PCI Functions

Described here are the functions that kernel-loaded drivers can use to get information about devices that are attached to the PCI bus. For more information on the PCI bus, refer to the PCI specification:

> *PCI Local Bus Specification*, revision 2.1, June 1, 1995, PCI Special Interest Group, PO Box 14070, Portland OR 97214, (800) 433-5177 or (503) 797-4207

Functions

get_nth_pci_info(), pci_info

Declared in: be/drivers/PCI.h

long **get_nth_pci_info**(long *index*, pci_info **info*)

typdef struct {...} **pci_info**

`get_nth_pci_info()` returns a `pci_info` structure for the *index*'th PCI device currently attached to the computer. Indices begin at 0; there are no gaps in the list.

The `pci_info` structure contains some common fields and a device-specific header:

Field	Meaning
ushort `vendor_id`	An identifier for the manufacturer of the device.
ushort `device_id`	An identifier for the device, assigned by the vendor.
uchar `bus`	The bus the device is on.
uchar `device`	The bus-relative device number.
uchar `function`	The function number in the device.
uchar `revision`	A device-specific version number, assigned by the vendor.

Field	Meaning
uchar class_api	The type of register-level interface to the device (the lower byte of the class code field).
uchar class_sub	The type of function the device performs (the middle byte of the class code field).
uchar class_base	The broadly-defined device type (the upper byte of the class code field).
uchar line_size	The size of the system cache line, in units of 32 bit words.
uchar latency	The latency timer for the PCI bus master.
uchar bist	The contents of the register for the built-in self test.
uchar header_type	The header type.
union u	A device-specific header structure.

The definition of the structures that the u union points to is given in *be/drivers/PCI.h*. You'll also find a number of constants that you can use to test various fields of a `pci_info` structure.

Return values:

B_NO_ERROR. The device was found.

B_ERROR. *index* is out-of-range.

read_pci_config(), write_pci_config()

Declared in: be/drivers/PCI.h

long **read_pci_config**(uchar *bus*, uchar *device*, uchar *function*,
                    long *offset*, long *size*)

void **write_pci_config**(uchar *bus*, uchar *device*, uchar *function*,
                    long *offset*, long *size*, long *value*)

These functions read from and write to the PCI configuration register space.

- The *bus*, *device*, and *function* arguments identify the device's configuration space. Their values can be gotten from the `bus`, `device`, and `function` fields of the `pci_info` structure provided by `get_nth_pci_info()`.

- *offset* is an offset to the location in the 256-byte configuration space that is to be read or written, and *size* is the number of bytes to be read from that location or written to it. Permitted sizes are 1, 2, and 4 bytes.

Plug and Play

WARNING

The information in this section will change in R4.

When the BeOS is booted, it automatically configures any Plug and Play peripherals that it finds. Drivers for these peripherals then query the BeOS for configuration information, including IRQs, DMA channels, and IO port ranges. From that point on, the driver need not worry about Plug and Play issues.

A driver queries the BeOS for configuration information through an `ioctl()` call on the special Plug and Play configuration that you access by `open()`'ing the special /pnp/config_mgr file. The `ioctl()` call lets the driver fetch the configuration of a particular device indexed by an integer ranging from 0 to N-1, where N is the number of plug and play devices installed in the system. The driver typically scans through the list of configurations until it finds the one matching its device as identified by the EISA product id. Typical usage of the Plug and Play `ioctl()` call is illustrated below:

```
isa_device_config config;
status_t ret;
int i, fd;

// open plug and play configuration manager
fd = open("/pnp/config_mgr", O_RDWR);

for (i=0;;i++) {
   // fetch the configuration of the i'th device
   *(uint *)&config = i;

   ret = ioctl(fd, CONFIG_MGR_GET_NTH_ISA_DEVICE_CONFIG,
      &config, sizeof(isa_device_config)
   if (ret == B_OK) {
      printf("Card: %s, Device: %s\n", config.card_name,
         config.logical_device_name);
   } else
      break;
}
```

The `ioctl()` call shown here returns an `isa_device_config` structure; the definition of the structure and the flags that you can use to examine its fields are given in /boot/develop/headers/be/device/isapnp.h.

Functions

ioctl()

Declared in: posix/unistd.h

   status_t **ioctl**(int *fd*, int *op*, isa_device_config **config*, int *size_config*)

   • *fd* is a file descriptor for the special file /pnp/config_mgr.

   • *op* is the constant CONFIG_MGR_GET_NTH_ISA_DEVICE_CONFIG, defined in *be/device/config_mgr.h*.

- *config*, on input, should contain in the first `sizeof(long)` bytes the index of the device whose configuration is to be fetched. On output, the memory will be filled with a `isa_device_config` structure containing the configuration information about the device. This structure is detailed in *be/device/isapnp.h*.

- *size_config* should always be `sizeof(isa_device_config)`.

The function returns `B_NO_ERROR` on success and `B_ERROR` on failure. Failure indicates that the index was out of range.

Macros

EQUAL_EISA_PRODUCT_ID()

Declared in: be/device/isapnp.h

EQUAL_EISA_PRODUCT_ID(EISA_PRODUCT_ID *id1*, EISA_PRODUCT_ID *id2*)

Compares two product id's, ignoring the revision value.

MAKE_EISA_PRODUCT_ID()

Declared in: be/device/isapnp.h

MAKE_EISA_PRODUCT_ID(EISA_PRODUCT_ID **ptr*, char *ch0*, char *ch1*, char *ch2*, uint12 *prod_num*, uint4 *rev*)

Properly gloms its parameters into a product id in little-endian format.

Building and Installing a Kernel Driver

The section tells you how to prepare, compile, and install your kernel driver.

- Export your driver's entry points by using the `__declspec()` macro:

```
__declspec(dllexport)
status_t init_hardware(void);
```

- Tell the linker to produce a shared library. If you're using the BeIDE, go to the **Settings** window, pop open the **Project** list, click on **PPC Project** or **x86 Project**, and select "Shared Library" in the **Project Type** popup menu. If you're using `make`, include the `-G` option.

- Disable the default behavior of linking against the shared system libraries. If you're using the BeIDE, remove the *libroot*, *libbe*, and *libdll* libraries from the project window. If you're using `make`, include the -nodefaults option.

- Add the kernel exports to the link list. On x86, this is located in */boot/develop/lib/x86/_KERNEL_.LIB*. On PowerPC, you must link against a copy of the kernel renamed to *_KERNEL_*.

When an attempt is made to open a device, the kernel first looks for the driver for that device among those already loaded into memory. Failing that, the kernel looks for a driver in the following directories (in this order):

1. */beos/system/add-ons/kernel/drivers* (on a floppy)

2. */boot/home/config/add-ons/kernel/drivers*

3. */boot/beos/system/add-ons/kernel/drivers*

Finished, publishable drivers should be installed in #2, */boot/home/config/add-ons/kernel/drivers*. Do *not* install in the *beos/system* directory.

Once your driver has been installed, it is available immediately; there is no need to restart the system, unless you are replacing a driver that has previously been installed and loaded into memory.

CHAPTER THIRTEEN

Network Add-ons

CHAPTER THIRTEEN

Network Add-ons

To add support for a new network device or protocol to the BeOS, you have to create and install an appropriate network add-on. These add-ons, which should be installed in the */boot/home/config/add-ons/net_server* directory (but see the warning below), can interface with the hardware through a lower-level kernel device driver or directly from the add-on, but the interface described in this chapter has to be followed.

WARNING

Currently, you have to install your network add-ons in */boot/beos/system/add-ons/net_server*. In a future release, the network add-on directory will be changed to the more appropriate location mentioned above.

There are two types of network add-ons:

- A *network device add-on* provides access to a network hardware interface so the BeOS can send and receive network traffic on that interface. To create a network device add-on, read the sections on the BNetConfig, BNetDevice, BIpDevice, BIpHandler, and BNetPacket classes.

- A *network protocol add-on* allows the BeOS to use a particular network data protocol on one or more interfaces. To learn how to create network protocol add-ons, read the sections on BNetProtocol and BNetPacket.

All the classes described in this chapter are pure virtual (with the exception of the BStandardPacket class, which is provided for convenience). You must create your own classes derived from these in your add-ons.

BCallbackHandler

Derived from: *none*

Declared in: be/addons/net_server/NetDevice.h

Library: libnetdev.so

The BNetConfig class's `Config()` function is called with a pointer to a BCallbackHandler object as one of its arguments. The BCallbackHandler class has one member function: `Done()`.

Your implementation of the `BNetConfig::Config()` function should call the callback handler's `Done()` function when configuration is complete and the user interface has been closed. You should only call done if your `Config()` function returned B_OK and the *autoconfig* argument wasn't specified as `true`. See the description of `Config()` in the BNetConfig class for more information.

Member Functions

Done()

virtual void Done(status_t *status*) = 0

When your `Config()` function's user interface has been closed, you should call the `Done()` function in the BCallbackHandler that was passed to `Config()`. The status parameter specifies whether or not configuration was successful; if you don't pass B_OK, it will be assumed that configuration failed.

BIpDevice

Derived from: *none*

Declared in: be/addons/net_server/IpDevice.h

Library: libnetdev.so

If the network server add-on you're writing communicates through IP packets, there is an extra step to go through while writing the add-on. Because the Network Server doesn't directly send and receive IP packets, you have to create a special layer that provides the interface between your network add-on's IP packets and the Network Server. The BIpDevice class defines the protocol for this special layer.

A network device of this kind requires the following three classes to define the interface with the BeOS:

BNetConfig	Lets the Network Server and others configure and obtain information about the device.
BNetDevice	Handles communication between the network and the Network Server.
BIpDevice	Represents the IP layer of the device. This object receives packets in the background and forwards them to the Network Server, and sends IP packets for the Network Server.

The Network Server determines that your add-on is for an IP device by calling the `IsIpDevice()` function of your add-on's BNetConfig-derived object.

Once the Network Server knows that the add-on represents an IP device, it will call the BNetDevice-derived object's `OpenIP()` function to obtain a pointer to an object derived from the BIpDevice class. Once this has been done, the Network Server will interact with your network add-on through the BIpDevice object and **not** the BNetDevice.

The IP protocol in the Network Server won't call into the BNetDevice if there's also a BIpDevice. However, other protocol add-ons might do so. For example, PPP exports a BIpDevice and a BNetDevice of type `B_PPP_NET_DEVICE`. Other protocol add-ons might use the BNetDevice for their own purposes.

If it doesn't make sense for your add-on's BNetDevice to be used by others (for example, if your add-on is a packet sniffer), you should set the BNetDevice's type to `B_NULL_NET_DEVICE`.

The Network Server will then call your BIpDevice's `Run()` function. `Run()` should spawn a thread to watch for incoming IP packets and forward them to the Network Server. This is done through the use of the BIpHandler object passed to the `Run()` function; the BIpHandler's `PacketReceived()` function should be called to do this.

If your IP device needs to manage timeouts, you should consider also inheriting from the BTimeoutHandler class.

Destructor

~BNetDevice()

virtual **~BNetDevice()**

Your derived class can implement the BIpDevice destructor, if necessary, to perform cleanup before objects of your derived class are deleted.

Member Functions

AllocPacket()

> virtual BNetPacket ***AllocPacket**(void) = 0

Your derived class should implement `AllocPacket()` to return a pointer to a newly-instantiated BNetPacket-derived object. As discussed further in the section on BNetPacket, you should never instantiate BNetPacket directly; it's an abstract class that you should subclass.

Unless you have special needs, usually you can return a BStandardPacket:

```
BNetPacket *AllocPacket(void) {
   return (new BStandardPacket());
}
```

Close()

> virtual void **Close**(void) = 0

Your derived class's implementation of `Close()` is called by the Network Server when your device is no longer in use. This function should close the device.

Flags()

> virtual uint **Flags**(void) = 0

You should implement the `Flags()` function to return the current flag settings for the IP device. Candidate flags are `B_FLAGS_POINT_TO_POINT` and `B_FLAGS_LINK_DOWN` (the latter isn't available in Release 3).

MaxPacketSize()

> virtual uint **MaxPacketSize**(void) = 0

Implement this function to return the size, in bytes, of the maximum packet size setting currently in effect.

Run()

> virtual void **Run**(BIpHandler *ipHandler) = 0

Your `Run()` function is called by the Network Server to tell your IP device add-on to begin receiving IP packets. Your `Run()` function should spawn a new thread that watches for incoming packets and forwards them on to the Network Server.

Because the Network Server doesn't handle IP traffic directly, you have to receive the packets in your add-on, then forward them to the Network Server by calling the *ipHandler* object's `PacketReceived()` function. *ipHandler* is, essentially, your interface to the Network Server:

```
/* we've received a packet - let the Network Server have it */
ipHandler->PacketReceived(thePacket, this);
```

Once you've done this, the packet belongs to the Network Server and you don't have to worry about it anymore.

SendPacket()

> virtual void **SendPacket** (uint32 *dest*, BNetPacket **packet*) = 0

Your derived class's implementation of `SendPacket()` is called to send the specified *packet* to the IP address specified by *dest*. Once the packet has been sent, you should delete it.

Statistics()

> virtual void **Statistics** (FILE **stat_file*) = 0

Your implementation of `Statistics()` should output device status information to the specified file. This will typically be called for debugging purposes, but can also be used to provide valuable status information to users.

BIpHandler

Derived from: *none*

Declared in: be/addons/net_server/IpDevice.h

Library: libnetdev.so

As discussed in the BIpDevice section, the Network Server doesn't directly receive packets from IP devices. Instead, those devices monitor the appropriate interface for IP packets and forward them to the Network Server for dispatching to the appropriate protocol handler. This is done using the BIpHandler class.

When you write a IP device add-on, you create a class, derived from the BIpDevice class, that represents your add-on to the Network Server. The Network Server tells your IP device add-on to begin monitoring the network for IP packets by calling the BIpDevice's `Run()` function. The `Run()` function should create a thread that watches for packets on the interface.

The BIpHandler class represents the interface between the Network Server and your IP device add-on; when your `Run()` function is called, you receive a pointer to a BIpHandler object whose member functions you can call to interact with the Network Server.

When the packet monitoring thread receives an IP packet, it needs to forward the packet to the Network Server. This is done by calling the `PacketReceived()` function in the BIpHandler object passed to the `Run()` function.

You can also determine your IP address, using the `Address()` function, and change your IP address by calling `SetAddress()`. The interface's netmask can be obtained by calling the `NetMask()` function.

Member Functions

Address(), SetAddress()

virtual uint32 **Address**(void) = 0
virtual void **SetAddress**(uint32 *address*) = 0
virtual uint32 **NetMask**(void) = 0

`Address()` returns the IP address of the interface from which your IP device is receiving packets.

`SetAddress()` lets you set the IP address you want to listen to. This allows your IP device to work with dynamic IP addresses.

`NetMask()` returns the netmask of the interface your IP device is connected to.

PacketReceived()

virtual void **PacketReceived**(BNetPacket **packet*, BIpDevice **ipDevice*) = 0

When your IP device handler receives a packet, it should use this function to forward the packet to the Network Server for dispatching. The *packet* parameter is a pointer to the packet itself, which must be of a class derived from BNetPacket (such as BStandardPacket or a custom packet class), and *ipDevice* must be a reference to your BIpDevice-derived object.

BNetConfig

Derived from: none

Declared in: be/addons/net_server/NetDevice.h

Library: libnetdev.so

Users occasionally install new networking interfaces, or reconfigure old ones. This is done using the **Network** preference application, which provides the basic user interface for configuring networking devices.

When your network add-on's `open_config()` static C function is called, it returns a pointer to an object of a class derived from BNetConfig. This is the interface by which the Network preference application gives users access to the configuration options available on your device.

An object derived from BNetConfig is also used to automatically select default preferences for your device when it is first installed, and to let the Network Server determine whether or not the add-on represents an IP device, which requires special handling.

User Configuration

The Network preference application lets the user install and customize network interfaces. A list of network interfaces is provided, and the user can click on one and hit the Modify button to configure that device more closely

In order to make this possible, your network device add-on has to implement the following static C function:

```
BNetConfig *open_config(const char *device);
```

`open_config()` must return an object of a class derived from BNetConfig. Your derived class must implement the following three functions:

- `IsIpDevice()` should return `true` if the device is an IP device; if it's not an IP device, it should return `false`. If you return `true`, the Network Server will call the BIpDevice's `OpenIP()` function and communicate through the BIpDevice object returned by that function.

- `Config()` is called by the Network preference application when the user clicks the Modify button to configure the interface. This can present a window or perform automatic configuration, depending on the needs of your add-on. This function is also called to automatically select default settings for the device when the device is first installed.

- `GetPrettyName()` should return the name of the device. This is the name that will be displayed in the Network preference application.

Let's look at a sample class, derived from BNetConfig:

```
class QuickNetConfig : public BNetConfig {
    public:
        int GetPrettyName(char *pretty_name, int buf_len) {
            int totlen = strlen(DRIVER_NAME)+1;
            if (buf_len < totlen) {
                return (-totlen);
            }
            strcpy(pretty_name, DRIVER_NAME);
            return totlen;
        }
        bool IsIpDevice(void) { return false };
        status_t Config(const char *ifname, net_settings *ncw,
                BCallBackHandler *callback, bool autoconf);
}
```

The QuickNetConfig class is pretty simple. `GetPrettyName()` is passed a pointer to a buffer and the length of the buffer, and fills that buffer with the name of the device. If the buffer is too small, we return the negative of the length actually needed. This lets the Network preference application know how much space is necessary for the name.

The device isn't an IP device, so `IsIpDevice()` returns `false`.

The `Config()` function is called with several parameters:

ifname	The name of the network interface.
ncw	A pointer to a `net_settings` structure; this is basically a magic cookie used when calling `find_net_setting()` and `set_net_setting()` to manage your saved configuration variables.
callback	A pointer to a BCallbackHandler object. This object has a single function, `Done()`, which you should call when your user interface has been closed. If you don't present a user interface, you don't have to call *callback*->`Done()`. `Done()` accepts one parameter, a `status_t`. Specify `B_OK` if the configuration was concluded successfully, or `B_ERROR` otherwise.
autoconf	A boolean; this is `true` if the `Config()` function should automatically configure the device to its default settings. If `false`, the user interface should be presented with the current settings intact. This is only used for IP devices.

```
extern "C" BNetConfig *open_config(const char *device) {
    system_info info;

    get_system_info(&info);
    if (info.platform_type == B_MAC_PLATFORM) {
        return NULL;
    }
    return (new QuickNetConfig());
}
```

This sample `open_config()` function checks to see if the add-on is running on a Macintosh; for whatever reason, the device doesn't need to be configured on a Mac, so it returns `NULL` to indicate that no configuration is necessary (or possible). Otherwise, a QuickNetConfig object is instantiated and returned.

Destructor

~BNetConfig()

> virtual **~BNetConfig()**

Your derived class can implement the BNetConfig destructor, if necessary, to perform cleanup before objects of your derived class are deleted.

Member Functions

Config()

> virtual status_t **Config**(const char *ifname*, net_settings *ncw*,
>   BCallbackHandler *callback*, bool *autoconfig* = false) = 0

Your derived class must implement the `Config()` function. This function is called by the Network preference application when the user selects your device and presses the Modify button (or double-clicks the device in the Network Interfaces list). In this case, the *autoconfig* parameter is `false`.

It is also called to automatically configure the device—for example, if the device has settings already saved in the network configuration, this function is calledwith autoconfig set to `true`. In response, your add-on should make the configuration specified by *ncw* the current configuration.

When *autoconfig* is `false`, you should present a user interface by creating a window containing controls for configuring the device. The callback parameter is a pointer to a BCallbackHandler; when your user interface is finished—when the user clicks an OK or Cancel button, for example—you should call BCallbackHandler's `Done()` function to let the caller know the configuration is complete.

Autoconfiguration is only supported for IP devices; if your device is not an IP device, and your `Config()` function is called with *autoconfig* `true`, you should return an error.

Also, if your device doesn't support autoconfiguration, or for any reason you can't autoconfigure the device, you should return an error.

The *device* parameter specifies the name of the device. You can use this string as the heading for `find_net_setting()` and `set_net_setting()` calls.

Return values:

   B_OK. No errors occurred.

   B_ERROR. Unable to open the user interface or autoconfigure the device.

See also: find_net_setting(), set_net_setting()

GetPrettyName()

   virtual int **GetPrettyName** (char *name_buffer*, int *buffer_len*) = 0

Your derived class will implement this function to return, in the buffer specified by *name_buffer*, the name of your device. This name is used in user interface displays, so it should be a user-friendly string. For instance, the standard BeOS NE-2000 Ethernet driver returns the string "Novell NE2000 compatible adapter (ISA)" in response to this call.

Before copying your device's name into the buffer, you should ensure that your string will fit in the buffer. Do this by comparing the name string's length to *buffer_len*. If the buffer is too small, you should return the negative of your string's length.

For example, if your string's length is 25 characters, but the buffer provided is only 12 bytes long, you should return -25.

If the string is successfully copied, return B_OK.

IsIpDevice()

   virtual bool **IsIpDevice** (void) = 0

Your derived class needs to implement the IsIpDevice() function to return true if the device is an IP device, and false if not. As discussed in the sections on BNetDevice and BIpDevice, IP devices are handled differently from other, non-IP devices.

Global C Functions

find_net_setting()

Declared in: be/net/net_settings.h

   char *find_net_setting(net_settings *ncw*, const char *heading*,
                  const char *setting_name*, char *buffer*, uint *buff_size*);

Reads a network setting into the specified *buffer*, which is *buff_size* bytes long. The setting to be read is identified by its *heading* (which can be thought of as a group name that identifies all the settings belonging to a particular application or add-on) and its *setting_name*, which is the name of the particular setting to be read into the buffer. If *ncw* is NULL, the setting is read from the network settings file. Otherwise, it is read from the net_settings record referenced by *ncw*.

The only time you should ever specify a value other than NULL for *ncw* is when the Network Server has provided you with a value to use. In particular, when a network device add-on's Config() function is called, the Network Server will provide you with a value to use for *ncw*.

set_net_setting()

Declared in: be/net/net_settings.h

> status_t **set_net_setting**(net_settings **ncw*, const char **heading*,
>   const char **setting_name*, char **buffer*)

Writes a network setting from the specified *buffer* into the network settings file specified by the *ncw* parameter. The *buffer* should be null-terminated.

The setting is stored in the group whose name is provided in the *heading* parameter, and is given the name *setting_name*. If a setting by that heading and name already exists, it is replaced with the new value.

If you wish to save the setting into the global network settings file, specify NULL for *ncw*. The only time you should ever specify a value other than NULL for *ncw* is when the Network Server has provided you with a value to use; you should usually pass NULL.

BNetDevice

Derived from: none

Declared in: be/addons/net_server/NetDevice.h

Library: libnetdev.so

When the Network Server loads your network device add-on and wants to begin using it, it needs to obtain a reference to an object derived from the BNetDevice class. BNetDevice is a pure virtual class that your add-on will subclass and flesh out.

To obtain a pointer to your BNetDevice, the Network Server calls your add-on's static C function open_device(). The protocol for this function is:

```
BNetDevice *open_device(const char *device_name);
```

This function should return a pointer to a BNetDevice object. For example:

```
extern "C" BNetDevice *open_device(const char *device_name) {
   MyNetDevice *dev;   * Pointer to BNetDevice-derived object */
```

```
    dev = new MyNetDevice();
    if (/* device initialized safely */) {
        return dev;
    }
    delete dev;
    return NULL;
}
```

In this example, MyNetDevice is the class we've derived from BNetDevice. We instantiate an object of this type and then try to start the device up. If the initialization fails, we delete the object and return NULL. If the device is started up safely, we return a pointer to the MyNetDevice object. Once this pointer has been returned, the Network Server knows how to communicate with our device.

If your network device add-on needs to manage timeout activity, you should consider inheriting from BTimeoutHandler as well as from BNetDevice.

Now that you know how the Network Server obtains a reference to your BNetDevice-derived object, let's investigate what needs to be implemented.

Starting Up and Shutting Down

These two functions need to be implemented to let the Network Server properly initialize and shut down your add-on:

- Close() should shut down your add-on, terminating its link with the network.

- OpenIP() should, if your device is an IP device, return a pointer to an object derived from BIpDevice. This object will be used for further networking by the Network Server. See BIpDevice for details on how to create IP devices If your device is not an IP device, or it's an IP device but you want to use the built-in IP device, you can just return NULL.

Device Information

Five functions must be implemented to provide access to information about the device your add-on represents, and to provide some additional configuration options:

- Address() should return the address of the device in the buffer provided by the caller. The format and size of the buffer is device-type specific; you can assume that the caller previously called Type() to determine the type of device your add-on represents and has established an appropriate buffer for you.

- MaxPacketSize() should be implemented to return the maximum packet size as currently configured.

- SetPromiscuous() turns on promiscuous mode when true is passed, and turns off promiscuity when false is passed. When your device is in promiscuous mode, it should accept incoming packets for any address; otherwise, it should only accept packets directed to the computer's address as well as broadcast and multicast packets.

- `Statistics()`, used primarily for debugging and network tuning, should output information about the device to the specified file.

- `Type()` should return the type of device your add-on represents.

Multicasting

If your network device supports multicasting, you must implement these two functions to allow other devices and protocols to add multicast addresses to (and remove them from) your device. If your device doesn't support multicasting, you can just return `B_ERROR` from these functions.

- `AddMulticastAddress()` subscribes your device to a multicast group on the network. When your `AddMulticastAddress()` function is called, this tells your device add-on to subscribe to the specified multicast address.

- `RemoveMulticastAddress()` should remove an address from the list of multicast groups your device is subscribed to.

Sending and Receiving Packets

Three functions must be implemented to send and receive packets via your device. Note that these may not be used by the Network Server if your device is an IP device, but must still be implemented. See BIpDevice for more details.

- `AllocPacket()` should allocate and return a pointer to a new packet. The packet returned must be of a class derived from BNetPacket (such as BStandardPacket, for example).

- `ReceivePacket()` should block until a packet arrives, then return a pointer to the packet.

- `SendPacket()` should transmit a packet over the network. Once the packet has been sent, `SendPacket()` should delete the packet.

Destructor

~BNetDevice()

virtual ~BNetDevice()

Your derived class can implement the BNetDevice destructor, if necessary, to perform cleanup before objects of your derived class are deleted.

Member Functions

AddMulticastAddress()

> virtual status_t **AddMulticastAddress** (const char *address) = 0

Your derived class must implement this function, even if it does nothing. This function is called to add a multicast address to your device. The address can be assumed to be in the correct format for the type of device your add-on supports.

Return values:
> B_OK. No errors occurred.
> *Other errors, as appropriate.*

Address()

> virtual void **Address** (char *address) = 0

Your derived class should implement `Address()` to stuff the specified buffer with the address of the interface. The format of this buffer is device type specific, and can be assumed to be the right size for the data you need to place into it.

AllocPacket()

> virtual BNetPacket ***AllocPacket** (void) = 0

Your derived class should implement `AllocPacket()` to return a pointer to a newly-instantiated BNetPacket-derived object. As discussed further in the section on BNetPacket, you should never instantiate BNetPacket directly; it's an abstract class that you should subclass.

Unless you have special needs, you can usually return a BStandardPacket:

```
BNetPacket *AllocPacket(void) {
   return (new BStandardPacket());
}
```

Close()

> virtual void **Close** (void) = 0

Your derived class' implementation of `Close()` is called by the Network Server when your device is no longer in use. This function should close the device.

MaxPacketSize()

> virtual uint **MaxPacketSize** (void) = 0

Implement this function to return the size, in bytes, of the maximum packet size setting currently in effect.

OpenIP()

>   virtual BIpDevice *OpenIP (void) = 0

Implement this function to open the IP device associated with the object's interface. If your device is an ethernet device, and you want to use the built-in IP device, you should return NULL. All other devices should return a pointer to an object of a type derived from BIpDevice.

The BIpDevice-derived object you return from this function will be used to send and receive IP packets on your network device; its Run() function will be called by the Network Server to cause it to begin monitoring the network for IP packets, and packets will be sent by calling its SendPacket() function. See the BIpDevice and BIpHandler sections for more information on implementing IP devices.

ReceivePacket()

>   virtual BNetPacket *ReceivePacket (void) = 0

The Network Server will call this function to receive a packet from the network interface defined by your add-on. This function should block until a packet arrives, then return a pointer to it.

RemoveMulticastAddress()

>   virtual status_t RemoveMulticastAddress (const char *address) = 0

Your derived class must implement this function, even if it does nothing. This function is called to remove a multicast address from your device. The address can be assumed to be in the correct format for the type of device your add-on supports.

Return values:
>   B_OK. No errors occurred.
>   *Other errors, as appropriate.*

SendPacket()

>   virtual void SendPacket (BNetPacket *packet) = 0

Your derived class's implementation of SendPacket() is called to transmit the specified *packet*. When this function is called, you should send the packet, then delete it.

SetPromiscuous()

> virtual status_t **SetPromiscuous** (bool *promiscuous*) = 0

This function is called to switch between promiscuous and non-promiscuous mode. When this function is called with *promiscuous* set to `true`, your add-on should switch the device into promiscuous mode. When *promiscuous* is `false`, you should ensure that promiscuous mode is disabled.

Return values:
> B_OK. No errors occurred.
> *Other errors, as appropriate.*

Statistics()

> virtual void **Statistics** (FILE **stat_file*) = 0

Your implementation of `Statistics()` should output device status information to the specified file. This will typically be called for debugging purposes, but can also be used to provide valuable status information to users.

Type()

> virtual net_device_type **Type** (void) = 0

This function returns the type of device your BNetDevice-derived class represents. The `net_device_type` can be one of the following:

B_NULL_NET_DEVICE	Not a real device.
B_ETHER_NET_DEVICE	Ethernet device.
B_PPP_NET_DEVICE	PPP device.
B_LOOP_NET_DEVICE	Loopback device.

This information is used by the Network Server, among other things, to determine the format of the device address and how the server should interact with your device add-on.

Global C Functions

deliver_packet()

> void **deliver_packet**(BNetPacket **packet*, BNetDevice **device*)

`deliver_packet()` delivers the specified *packet* to the Network Server. You should place a pointer to your add-on's own BNetDevice-derived object in the *device* parameter. This would be necessary if you implement a device, such as PPP, that receives packets from one interface (like a serial port) and needs to forward them to the Network Server to be processed. The Network Server, in return, will forward the packet to each packet handler that's registered as being interested in getting packets from your device.

BNetPacket

Derived from: *none*

Declared in: be/addons/net_server/NetPacket.h

Library: libnetdev.so

Network packets are represented by objects derived from the BNetPacket pure virtual class. Your device or protocol add-on must implement a subclass of BNetPacket that represents the packets your device or protocol manages. One derivation of BNetPacket, called BStandardPacket, is provided for you.

When a packet is received, the BNetDevice will allocate a new BNetPacket and fill it with the incoming packet data by using calls defined in this class. Likewise, when someone wants to send a packet, they'll call BNetDevice's `AllocPacket()` function to allocate an appropriate BNetPacket-derived object, then the functions described here to fill the packet with data.

Reading and Writing Packets

Once an object derived from BNetPacket is instantiated, data can be placed into the packet buffer by calling `Write()`, or by calling `DataBlock()` to get a pointer to the range of data the caller wants to change. Likewise, `Read()` is used to fetch data from the packet buffer, and `DataBlock()` returns a pointer so the buffer can be read directly.

Base and Size

An important component of your packet object is the buffer that actually contains the data in the packet. This buffer consists of a virtual block of memory—which doesn't have to be contiguous—and two values: *base* and *size*.

The base is the offset to the byte within the buffer that is currently considered to be the first byte of data in the buffer. This may sound like a strange concept, but it's actually a convenience—if you need to dodge headers and the like stashed in the data buffer, you can simply adjust the base offset. The offset into the buffer you specify when calling `Read()`, `Write()`, or `DataBlock()` is an offset from the current base.

The size is the number of bytes between the current base and the end of the packet buffer. That means that every time the base changes, the size changes as well, to reflect the new length of the data in the range from the base to the buffer's end.

There are two functions that you need to implement for each of these two values:

- `Base()` should return the current base.
- `SetBase()` should be implemented to set the current base and to adjust the size. The parameter to this function is an offset from the current base.
- `Size()` should return the current size. This value should be buffer_size - base.
- `SetSize()` should be implemented to set the size of the buffer. Note that this is relative to the current base.

The `SetBase()` function you implement might look something like this:

```
void MyNetPacket::SetBase(int offset) {
   base += offset;
   size -= offset;
}
```

Your `SetSize()` function should do something like this:

```
void MyNetPacket::SetSize(uint newsize) {
   ResizeBuffer(buffer, base+newsize);
   size = newsize; /* save the new size */
}
```

This example assumes that the `ResizeBuffer()` function resizes the buffer to the size specified. The total size of the buffer should be the requested size plus the current base.

Obviously these examples skimp a bit on details; that's because the specifics depend largely on how your add-on works internally.

Constructor and Destructor

BNetPacket()

BNetPacket(void)

Your derived class can implement the BNetPacket constructor, as desired.

~BNetPacket()

> virtual ~BNetPacket()

Your derived class can implement the BNetPacket destructor, as desired.

Member Functions

Base(), SetBase()

> virtual uint **Base** (void) = 0
> virtual void **SetBase**(int *offset*) = 0

Your derived class should implement `Base()` to return the offset into the packet at which data actually begins. The value returned by this function is an absolute offset into the packet data.

The `SetBase()` function should be implemented to set the base as an **offset** from the current base.

Together, these functions can be used to hide packet headers without actually stripping them out of the packets. Note that changing the base offset also should affect the value returned by `Size()`; if you add 15 to the base, you need to subtract 15 from the size to keep things in balance.

DataBlock()

> virtual char *DataBlock (uint *offset*, uint *size*) = 0

Your derived class should implement this function to return a pointer to the byte of data located at the specified *offset* into the packet's data. Before calling `DataBlock()`, the caller has in the variable pointed to by *size* the number of bytes they'd like to read. Your implementation of `DataBlock()` should replace this with the actual number of bytes of data between *offset*+`Base()` and the end of the contiguous block. This value should only differ from the original value if there are fewer bytes remaining in the packet than the caller requests.

NOTE

The *offset* should be added to the base specified by the last `SetBase()` call.

If the packet buffer is comprised of multiple non-contiguous blocks of memory, `DataBlock()` does not cross block boundaries. For example, if the buffer consists of three 1,000-byte buffers, and `DataBlock()` is called, with offset 500, requesting 1,000 bytes of data), only 500 bytes—the data between the offset 500 and the end of the first block—are returned. `DataBlock()` will have to be called multiple times to scan through all three blocks.

Your `DataBlock()` implementation should return `NULL` when the offset is at the end of the buffer. This indicates to the caller that there is no data left. You should never return 0 in *size*.

NOTE

The data is not copied by this function; it only returns a pointer to the data and the number of bytes of data from the specified *offset* to the end of the contiguous block of data in which the specified *offset* resides.

Read(), Write()

virtual void **Read** (uint *offset*, char **buffer*, uint *count*) = 0
virtual void **Write**(uint *offset*, const char **buffer*, uint *count*) = 0

Your derived class should implement `Read()` to copy data from the specified *offset* in the packet's data to the address pointed to by *buffer*. Up to *count* bytes should be copied. If *count* is larger than the number of bytes between *offset* and the end of the packet, then that portion of the packet is transferred.

`Write()` should be implemented to write *count* bytes of data from the specified *buffer* to the specified *offset* in the packet data.

Default versions of `Read()` and `Write()` are provided for you; you probably won't have to implement them yourself.

SetSize(), Size()

virtual void **SetSize** (uint *size*) = 0
virtual uint **Size**(void) = 0

Your derived class should implement `SetSize()` to allow the caller to specify the size of the packet data that can be represented by the object. This size should be the size of the data *following* the current base offset, so if the current base is 32, you should set the size of the packet buffer to *32+size*.

The `Size()` function should return the current packet size.

Note that the size of the packet buffer will fluctuate as the base offset is moved around using the `SetBase()` function. The `Size()` and `SetSize()` functions manipulate the size of the data between the current base and the end of the packet buffer.

Global C Functions

copy_packet()

> void **copy_packet**(BNetPacket *srcpacket*, uint *srcoffset*, BNetPacket *dstpacket*,
> uint *dstoffset*, uint *size*)

`copy_packet()` copies data from a source packet to a destination packet. *size* bytes of data are copied beginning at the specified *srcoffset* within the packet specified by *srcpacket* and stored starting at the specified *dstoffset* within the packet pointed to by the *dstpacket* parameter.

BNetProtocol

Derived from: *none*

Declared in: be/addons/net_server/NetProtocol.h

The BNetProtocol class is an abstract class that defines the basic interface between the Network Server and your protocol.

When the Network Server loads your protocol add-on, its `open_protocol()` global function will be called. This function should return a pointer to an object of a class derived from BNetProtocol. For example, if the class QuickProtocol is derived from BNetProtocol, our `open_protocol()` function might look like this:

```
extern "C" BNetProtocol *open_protocol(const char *devname) {
   ...
   return new QuickProtocol();
}
```

The `open_protocol()` function might also spawn a new thread or perform other activities, but the key issue is that it must return a pointer to a BNetProtocol-derived object to let the Network Server know how to communicate with it.

Once the Network Server knows how to get in touch with your protocol add-on, it will call the protocol's `AddDevice()` function once for each network interface. You can implement this function to examine each device and determine whether or not your protocol should receive packets from that device. If you want to get packets from the device, call `register_packet_handler()` to register a packet handler for that device:

```
void QuickProtocol::AddDevice(BNetDevice *device,
                const char *name) {
   if (device->Type() == B_ETHER_NET_DEVICE) {
      register_packet_handler(myHandler, device);
   }
}
```

myHandler is a pointer to an object of a class derived from BPacketHandler. This object's `PacketReceived()` function will be called for each packet received by your protocol. See the BPacketHandler section for further details.

If your protocol requires that timeouts be managed and served, your BNetProtocol-derived class can also inherit from the BTimeoutHandler class, which provides these services in a convenient and easy-to-use form.

Destructor

~BNetProtocol()

> virtual **~BNetProtocol()**

Your derived class can implement the BNetProtocol destructor, if necessary, to perform cleanup before objects of your derived class are deleted.

Member Functions

AddDevice()

> virtual void **AddDevice** (BNetDevice *device*, const char *name*) = 0

Your derived class must implement this function. It's called by the Network Server once for each network device, so that you can determine whether or not your protocol wishes to receive packets from the device.

If you wish to receive packets from this device, call `register_packet_handler()` to register with the Network Server as a party with an interest in the device:

```
if (device->Type() == B_ETHER_NET_DEVICE) {
   register_packet_handler(myHandler, device);
}
```

In this example, our protocol only wants to receive packets from ethernet devices, so it checks the device to see if it's of type `B_ETHER_NET_DEVICE` before registering to receive packets.

Global C Functions

register_packet_handler()

> void **register_packet_handler**(BPacketHandler *handler*, BNetDevice *device*,
>   int *priority* = 0)

Registers the specified packet handler with the Network Server. A BNetProtocol-derived object's `AddDevice()` function should call this function to register itself to receive packets from the specified device. The *priority* specifies the order in which the handlers will receive packets; the higher the value, the higher-priority the handler. Most devices should use 0, the default. Packet sniffers and other debugging aids should set the priority to 1 so they don't risk missing packets that other packet handlers might accept.

See also: BNetProtocol::AddDevice()

unregister_packet_handler()

void **unregister_packet_handler**(BPacketHandler *handler*, BNetDevice *device*)

Tells the Network Server to stop sending packets from the specified *device* to your packet handler.

BPacketHandler

Derived from: *none*

Declared in: be/addons/net_server/NetProtocol.h

Library: libnetdev.so

When you register a protocol with the Network Server (by calling register_packet_handler()), you establish a connection between the Network Server and a packet handler object.

Your protocol add-on should include a class derived from BPacketHandler. An object of this class is then passed to register_packet_handler() to tell the Network Server how to dispatch packets to your protocol.

Once your packet handler has been registered with the Network Server, packets will be sent to your packet handler. The Network Server does this by calling the packet handler's PacketReceived() function:

virtual bool **PacketReceived**(BNetPacket *packet*, BNetDevice *device*) = 0

Your PacketReceived() implementation can analyze the contents of the *packet* and the *device* on which the packet was received and decide whether or not the packet is one that your protocol will handle, returning true if the packet was handled and false if it was not. If you handle the packet (and return true), you must also delete the packet.

Let's look at a sample BPacketHandler-derived class:

```
class QuickPacketHandler : public BPacketHandler {
  public:
      virtual bool PacketReceived(BNetPacket *packet,
```

```
                    BNetDevice *device);
        void ProcessPacket(BNetPacket *packet);
}

bool QuickPacketHandler::PacketReceived(BNetPacket *packet,
            BNetDevice *device) {
   if (/* packet is one we want */) {
       ProcessPacket(packet);
       delete packet;
       return true;
   }
   return false;
}
```

In this sample, we first check to see if the packet is one that our handler wants to
receive. If it is, we process the packet in some way, delete the packet, and return
true, which indicates to the Network Server that the packet has been handled. If we
don't want the packet, we return false, so the Network Server knows to send the
packet to the next protocol add-on.

Member Functions

PacketReceived()

> virtual bool **PacketReceived** (BNetPacket *packet*, BNetDevice *device*) = 0

Your derived class must define this function. The Network Server calls it when a
packet is received by an interface with which your protocol has registered. If your
protocol handles the packet, you should delete it and return true. If you don't
accept the packet, return false so the Network Server knows to pass it along to
another protocol.

The *packet* parameter points to the actual packet that has been received by your
protocol add-on. The *device* parameter is a pointer to the device add-on that received
the packet.

BStandardPacket

Derived from: BNetPacket

Declared in: be/addons/net_server/NetPacket.h

Library: libnetdev.so

The pure abstract class BNetPacket defines a network packet in the most generic
possible terms. In fact, it's so generic that you have to implement your own derived
class to actually manipulate network packets.

The BStandardPacket class is provided as a default BNetPacket-derived class that you can use in many cases; unlike the BNetPacket class, BStandardPacket provides useful implementations of its member functions (BNetPacket implements only the `Read()` and `Write()` functions, which are useless without the other functions being implemented as well), so this is often a better starting place than BNetPacket itself.

For a more detailed view into the lives and loves of network packets, read the BNetPacket section.

Constructor and Destructor

BStandardPacket()

    BStandardPacket (uint *size* = 0)

Constructs a new BStandardPacket object, which can contain data of up to *size* bytes.

NOTE

Packet sizes smaller than 1,536 bytes are handled slightly more efficiently by the BStandardPacket class.

~BStandardPacket()

    ~BStandardPacket()

Deallocates the packet data buffer and destroys the object.

Member Functions

Base(), SetBase()

    uint **Base** (void)
    void **SetBase**(int *offset*)

`Base()` returns the offset into the packet at which data is considered to begin. The value returned by this function is an absolute offset into the packet data.

The `SetBase()` function sets the base as an **offset** from the current base; to move the base forward 12 bytes, you would call:

    packet->SetBase(12);

To move the base backward 8 bytes, you would call:

    packet->SetBase(-8)

Together, these functions can be used to hide packet headers without actually stripping them out of the packets. Note that changing the base offset also affects the value returned by `Size()`; adding 15 bytes to the base likewise reduces the size of the available data by 15 bytes (since the distance between the base and the end of the data has been reduced by 15 bytes).

DataBlock()

char *__DataBlock__ (uint *offset*, uint **size*)

This function returns a pointer to the byte of data located at the specified *offset* into the packet's data. Keep in mind that the *offset* specified here is added to the current base offset.

Before calling `DataBlock()`, store the number of bytes you want to read in the *size* varaible. When the function returns, the value of *size* will be changed to the number of bytes actually available beginning at the returned address. The value of *size* will only change if there are fewer bytes left in the packet's data than you asked for.

WARNING

If the offset would index out of the packet's data buffer, `DataBlock()` invokes the system debugger.

Read(), Write()

void __Read__ (uint *offset*, char **buffer*, uint *count*)
void __Write__(uint *offset*, const char **buffer*, uint *count*)

`Read()` copies data from the specified *offset* in the packet's data to the address pointed to by *buffer*. Up to *count* bytes are copied. If *count* is larger than the number of bytes between *offset* and the end of the packet, then that portion of the packet is transferred.

`Write()` copies *count* bytes of data from the specified *buffer* to the specified *offset* in the packet data.

Again, keep in mind that the specified *offset* values are added to the current base offset before the read or write operation is performed.

SetSize(), Size()

void __SetSize__ (uint *size*)
uint __Size__(void)

`SetSize()` lets the caller specify the size of the packet data that can be represented by the object. This call changes the number of bytes between the current base and the end of the packet data buffer.

The `Size()` function returns the current packet size—the number of bytes between the base and the end of the packet buffer.

Note that the size of the packet buffer will fluctuate as the base is moved around using the `SetBase()` function. The `Size()` and `SetSize()` functions manipulate the size of the data between the current base and the end of the packet buffer.

BTimeoutHandler

Derived from: *none*

Declared in: be/addons/net_server/NetPacket.h

Library: libnetdev.so

As you're writing your fantastic new network add-on, you're liable to need to cope with situations in which timeouts can occur. Maybe an expected packet has taken too long to arrive, or a kernel-level device driver isn't responding fast enough. There are several possible cases in which your add-on will need to be able to time out if something doesn't occur in a reasonable amount of time.

To make handling timeout situations easier, you can use the BTimeoutHandler class. When you create your protocol or network device object, or your packet handler, you can also inherit from BTimeoutHandler to gain access to an easy-to-use timeout mechanism:

```
class QuickPacketHandler : public BPacketHandler,
              public BTimeoutHandler {
  public:
      virtual bool PacketReceived(BNetPacket *packet,
              BNetDevice *device);
      virtual void TimedOut(uint32 receipt);

      uint32 mainTimeoutReceipt;
      uint32 otherTimeoutReceipt;

}
```

You can then use the `set_timeout()` function to register a timeout with the Network Server. For instance, if you want a timeout to occur after 1000 microseconds:

```
QuickPacketHandler *packetHandler;

packetHandler = new QuickPacketHandler();
packetHandler->mainTimeoutReceipt = set_timeout(packetHandler, 1000);
packetHandler->otherTimeoutReceipt = 0;/* no timeout set */
```

The value returned by `set_timeout()` is the receipt—a unique 32-bit integer that identifies the timeout you've just set. This is passed to `TimedOut()` when a timeout occurs, and you can pass it to `cancel_timeout()` to cancel a pending timeout. The receipt is never zero, so you can use a value of zero to represent "timeout not set" if you wish.

If the timeout isn't canceled before 1000 microseconds have passed, the Network Server will automatically call your `TimedOut()` function. Let's look at a brief example of a `TimedOut()` function:

```
void QuickPacketHandler::TimedOut(uint32 receipt) {
    if (receipt == mainTimeoutReceipt) {
        /* handle the main timeout */
    }
    else if (receipt = otherTimeoutReceipt) {
        /* handle the other timeout */
    }
}
```

When a timeout occurs and your `TimedOut()` function is called, the timeout is canceled for you; you don't have to cancel the timeout in this situation. However, if you need to cancel the timeout (if, for example, the packet you're waiting for arrives), you can call `cancel_timeout()`:

```
cancel_timeout(packetHandler->receipt);
```

Note that `cancel_timeout()` returns `true` if the timeout was canceled and `false` if the timeout couldn't be canceled. If `false` is returned, you **must** wait for the timeout to occur before deleting the BTimeoutHandler. If you delete the object before the timeout occurs, a crash is likely to follow.

Member Functions

TimedOut()

> virtual void **TimedOut**(uint32 *receipt*) = 0

Your derived class must define this function. The Network Server calls it when a timeout occurs.

The *receipt* parameter tells you which timeout occurred; if you registered more than one timeout, you can tell which one occurred by examining this value.

Global C Functions

cancel_timeout()

> bool **cancel_timeout**(uint32 *receipt*)

Cancels the timeout specified by *receipt*. This value is returned by the `set_timeout()` function when you register a BTimeoutHandler with the Network Server.

`cancel_timeout()` returns `true` if the timeout was successfully canceled, and `false` if the timeout could not be canceled. If `false` is returned, you should wait until the timeout is handled, then call `cancel_timeout()` again.

set_timeout()

uint32 **set_timeout**(BTimeoutHandler **handler*, bigtime_t *howlong*)

Sets a new timeout, which will occur after *howlong* microseconds. When the timeout occurs, the specified *handler*'s `TimedOut()` function will be called.

`set_timeout()` returns a receipt, which is a unique 32-bit unsigned integer that identifies the newly-created timeout. This value will be passed to `TimedOut()` when the timeout occurs, and should be passed to `cancel_timeout()` to cancel the timeout.

Index

 # More Titles from O'Reilly

Web Authoring and Design

Designing with JavaScript

By Nick Heinle
1st Edition September 1997
256 pages, Includes CD-ROM
ISBN 1-56592-300-6

Written by the author of the "JavaScript Tip of the Week" web site, this new Web Review Studio book focuses on the most useful and applicable scripts for making truly interactive, engaging web sites. You'll not only have quick access to the scripts you need, you'll finally understand why the scripts work, how to alter the scripts to get the effects you want, and, ultimately, how to write your own groundbreaking scripts from scratch.

GIF Animation Studio

By Richard Koman
1st Edition October 1996
184 pages, Includes CD-ROM
ISBN 1-56592-230-1

GIF animation is bringing the Web to life—without plug-ins, Java programming, or expensive authoring tools. This book details the major GIF animation programs, profiles work by leading designers (including John Hersey, Razorfish, Henrik Drescher, and Erik Josowitz), and documents advanced animation techniques. A CD-ROM includes freeware and shareware authoring programs, demo versions of commercial software, and the actual animation files described in the book. *GIF Animation Studio* is the first release in the new Web Review Studio series.

Shockwave Studio

By Bob Schmitt
1st Edition March 1997
200 pages, Includes CD-ROM
ISBN 1-56592-231-X

This book, the second title in the new Web Review Studio series, shows how to create compelling and functional Shockwave movies for web sites. The author focuses on actual Shockwave movies, showing how the movies were created. The book takes users from creating simple time-based Shockwave animations through writing complex logical operations that take full advantage of Director's power. The CD-ROM includes a demo version of Director and other software sample files.

Photoshop for the Web

By Mikkel Aaland
1st Edition April 1998
238 pages, ISBN 1-56592-350-2

Photoshop for the Web shows you how to use the world's most popular imaging software to create Web graphics and images that look great and download blazingly fast. The book is crammed full of step-by-step examples and real-world solutions from some of the country's hottest Web producers, including *HotWired*, c|net, *Discovery Online*, *Second Story*, *SFGate*, and more than 20 others.

Designing with Animation

By J. Scott Hamlin
1st Edition November 1998 (est.)
250 pages (est.), ISBN 1-56592-441-X

Designing with Animation treats the subject of Web animation with a level of sophistication that both meets the needs of today's demanding professionals and pushes the envelope for amateur animators. Topics include GIF animation, advanced animation techniques, seamless integration of animation, creative interactive animation with Java, JavaScript, and Macromedia Flash, vector-based and 3D animation, adding sound to animation, and animation techniques with Photoshop.

Web Navigation: Designing the User Experience

By Jennifer Fleming
1st Edition September 1998 (est.)
300 pages (est.), Includes CD-ROM
ISBN 1-56592-351-0

Web Navigation: Designing the User Experience offers the first in-depth look at designing web site navigation. Through case studies and designer interviews, a variety of approaches to navigation issues are explored. The book focuses on designing by purpose, with chapters on entertainment, shopping, identity, learning, information, and community sites. The accompanying CD-ROM includes a tour of selected sites, a "netography," and trial versions of popular software tools.

Web Authoring and Design

Information Architecture for the World Wide Web

By Louis Rosenfeld & Peter Morville
1st Edition January 1998
226 pages, ISBN 1-56592-282-4

Learn how to merge aesthetics and mechanics to design web sites that "work." This book shows how to apply principles of architecture and library science to design cohesive web sites and intranets that are easy to use, manage, and expand. Covers building complex sites, hierarchy design and organization, and techniques to make your site easier to search. For webmasters, designers, and administrators.

HTML: The Definitive Guide, 2nd Edition

By Chuck Musciano & Bill Kennedy
2nd Edition May 1997
552 pages, ISBN 1-56592-235-2

This complete guide is chock full of examples, sample code, and practical, hands-on advice to help you create truly effective web pages and master advanced features. Learn how to insert images and other multimedia elements, create useful links and searchable documents, use Netscape extensions, design great forms, and lots more. The second edition covers the most up-to-date version of the HTML standard (HTML version 3.2), Netscape 4.0 and Internet Explorer 3.0, plus all the common extensions.

Designing for the Web: Getting Started in a New Medium

By Jennifer Niederst
with Edie Freedman
1st Edition April 1996
180 pages, ISBN 1-56592-165-8

Designing for the Web gives you the basics you need to hit the ground running. Although geared toward designers, it covers information and techniques useful to anyone who wants to put graphics online. It explains how to work with HTML documents from a designer's point of view, outlines special problems with presenting information online, and walks through incorporating images into web pages, with emphasis on resolution and improving efficiency.

Web Programming

CGI Programming on the World Wide Web

By Shishir Gundavaram
1st Edition March 1996
450 pages, ISBN 1-56592-168-2

This book offers a comprehensive explanation of CGI and related techniques for people who hold on to the dream of providing their own information servers on the Web. It starts at the beginning, explaining the value of CGI and how it works, then moves swiftly into the subtle details of programming.

JavaScript: The Definitive Guide, 3rd Edition

By David Flanagan & Dan Shafer
3rd Edition June 1998
800 pages, ISBN 1-56592-392-8

This third edition of the definitive reference to JavaScript covers the latest version of the language, JavaScript 1.2, as supported by Netscape Navigator 4.0. JavaScript, which is being standardized under the name ECMAScript, is a scripting language that can be embedded directly in HTML to give web pages programming-language capabilities.

Learning VBScript

By Paul Lomax
1st Edition July 1997
616 pages, includes CD-ROM
ISBN 1-56592-247-6

This definitive guide shows web developers how to take full advantage of client-side scripting with the VBScript language. In addition to basic language features, it covers the Internet Explorer object model and discusses techniques for client-side scripting, like adding ActiveX controls to a web page or validating data before sending it to the server. Includes CD-ROM with over 170 code samples.

O'REILLY™

TO ORDER: **800-998-9938** • **order@oreilly.com** • **http://www.oreilly.com/**
OUR PRODUCTS ARE AVAILABLE AT A BOOKSTORE OR SOFTWARE STORE NEAR YOU.
FOR INFORMATION: **800-998-9938** • **707-829-0515** • **info@oreilly.com**

Web Programming

WebMaster in a Nutshell, Deluxe Edition

By O'Reilly & Associates, Inc.
1st Edition September 1997
374 pages, includes CD-ROM & book
ISBN 1-56592-305-7

The Deluxe Edition of *WebMaster in a Nutshell* is a complete library for web programmers. It features the Web Developer's Library, a CD-ROM containing the electronic text of five popular O'Reilly titles: *HTML: The Definitive Guide*, 2nd Edition; *JavaScript: The Definitive Guide*, 2nd Edition; *CGI Programming on the World Wide Web*; *Programming Perl*, 2nd Edition—the classic "camel book"; and *WebMaster in a Nutshell*, which is also included in a companion desktop edition.

Dynamic HTML: The Definitive Reference

By Danny Goodman
1st Edition July 1998
1088 pages, ISBN 1-56592-494-0

Dynamic HTML: The Definitive Reference is an indispensable compendium for Web content developers. It contains complete reference material for all of the HTML tags, CSS style attributes, browser document objects, and JavaScript objects supported by the various standards and the latest versions of Netscape Navigator and Microsoft Internet Explorer.

Web Client Programming with Perl

By Clinton Wong
1st Edition March 1997
228 pages, ISBN 1-56592-214-X

Web Client Programming with Perl shows you how to extend scripting skills to the Web. This book teaches you the basics of how browsers communicate with servers and how to write your own customized web clients to automate common tasks. It is intended for those who are motivated to develop software that offers a more flexible and dynamic response than a standard web browser.

Frontier: The Definitive Guide

By Matt Neuburg
1st Edition February 1998
618 pages, 1-56592-383-9

This definitive guide is the first book devoted exclusively to teaching and documenting Userland Frontier, a powerful scripting environment for web site management and system level scripting. Packed with examples, advice, tricks, and tips, *Frontier: The Definitive Guide* teaches you Frontier from the ground up. Learn how to automate repetitive processes, control remote computers across a network, beef up your web site by generating hundreds of related web pages automatically, and more. Covers Frontier 4.2.3 for the Macintosh.

WebMaster in a Nutshell

By Stephen Spainhour & Valerie Quercia
1st Edition October 1996
374 pages, ISBN 1-56592-229-8

Web content providers and administrators have many sources for information, both in print and online. WebMaster in a Nutshell puts it all together in one slim volume for easy desktop access. This quick reference covers HTML, CGI, JavaScript, Perl, HTTP, and server configuration.

How to stay in touch with O'Reilly

1. Visit Our Award-Winning Web Site

http://www.oreilly.com/

★ "Top 100 Sites on the Web" — *PC Magazine*
★ "Top 5% Web sites" — *Point Communications*
★ "3-Star site" — *The McKinley Group*

Our web site contains a library of comprehensive product information (including book excerpts and tables of contents), downloadable software, background articles, interviews with technology leaders, links to relevant sites, book cover art, and more. File us in your Bookmarks or Hotlist!

2. Join Our Email Mailing Lists

New Product Releases

To receive automatic email with brief descriptions of all new O'Reilly products as they are released, send email to:
listproc@online.oreilly.com
Put the following information in the first line of your message (*not* in the Subject field):
subscribe oreilly-news

O'Reilly Events

If you'd also like us to send information about trade show events, special promotions, and other O'Reilly events, send email to:
listproc@online.oreilly.com
Put the following information in the first line of your message (*not* in the Subject field):
subscribe oreilly-events

3. Get Examples from Our Books via FTP

There are two ways to access an archive of example files from our books:

Regular FTP

- ftp to:
  ftp.oreilly.com
  (login: anonymous
  password: your email address)
- Point your web browser to:
  ftp://ftp.oreilly.com/

FTPMAIL

- Send an email message to:
  ftpmail@online.oreilly.com
  (Write "help" in the message body)

4. Contact Us via Email

order@oreilly.com
To place a book or software order online. Good for North American and international customers.

subscriptions@oreilly.com
To place an order for any of our newsletters or periodicals.

books@oreilly.com
General questions about any of our books.

software@oreilly.com
For general questions and product information about our software. Check out O'Reilly Software Online at **http://software.oreilly.com/** for software and technical support information. Registered O'Reilly software users send your questions to: **website-support@oreilly.com**

cs@oreilly.com
For answers to problems regarding your order or our products.

booktech@oreilly.com
For book content technical questions or corrections.

proposals@oreilly.com
To submit new book or software proposals to our editors and product managers.

international@oreilly.com
For information about our international distributors or translation queries. For a list of our distributors outside of North America check out:
http://www.oreilly.com/www/order/country.html

O'Reilly & Associates, Inc.
101 Morris Street, Sebastopol, CA 95472 USA
TEL 707-829-0515 or 800-998-9938
        (6am to 5pm PST)
FAX 707-829-0104

Titles from O'Reilly

International Distributors

UK, EUROPE, MIDDLE EAST AND NORTHERN AFRICA (EXCEPT FRANCE, GERMANY, SWITZERLAND, & AUSTRIA)

INQUIRIES
International Thomson Publishing Europe
Berkshire House
168-173 High Holborn
London WC1V 7AA
United Kingdom
Telephone: 44-171-497-1422
Fax: 44-171-497-1426
Email: itpint@itps.co.uk

ORDERS
International Thomson Publishing Services, Ltd.
Cheriton House, North Way
Andover, Hampshire SP10 5BE
United Kingdom
Telephone: 44-264-342-832 (UK)
Telephone: 44-264-342-806 (outside UK)
Fax: 44-264-364418 (UK)
Fax: 44-264-342761 (outside UK)
UK & Eire orders: itpuk@itps.co.uk
International orders: itpint@itps.co.uk

FRANCE

Editions Eyrolles
61 bd Saint-Germain
75240 Paris Cedex 05
France
Fax: 33-01-44-41-11-44

FRENCH LANGUAGE BOOKS
All countries except Canada
Telephone: 33-01-44-41-46-16
Email: geodif@eyrolles.com
English language books
Telephone: 33-01-44-41-11-87
Email: distribution@eyrolles.com

GERMANY, SWITZERLAND, AND AUSTRIA

INQUIRIES
O'Reilly Verlag
Balthasarstr. 81
D-50670 Köln
Germany
Telephone: 49-221-97-31-60-0
Fax: 49-221-97-31-60-8
Email: anfragen@oreilly.de

ORDERS
International Thomson Publishing
Königswinterer Straße 418
53227 Bonn, Germany
Telephone: 49-228-97024 0
Fax: 49-228-441342
Email: order@oreilly.de

JAPAN

O'Reilly Japan, Inc.
Kiyoshige Building 2F
12-Banchi, Sanei-cho
Shinjuku-ku
Tokyo 160-0008 Japan
Telephone: 81-3-3356-5227
Fax: 81-3-3356-5261
Email: kenji@oreilly.com

INDIA

Computer Bookshop (India) PVT. Ltd.
190 Dr. D.N. Road, Fort
Bombay 400 001 India
Telephone: 91-22-207-0989
Fax: 91-22-262-3551
Email: cbsbom@giasbm01.vsnl.net.in

HONG KONG

City Discount Subscription Service Ltd.
Unit D, 3rd Floor, Yan's Tower
27 Wong Chuk Hang Road
Aberdeen, Hong Kong
Telephone: 852-2580-3539
Fax: 852-2580-6463
Email: citydis@ppn.com.hk

KOREA

Hanbit Media, Inc.
Sonyoung Bldg. 202
Yeksam-dong 736-36
Kangnam-ku
Seoul, Korea
Telephone: 822-554-9610
Fax: 822-556-0363
Email: hant93@chollian.dacom.co.kr

SINGAPORE, MALAYSIA, AND THAILAND

Addison Wesley Longman Singapore PTE Ltd.
25 First Lok Yang Road
Singapore 629734
Telephone: 65-268-2666
Fax: 65-268-7023
Email: daniel@longman.com.sg

PHILIPPINES

Mutual Books, Inc.
429-D Shaw Boulevard
Mandaluyong City, Metro
Manila, Philippines
Telephone: 632-725-7538
Fax: 632-721-3056
Email: mbikikog@mnl.sequel.net

CHINA

Ron's DataCom Co., Ltd.
79 Dongwu Avenue
Dongxihu District
Wuhan 430040
China
Telephone: 86-27-83892568
Fax: 86-27-83222108
Email: hongfeng@public.wh.hb.cn

ALL OTHER ASIAN COUNTRIES

O'Reilly & Associates, Inc.
101 Morris Street
Sebastopol, CA 95472 USA
Telephone: 707-829-0515
Fax: 707-829-0104
Email: order@oreilly.com

AUSTRALIA

WoodsLane Pty. Ltd.
7/5 Vuko Place, Warriewood NSW 2102
P.O. Box 935
Mona Vale NSW 2103
Australia
Telephone: 61-2-9970-5111
Fax: 61-2-9970-5002
Email: info@woodslane.com.au

NEW ZEALAND

Woodslane New Zealand Ltd.
21 Cooks Street (P.O. Box 575)
Waganui, New Zealand
Telephone: 64-6-347-6543
Fax: 64-6-345-4840
Email: info@woodslane.com.au

THE AMERICAS

McGraw-Hill Interamericana Editores,
S.A. de C.V.
Cedro No. 512
Col. Atlampa 06450
Mexico, D.F.
Telephone: 52-5-541-3155
Fax: 52-5-541-4913
Email: mcgraw-hill@infosel.net.mx

SOUTH AFRICA

International Thomson Publishing
South Africa
Building 18, Constantia Park
138 Sixteenth Road
P.O. Box 2459
Halfway House, 1685 South Africa
Telephone: 27-11-805-4819
Fax: 27-11-805-3648